Contents

Introduction

'Everyone was out on the streets, waving their flags, banging drums, dancing, singing, crying. It was the first time I'd seen members of the two main political parties cheering the same president! Everyone was full of hope that this was the start of something new. We'd lost so much in all those years. It wasn't enough for things to go back to how they were before the barbarism of the dictatorship, we wanted something better.'

Ana María (Argentina)

On 10 December 1983 hundreds of thousands of Argentines filled the streets of Buenos Aires to celebrate the inauguration of the newly-elected president, Raúl Alfonsín, and the end of a seven-year military dictatorship which had become synonymous with death squads, concentration camps and murder. As the president appeared on the balcony of the presidential palace the crowds roared its approval, waving political banners and blue and white national flags and chanting, 'Argentina today, Chile and Uruguay tomorrow'. Uruguayans had to wait another two years for the end of military rule and it was not until 1990, after more than 16 years in power, that General Pinochet finally handed over to an elected president in Chile. 1989 saw the overthrow of Latin America's longest surviving dictator, General Stroessner, ruler of Paraguay since 1954.

In all four countries of the southern cone area of Latin America women led the struggle for democracy, showing extraordinary courage and determination in confronting the brutality of military repression. In Argentina, the Mothers and Grandmothers of the victims of the regime's concentration camps mounted the first public challenge to military rule, breaking the silence imposed by the terror of 'disappearances' with their weekly marches in Plaza de Mayo (May Square) in the heart of Buenos Aires. Driven by desperation, they

2 Out of the Shadows

risked their lives to take to the streets to demand the return of their missing children and grandchildren. In Paraguay, peasant women organised their first public demonstration and the largest gathering of women in the country's history to demand land and democracy. But it was not only in public protests that women played a crucial role in the opposition movement to dictatorship. Behind the scenes, in shanty towns and poor communities, women fought a private daily battle for the survival of their families in the face of the devastation caused by the economic policies of the military. With communal kitchens, canteens and health projects, they helped keep working-class organisation alive and built networks of resistance to military rule.

It was a challenge that took the military rulers by surprise. Before the coups most of these women had been housewives, tied to the home by children, with no political experience and little interest in the world outside their homes and families. Military rule shattered this world, forcing them to take on a more active role in public affairs. As male breadwinners fell victim to a wave of unemployment, women were forced to find paid work; as savage cuts in government spending put medical care out of the reach of working-class families, women started their own health campaigns; when hunger and despair struck their communities, they combined their efforts, setting up communal self-help projects to feed their families; and when members of their families fell victim to political persecution and 'disappearance', they organised public protests that brought the attention of the international community to their cause. In the name of motherhood and the family, women extended their domestic role into the public arena, and in the process they transformed not only politics, but also challenged traditional ideas about women. They became aware of their own interests not only as members of the poor and working-class sectors of society, but also as women. The slogans 'democracy in the country and democracy in the home' and 'without women there's no democracy' which appeared in the pre-election rallies in Chile and Uruguay expressed women's determination to make a permanent place for themselves and their interests in the world of politics.

Ironically, the immediate effect of the return of 'democratic' politics was a fall in women's political activity, as male-dominated political parties and trade unions took the centre stage and national and local government moved into the areas in which women had worked. Few women candidates were put forward by political parties and they were only a tiny minority of those elected to the new parliaments. In the Uruguayan parliament there were no women at all. Women did not give up and return to the home, however, and this book tells the story of their battle, not only for the survival of their families in the face of continued economic hardship, but also against inequality and discrimination in the trade unions, political parties and society at large.

While there is a great variation in the position of women depending on the country and geographical region in which they live and on the particular religious, ethnic and social group to which they belong, what is striking about the testimonies of the women in this book are the similarities in their everyday lives. Much of the uniformity in the lives of women of all four countries is the result of the particularly oppressive version of sexism which permeates Latin American culture, known as *machismo.*

Machismo

Machismo is an ideology which owes much to Spanish colonial ideas about women (they were classified in colonial legal codes as 'imbeciles by nature') and the teachings of the Roman Catholic Church. Gender is the term used to refer to the different roles that societies and cultures ascribe to men and women, as opposed to sex which refers only to biological differences. *Machismo* is a system of gender relations which exaggerates the differences between men and women according to their so-called 'natural' qualities and determines what is acceptable behaviour from each. Although these differences are supposed to complement each other, *machismo* clearly asserts the superiority of the male over the female. The stereotypical macho male is strong, aggressive and virile while women are dependent, self-sacrificing, submissive and emotional; men are unfaithful by nature and women are monogamous and devoted to the family. Men and women are destined to different roles in society: men in the outside world of work, money and politics and women in the unpaid work of the home. Most women are brought up with the idea that their natural role in life is to become a mother and that their place is inside the home. The female equivalent of *machismo*, known as *marianismo*, refers to the exalted respect women command as mothers and has sometimes led to the misconception that countries such as Paraguay and Chile are 'matriarchal' societies, or societies ruled by women.

The lives of most women, of course, have never conformed to these caricatures. Necessity has dictated that a significant proportion of working-class women, for example, have always worked outside the home and most of those interviewed here had paid jobs at some time in their lives. In the past thirty years economic and social factors have transformed the position of many women in the Southern Cone. Most women in Argentina, Uruguay and Chile now live in cities, they have fewer children and there has been an explosion in the number of women in education and paid work. Nevertheless, *machismo* continues to exert a strong influence over women, creating a whole series of obstacles to their participation in society and limiting the choices they can make in their lives.

Cultural barriers combine with the teachings of the Church and family and civil law to consolidate discrimination against women. The influence of *machismo* can still be seen in many laws, particularly in relation to married women and reproductive rights. In a continent where most of the population are registered as Catholic, the teachings of the traditional Roman Catholic Church reinforce and perpetuate the subordination of women. Women are seen as protectors of the faith and virtue and encouraged to endure silently unhappy marriages and poverty. Although one in five households in Latin America is headed by a woman, the Church has been one of biggest obstacles to the introduction of divorce. When divorce and equal rights for children born outside marriage were introduced briefly in Argentina in the 1950s under President Perón, the withdrawal of church support for his government helped legitimise the coup which toppled him. In Chile and Paraguay divorce is available only in very exceptional circumstances and has only recently been legalised in Argentina. Only in Uruguay has divorce been available since early in the century.

Until recently, Uruguay was also the only exception to a system where men had privileged legal rights over marital decisions, children and property. Until 1985 Argentina still had the system of *patria potestad*, which gave men the final decision over issues concerning children, even after the couple had separated. In Chile the concept of women's obedience to their husbands is still enshrined in family law. In Paraguay the freedom of married women to work outside the home is also limited by law. Paraguayan husbands still have control over matrimonial property and women have to obtain the consent of their husbands before entering into economic activity. A woman's duty to be sexually faithful to her husband is also embodied in legal systems as in Chile, where a woman commits adultery if she is found having sex with any man other than her husband, while for men adultery only applies if the sexual act takes place inside the marital home. In Paraguay the law exempts a man from punishment if he murders his wife when she is found in the act of adultery.

Contraception is legal, although not always widely available to women. Its availability has been, and to a large extent continues to be, determined by access to medical services and by the woman's ability to pay. In Argentina in 1974, for example, during the government of Isabel Perón, over-the-counter sales of contraceptives were banned. Rural women in particular have little access to contraception and to the medical supervision they require and this partly explains the higher birth rates in rural areas. Moreover, decisions about having children are still often taken out of women's hands by their partners and by the Church: men often object to women using contraception, seeing a large family as proof of their virility, and the Church campaigns actively against the use of artificial methods of birth control. Eulogia, a peasant from Paraguay where families of ten or more children are not uncommon, recalls, 'I've had 15 children. The eleventh time I was pregnant with twins and I went to the priest and told him that we couldn't support any more children. He told me it was wicked to think of stopping pregnancies and that we would be punished, so I never went back to him and I went on having children.'

One consequence of the unavailability of contraception is a high abortion rate. Despite the huge number of illegal, backstreet and self-induced terminations carried out in Latin America and the high number of maternal deaths and injury that result from them, abortion remains a taboo issue. Statistics on illegal abortions are obviously unreliable, but some studies suggest that up to forty per cent of pregnancies in Latin America end in abortion. Uruguay is believed to have one of the highest rates of abortion in Latin America — 150,000 a year in a country of three million, resulting in over a hundred deaths a year. Research in the early 1970s suggests that nearly half of all pregnancies in Chile ended in abortion. In one survey in Paraguay, 35 per cent of women interviewed admitted having had one or more abortions and a study of 13 Third World countries showed Paraguay with the highest maternal mortality as a result of backstreet abortions.

Several of the women interviewed in this book talked of having performed abortions on themselves and recognised it as a serious problem in their neighbourhoods. In the words of one Argentine woman, 'In my neighbourhood a woman with five little children has just died trying to do an abortion on herself. There was another case of a fifteen year old who did an abortion with a parsley root, which is very common and very dangerous, because it rots inside and causes an infection'. According to a Chilean woman, 'Women don't want to talk about abortion because it's against the teachings of the Church and also because it's against the law, but nearly all women have them'. Abortion is illegal in Chile and Paraguay, except to save the mother's life, and permitted only on exceptional grounds in Argentina and Uruguay. A woman who has an abortion in Paraguay can be sentenced to 18 months in prison and in Chile she can receive a sentence of between three and five years.

Machismo also influences attitudes to women and work and creates a whole series of obstacles to their participation in the labour market. Housework and children are considered to be the 'natural' responsibility of women. An International Labour Organisation study carried out in 1984 showed that the average Argentine housewife worked ten hours a day, seven days a week, on housework while other members of the family contributed an average of 15 minutes a day. In the Paraguayan countryside, where the majority of families live without the benefits of running water and electricity, the preparation of food, cleaning and washing are infinitely more burdensome. These household tasks however, are not considered to be 'real' work and neither are the mass of jobs women do to assist family businesses and farms. The invisibility of this unpaid work is reflected in the statistics of women's economic activity, which measures the proportion of women of working age actually in paid employment plus those searching for work, but exclude housework, childcare and women's role in family businesses and farming.

Women's work inside the home seriously restricts the paid jobs they can do. Latin American men, in general, avoid housework and childcare, and there is little in the way of nursery school or creche provision. As a result married women with young children form a low proportion of the workforce. The majority of women in paid employment are single, separated or divorced and most have to combine paid work with housework in what has become known as the 'double shift'.

The dramatic increase in educational opportunities in the last thirty years has meant that working-class women are much more likely than their mothers to finish primary school and have some secondary education. The differences in educational backgrounds of young and older women came out clearly in the interviews. Of the older women, the majority had little schooling and were brought up with the idea that, since the woman's main role in life is to become a wife and mother, education and training were not a priority for them. This attitude still reigns in rural areas of Paraguay, where in 1982 32 per cent of all Paraguayan women were illiterate while the figure for men was 26 per cent. This reflects not only the lack of educational provision in Paraguay's rural areas but also the continued existence of a particularly severe form of social and cultural discrimination against rural women. When a peasant girl reaches puberty it is no longer acceptable for her to leave the house alone and she can only go to school if she has brothers of school age willing to take her. Only one in three Paraguayan university students are women and most of these are women from the towns and cities.

Women in Argentina, Uruguay and Chile are only slightly more likely to be illiterate than men and there is little difference between men and women's schooling at all levels of the educational system. Since the 1960s there has been a huge expansion in the numbers of women entering higher education. In Argentina and Uruguay nearly

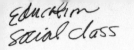
education
social class

half of university students are women and in Chile the proportion is only slightly lower. In all these countries, however, women are less likely to receive vocational training and less likely to be found studying typically 'male' subjects, such as science, engineering and technology.

In all countries except Paraguay there has been a large increase in women in paid employment. The proportion of Paraguayan women in or available for paid work showed a fall from the 1950s due to a drop in rural employment opportunities. In 1985, when the rate of female economic activity for Great Britain was 39 per cent, the figure for Paraguay, where statistics are notoriously unreliable, was 19 per cent. Uruguay and Argentina's rates of around 28 per cent were among the highest in the continent and in Chile the figure was 25 per cent. Most of the new opportunities were for educated women in the growing state sector, mainly in areas for which their home life was deemed to give them 'natural' qualifications, such as teaching, nursing, public administration and community and social services. Women on average earned about half a man's average wage, even though women had higher educational levels than men in comparable jobs. Argentina and Uruguay have, on paper at least, the most advanced labour legislation in Latin America in relation to women. In Argentina, for example, maternity leave provision is superior to Britain's, but women are often unable to claim their legal entitlement.

For the mass of women in paid work, labour legislation is a nicety from which they rarely benefit. These women, with little formal education or training, have seen their job opportunities diminish as the traditional sources of women's employment in textiles and food industries have contracted. Many have been forced to work on the 'informal' labour market, working cash-in-hand in small, often illegal enterprises which offer no job security or welfare benefits. In 1979 half of all urban female employees in Latin America were domestic servants, whose pay and conditions of work rank among the worst of all Latin American workers.

Social class plays a major role in determining the nature of gender inequalities and their effect on women's lives. While upper- and middle-class women may also have the chief responsibility for the home and children, they are less constrained by housework and childcare, which is frequently carried out by working-class women employed as domestic servants. An Argentine professional woman and her domestic servant, often Paraguayan, inhabit different worlds. Middle-class women have greater access to education and more opportunities for better paid work. Money can buy better healthcare and even abortion laws can be bypassed by private arrangements.

The sharp class differences which divide women were reflected in the nature of the women's movements which grew up in the early twentieth century. With few exceptions, the women interviewed had never been involved in women's rights organisations prior to the 1970s. Working-class women, often not legally married to their partners and struggling to feed their families, saw the demands of these movements for higher education, equal rights in marriage and even the vote, as middle-class affairs. They took little part in the important female suffrage and civil rights movements which grew up in Argentina, Uruguay and Chile. The independent women's movement in all three countries dissolved after achieving their goals. Uruguayan women won the vote in 1932 and equal civil rights in the 1940s, and in Chile women's suffrage began in 1949. In Argentina the independent women's movement began to decay even before the vote was granted and suffrage organisations were not even able to claim success for their decades-long struggle. Their demands were hijacked by Perón who saw women as a huge untapped source of support for his political ambitions. With his wife Evita Perón as his appointed spokesperson for women's rights, the struggle for the vote in Argentina became a genuinely mass affair. When they were awarded the vote in 1947, tens of thousands of women filled the streets of the centre of Argentina's capital, Buenos Aires.

Paraguayan women were the last in Latin America to get the vote, in 1961. Women organised inside approved political parties which were strictly controlled by the Stroessner dictatorship and political repression prevented the emergence of any significant independent movement.

But political rights for women did not mean political power. None of the countries beat the record set in 1951 when, in the first election in which Argentine women could vote, 24 women deputies and seven women senators were elected to parliament. Of the women interviewed, only in Argentina and Uruguay had women held positions in political parties or trade unions before the coups, although these were always minor positions. From national government and local councils to community organisations and trade unions, with a few notable exceptions, men have occupied the key positions of power and decision-making. Consequently gender issues have rarely reached the agendas of political parties. Apart from some formal gains in the area of labour legislation, there was little progress from the 1940s to the early 1970s, even in Uruguay and Chile, countries not under military governments. Parties of the left and trade unions have tended to see women's demands as divisive to working-class unity and of secondary importance to the class struggle. Parties of the right have appealed to women in their traditional role as mothers and home-makers and paid little attention to issues such as education and job opportunities.

This is not to suggest that women have played no part in popular movements for social change, but rather that they have been excluded from leadership positions and that their contributions have been underestimated or 'invisible'. Research by Latin American feminists is only now beginning to uncover the crucial, if hidden, role women have played across the political spectrum. In Chile, for example, many working-class women, including some interviewed here, were active in the social and health campaigns of President Allende. At the same time some middle- and upper-class Chilean women were vocal in their opposition to Allende and in their support of the military coup which toppled him. In Argentina the key role played by women in the resistance to military rule and popular social movements did not go unnoticed; nearly one third of those who 'disappeared' under the military regimes of 1976-83 were women.

Military Rule

When the United Nations declared a Women's Decade in 1975, three of the four countries in this study were under military rule; Argentina fell a year later. Millions of women were living in the shadow of dictatorship, disappearances, torture, murder and poverty. When the tanks rolled out onto the streets of Chile (1973), Uruguay (1973) and Argentina (1976) it was on the pretext of a threat to the 'Western and Christian way of life'. In Chile sections of the labour movement had begun organising massive strikes to press for more radical policies from the Popular Unity government of the Marxist President Allende. In Uruguay and Argentina the threat came from a combination of working-class militancy and a number of small guerrilla organisations. The militaries' promises to restore order and stability won the support of significant sections of the middle and upper classes and right-wing movements in all three countries. Few could have predicted the barbarism that was to follow.

The regimes which seized power in the Southern Cone in the 1970s were all pro-Western in foreign policy, defenders of the free market on the economic front and virulently anti-communist in domestic politics. In all countries the military violently crushed any potential opposition, closing political parties and trade unions, banning public meetings and controlling information through censorship, not only of the media but also in universities and throughout the education system. In Argentina, for example, this not only included the outlawing of communist texts but also the works of Freud and the teaching of psychology. All four military regimes adhered to the guiding principle of United States policy in Latin America, the doctrine

of National Security. This doctrine, developed in the wake of the Cuban
Revolution in 1959, assigned the armed forces of Latin America the
role of safeguarding internal security and waging war against
'subversive elements' within their borders. Many Latin American
military officers had been trained in counter-insurgency methods in
the US army School of the Americas in Panama where the curriculum
included courses on the theory and practice of torture. The armed
forces of all four countries co-operated with each other in a
combination of legal and illegal methods ranging from persecution
and illegal detention to torture and murder in order to wipe out any
possible resistance to their rule.

In Paraguay, since the coup of 1954 this had taken the form of
'nipping in the bud' any nascent opposition, normally by huge 'search
and kill' operations. This was the fate of a church-supported peasant
movement in 1976, the only significant popular opposition to emerge
during the Stroessner years. The bloodbath which followed the coup
in Chile was just the first stage of a repressive strategy that cost
thousands of lives and forced tens of thousands into exile. In Uruguay
one in thirty of the population passed through prison and some half
a million people left the country. The Argentine military, anxious to
avoid the international outcry which followed the Chilean coup, built
a massive network of 350 concentration camps into which, according
to the estimates of human rights organisations, between 20-30,000
victims simply 'disappeared' from the eyes of the world. Some 5,000
others were killed and hundreds of thousands went into exile.

A crushed opposition and a population paralysed by terror were the
prerequisites for the imposition of economic projects based on the free
market economics of the Chicago monetarist school. For the economy
this meant cuts in real wages and government expenditure, incentives
for foreign investors and increased borrowing from international
banks. For the majority of the population it meant growing
unemployment, deteriorating social services and a drastic fall in living
standards. When foreign markets contracted with the world recession
in the early 1980s, the situation became critical for wide sectors of
society in all four countries. Export earnings crashed at the same time
as US interest rates rose, making interest payments on the massive
foreign debts only possible by further borrowing. Governments turned
to the International Monetary Fund whose condition for credit was a
package of austerity measures which raised the price of food, while
cutting wages and social services still further. Extreme poverty became
visible for the first time in countries like Argentina and Uruguay. In
Chile, where monetarist polices were implemented in their most
undiluted form, unemployment reached between 25-30 per cent in
1983, when an estimated thirty per cent of all Chilean families were

living in 'extreme' poverty. In 1986 half the population of Paraguay were estimated to be living below the poverty line and in some regions over a third of the population were suffering from malnutrition.

Women's lives were not only affected by the general political and economic conditions created by the dictatorships, but also by the ideological offensive directed at them by the military rulers. In the words of Chile's General Pinochet, 'the more a woman is feminine, the more she is admirable'. Calls for a return to traditional Christian and family values accompanied the military seizures of power and in this the military regimes were supported by powerful sections of the Church. Women were to revert to their traditional roles as guardians of the faith, the family and morality and to their proper place, the home. Attempts were made to limit, if not eliminate, a public role for women; many of the gains of the previous years, such as maternity benefits and labour rights, were revoked, and in Chile they even went as far as trying to ban women from wearing trousers.

The role that women were to play in the years of dictatorship was not that envisaged by the military when they extolled the virtues of motherhood and the family. Ironically it was the regimes' own economic and political programmes which provoked the surge in women's public participation in those years and most women defended their activities as those of good mothers and wives. Falling living standards forced many women out of the house and into paid work for the first time and chronic poverty forced others to look for community solutions to the problem of feeding their families. Many women had their first real contact with the outside world of politics when the army burst into their homes and seized family members or when husbands were sacked for political or union activity. The repression of political parties and unions brought political life to the community where it was more accessible to women and in all four countries women became a key force in resistance to military rule.

In Chapter One, Chilean housewives from the shanty towns around Santiago describe the devastation caused to their communities by the brutality of the military coup of 1973 and the 'shock' economic policies the regime imposed. They describe how the new organisations they created to combat widespread unemployment and chronic poverty put them in the firing line of a regime determined to crush all working-class organisation. Their courageous defence of their communal kitchens and canteens, shopping collectives and sewing workshops not only ensured the survival of their families, but also offered women a new role in community life. The value they attach to the opportunities for companionship, self-education and personal development offered by their new organisations helps explain their persistence, even as the economic situation has become less critical.

Throughout the Southern Cone, economic crisis forced growing numbers of women into paid work, a phenomenon which was most pronounced in Uruguay. In Chapter Two, Uruguayan women describe their 'double day' of work, inside and outside the home, and their role in the struggle to re-establish trade unions under the military regime. With the return of constitutional rule they found themselves engaged in another battle, this time to force the male world of trade unions to introduce women's concerns into union policy and to create a new kind of trade unionism, more attractive and accessible to women. Working closely with the wider women's movement, they recount the successes of new women's commissions in areas such as equal pay and opportunities, childcare, health education and training.

The voices of peasant women from the Paraguayan Peasants Movement appear for the first time in English in Chapter Three. Their testimonies tell of their fight not only against landlessness and poverty, but also against the particularly oppressive form of discrimination they face as Paraguayan women. They describe their battle within the peasant's movement to establish a women's commission to promote equal rights for women, both inside the movement and in their homes and communities. The testimonies of women from a new peasant community, Limoy, show the effect of the commission on women's lives and their remarkable achievements in the face of extreme poverty and the deeply-embedded *machismo* of peasant men.

In Chapter Four, Argentina's Mothers and Grandmothers of Plaza de Mayo describe how their desperation for information about their 'disappeared' children led them to organise the first public protest against one of the most brutal dictatorships Latin America has witnessed. The discovery of the military's secret network of concentration camps and the disappearance of three Mothers only reinforced their determination to continue a remarkably courageous struggle, which became an inspiration for the human rights movements throughout the continent.

Argentina, for many years one of the richest Latin American nations, was unfamiliar with the kind of hunger suffered in much of the continent during the military period. Chapter Five looks at the varied ways Argentine women responded to the economic crisis of the early 1980s, from the shopping strikes of militant housewives' groups to the creation of the world's first housewives' trade union calling for wages for housework. With the dramatic decline in the Argentine economy and the adoption of austerity measures by constitutional governments, this chapter looks at one of the first examples of women's self-help groups in the poor neighbourhoods of Buenos Aires.

Working-class women's resistance to military rule has made them more conscious of discrimination against them as women, at work, in the world of politics and inside the home. Domestic violence, women's sexuality, education and childcare, as well as the immediate problems of caring for their families, have become issues for many women's organisations. Most reject the label 'feminist'. An exception is Chile, where women in the shanty towns have begun to make their needs a priority, a process which has led them to question the traditional roles of men and women. Chapter Six looks at the growth of grassroots feminism in Chile and the differences they perceive between 'middle-class' women's organisations and their own brand of feminism.

The book is based on extensive interviews with women in all four countries. Sometimes names and places have been changed to protect the women involved. Most women belonged to organisations which had been mentioned in passing in the local press or had been suggested by women who worked in the field, including aid workers from CAFOD and Oxfam. The themes discussed reflect key areas of grassroots activity by women in each of the four countries. This does not mean that they are the only areas of women's activity in those countries. All four countries, for example, had human rights movements in which women played the key role; women's commissions are appearing in trade unions throughout the region and women's neighbourhood organisations are becoming a common feature of community life in the Southern Cone. Remarkably, some of these groups have so far received little publicity in their own countries and little has been written about them. For these groups in particular, it is important that their voices be heard and their words recorded. Without their testimonies, their work and achievements may, like many women's struggles in the past, disappear from history.

Many of the women interviewed were the leaders of organisations. Men were almost never present during the interviews. Almost all the women had faced problems with their husbands in the beginning, but most said they have now established their right to time for their own activities. Most had experience of talking about their work, even to foreigners. Organisations for which international solidarity has been crucial, such as the Mothers of the Plaza de Mayo, and community groups which receive financial support from foreign aid organisations, welcomed the continued interest in their work. In some ways being a foreigner made the task of talking to these women easier, a fact pointed out by several Argentine and Paraguayan colleagues. Not being involved in local party politics, nor part of a local feminist movement that they often perceived as being middle-class, was an advantage when dealing with groups who were anxious to preserve their independence or class identity.

With women who were new to the organisations, there was clearly less understanding of why a 'gringo' should be interested in their affairs. For most women in the village of Limoy in rural Paraguay, for example, it was the first time they had spoken to a foreigner. Their broken Spanish meant interviews had to be carried out with the help of those among them who were bilingual in Spanish and the native Guaraní. There was a great deal of curiosity about me, about life in the UK and considerable amusement at my ignorance of British farming techniques.

All the women were extremely kind and patient, and generous with their time and affections. Most of the interviews were carried out while they were working, in the gaps between workshops at summer schools, as in Chile or while they were organising new campaigns, as with the Mothers. Even though many of the groups now have their own premises, the interviews often took place in their homes, which was frequently where they also carried out their paid jobs and where meetings of their organisations were held. They talked while they cooked for their families and for the communal kitchens, while customers came to buy from their communal shops, while organising games for forty children in a creche or while they attended to streams of visitors. They found the time to show me around their neighbourhoods, deliver me to and from buses, and often insisted on feeding me. I usually left with samples of their work: bread and cakes from communal bakeries, needlework from their workshops and in Paraguay they loaded me up with watermelons, grapes and honey. The Paraguayan men and women shared their homes with me, went to great lengths to make me comfortable and enthusiastically accompanied me on long treks across the countryside.

This book is dedicated to these women, to the strength, humour and optimism they show in the face of severe hardship and to their creative and courageous struggle for social justice.

16

Chile
Chronology

1949 Women win the vote.

1970 Salvador Allende becomes the world's first elected Marxist president.

1973 President Allende killed during the bloody military coup which brings General Pinochet to power. Coup provokes international condemnation.

1974 Association of Relatives of the Detained and Disappeared is formed. Church sponsors neighbourhood groups to look after the victims of military persecution and unemployment.

1982 Movement of Women Slum Dwellers (MOMUPO) is created to unite and co-ordinate the activities of grassroots women's groups. More than 50,000 people in Greater Santiago belong to 494 grassroots organisations set up to combat poverty.

1983 One third of the population is out of work. First mass street protests against Pinochet regime. Several federations are set up to co-ordinate women's opposition to military rule.

1986 Creation of the Communal Kitchen Command. Two hundred grassroots organisations join trade unions and political parties in the Civil Assembly and organise a two day national strike. Assassination attempt on General Pinochet. Military impose a state of siege to clamp down on resistance in the shanty towns.

1988 Pinochet defeated in the plebiscite by which he sought to maintain power for another ten years.

1989 First free elections for 19 years. Christian Democrat Patricio Aylwin leads opposition coalition which wins elections. General Pinochet remains as commander-in-chief of the armed forces. 270,000 Chileans belong to some 3,000 grassroots organisations.

1990 The government creates the National Women's Service (SERNAM) to develop and promote women's programmes.

1991 The government publishes the report of the Committee of Truth and Reconciliation which chronicles the murders of 2,279 people by the military in the aftermath of the coup.

1

'The Kitchen Never Stopped'

Women's self-help groups in Chile's shanty towns

LUZ MARIA: When they began to interrogate my husband, being an uncultured woman you could say, not educated for anything, I had the guts to stand by his side and answer their questions. My husband couldn't speak because he was in total shock. He forgot everything, even his date of birth, where he'd worked, why he'd left. They asked the opposite — why he'd been sacked — but we'd been lucky because a relative had found him another job. They asked one question after another, repeating the questions, changing them around, trying to confuse me and after they'd asked so many things so many times I went to get the bag of documents that I've always kept and I put everything on the table so they could see he hadn't been sacked for being a militant, that he'd left of his own accord and that now he was in a better job.

From then on my husband never wanted to participate in anything again. He fell to pieces. But I reacted differently. Before, he always told me that I was a woman who didn't understand anything, that it wasn't worth having a conversation with me and that I was a brute because I come from the south. He had undervalued me, put me down all my life. Now I realised that he was only alive thanks to me. If I'd been so stupid, so brutish, I'd have been crying, or created a scandal or a wrong word would have come out. If I'd said one wrong thing or said something badly, they would have taken him and I'd never have seen him again. It was then that I thought, 'I'm worth something'. I said to him then, 'You're not going to tell me I'm useless again. Things are going to be different now. Now I'm going to go out, work with the church, get involved'.

The courage and strength with which thousands of working-class housewives like Luz María faced the violence and poverty inflicted by military rule on a wide sector of Chilean society provided the backbone of resistance to the regime which seized power in 1973. When massive street protests broke out in 1983, what captured the attention of onlookers throughout the world was the number of women confronting the tear gas, water cannon and bullets of the armed forces. This, however, was only the public face of a long drama that had been unfolding behind the scenes in the poor neighbourhoods of Santiago where women played a crucial role in the day-to-day survival of their families and communities. Women like Luz María were the key actors in the network of workshops, communal kitchens (comedores), popular canteens, housing, cultural and human rights organisations, created as part of the battle against poverty and despair.

The coup of 1973 ended four decades of stable parliamentary government in Chile. The strong trade unions and communist and socialist parties of the working class and peasants were radical but not revolutionary. They accepted the rules of the parliamentary game, participating in the political system, contesting elections and gaining seats in congress. This heritage of parliamentary democracy was a powerful factor in allowing the Marxist, Salvador Allende, to be elected president in 1970. It was not until the working class began to demand more radical policies from Allende's government that the military stepped in.

The bloodbath which followed the coup provoked a wave of international condemnation. On the morning of 11 September 1973, President Allende broadcast his defiant farewell speech from La Moneda, the presidential palace, shortly before it was bombed by the Chilean airforce and the president himself was killed. Political parties were closed down, trade unions were declared illegal and the tanks rolled out onto the streets in search of any potential opponents to the regime. Chile's main football stadium became the scene of mass murder and torture as some 3,000 people were slaughtered or 'disappeared'. Having smashed Chile's political system, the regime launched an economic onslaught based on the monetarist policies of the Chicago school, the production of raw materials for export, free markets, privatisation, massive cuts in welfare expenditure, the privatisation of health and education services and the destruction of a large part of the country's industry. The immediate results were unemployment, poverty and unprecedented misery for a wide sector of Chilean society. Some of the worst effects of military rule were felt in the poblaciones, the slums of the vast urban belt around Chile's capital Santiago. About two million people, half Santiago's population, live in the *poblaciones*. The changing fortunes of Chile's working classes and poor are reflected in the half-built concrete and brick structures, patched with corrugated iron and wooden planks, the semi-paved or dirt streets and the deteriorating schools and clinics. Vast areas of cardboard, wooden and metal makeshift shelters are tacked on to the borders of the *poblaciones*, where the poorest of Chile's poor live with no piped water, street lighting or sewerage facilities. During the first two years after the coup many of these *poblaciones* were occupied by the military in their attempts to search out union, political and neighbourhood leaders who formed the basis of support for the Allende government.

Forty minutes by bus from the centre of Santiago to the northern zone of the city, just off the main road, lies a *población* of 12,000 inhabitants where Luz María lives with her husband and four children.

Luz María: We were woken up by the sound of the tanks on the streets and the deafening noise of the helicopters which seemed like they were touching the roof of our house. On the radio they were saying that there was going to be a state of siege, and they were giving us instructions about what we had to do, that foreigners had to present themselves to the authorities to be sent home. Everything they said was full of threats. You could hear the bombs hitting La Moneda and I heard the president speaking on the radio. They were searching houses. The neighbours told me to buy food because the shops were going to be closed and to keep the children indoors and we all started dashing about in a panic. I didn't have any idea what a coup was — I don't think any of the women did. There'd never been one before. Then I heard that they were taking people to the stadium and I began to realise what it all meant.

My husband, like most of the men in this neighbourhood, worked in the local factory. He was a union militant. On the day of the coup the workers occupied the factory so the army wouldn't take it over and they began to burn all their records so that they couldn't find out the names of the militants. My husband was lucky because his brother stayed in the factory until the end and burnt his files. If he hadn't, my husband would have disappeared with the hundreds of others who were taken from the factory.

After the coup they closed the factory, changed its name and reopened it. They called some of the people back to work, including my husband and he went back not knowing what was going to happen to him. DINA (the secret police) used to go to the factory and take away workers and the next day their bodies were found in the river. DINA made the other workers pull out the corpses. My husband became more and more terrified but he had to go on working because we had the children to feed. The working class doesn't have the option of exile. He had to go on working, seeing that every day his workmates were disappearing.

They raided our house on 11 September 1974, the first anniversary of the coup. Every 11 September we relived the coup because they closed the streets and the army appeared in battle gear, with their faces painted, frightening the children. They came to my house at seven in the morning. In those years they just kicked open the door and walked straight in. I was getting dressed, I was pregnant with my little girl. I was alone with the children. My husband was working the night shift. They said they were from DINA and they wanted to know what the vehicle was that had been at my house on a certain day. Thank God I didn't have a nervous attack. I answered all the questions calmly while another man turned over the house. They looked everywhere — in the latrine, the well, they dug up the yard to see if there was anything buried. Others were asking the neighbours questions — what was my husband like, where were the weapons. They treated many people very badly, but they were OK with me and I was very polite with them. I told them that my husband was working and that if they wanted they could wait. Of course they were going to wait anyway. The area was full of vehicles as if they'd come to get hundreds of people. Then my husband arrived. I didn't know that people had gone to the bus stop to meet him. He had two choices — to go home or to run. Everyone told him not to go home, but he was brave enough to come home and they interrogated him. The DINA men said, 'Now it depends on the neighbours whether he stays alive or whether you become a widow'. The neighbours all tried to protect him, saying he was a very quiet man, a good neighbour, a good sportsman, things like that. They took a long time, I think it was an hour, but it seemed like a century and when they came back they said they had nothing against him and left.

Olga lives in the *población* of La Victoria, five blocks down from the main street in a narrow dirt road lined with one storey houses built of brick, sheets of corrugated iron and wooden boards. She is in her early sixties and has lived alone since the death of her husband, a former community leader, four years ago.

OLGA: I'd never seen anything like it in my life. In the first raid they took away all the men. At six in the morning, when it was still dark, we woke up with the noise of helicopters which sounded like they were landing on the houses. They were calling out over the loudspeakers that all the men between the ages of 18 and 60 had to go out onto the streets. When we went outside we saw that everything was surrounded by the military, lorries, police, tanks and soldiers. They led the men off to a nearby football stadium, hitting them with sticks. The women followed behind. The streets were full of women and we were all shouting 'murderers!'. They kept the men for days in the stadiums without food and some never came back. It went on for a week, the neighbourhood surrounded, police and army everywhere, the shooting. We couldn't go outside because they were firing bullets from the main road into the neighbourhood. They raided many houses, went through everything, did anything they wanted. They were looking for weapons, they said, and leaders.

They came to our house another two times for my husband. The first time I told them I didn't know where he was because he'd gone off with another woman and they left. The second time was in 1974 when they took me and my husband to a concentration camp. They came at 8.30 one evening, when we were asleep. They knocked at the door and my husband got up to see who it was. He was in his pyjamas and they took him like that. I was in bed and they came into the house and told me to get up. When I asked why, they swore at me. They said I had to get dressed in front of them. Then they blindfolded me so I didn't see anything but I think they were from the air force. They turned the whole house over, broke everything, threw out all the clothes and stole my glasses and all the money. It was Saturday and my husband had just been paid.

At first we were in a police station in Santiago and then they took us to Tejas Verdes which was a summer camp. All the holiday cabins were full of prisoners. They put me in a room where there were about forty other women, all asleep on big mattresses. They kept us all in the cabin and only took us out to go to the toilet or for interrogation. They took us for interrogation at seven in the morning, and brought us back at ten at night. When it was the men's turn you could hear them being tortured with the electricity — you could hear them screaming. They tortured them right in front of us. They tortured my husband. They tortured the women too. When they took a woman for interrogation we all said 'be brave' and she came back crying, in a terrible state. They put us in a tiny room, like a bathroom, full of damp papers and when they took us back at night we were all wet and frozen and beaten. We were all terrified.

They asked if I knew certain people, what I did, what my husband did, what the people in La Victoria did, why people visited my house so much. At that time I made skirts so I told them I was a dressmaker and that's why people came to my house. They accused me of being a communist so I said 'If you say I'm a communist, perhaps I am' and then they hit me. I let them hit me, what could I do? Then they said they wouldn't hit me again and they didn't.

I spent two months in that room. I remember there was an earth tremor and everything was shaking but they wouldn't let us out. We never gave anything away, we didn't say a word and they couldn't find anything against us so they let us go. We were lucky to get out alive. Very few people got out.

That the military subjected entire *poblaciones* to this kind of terror reflects the high degree of community organisation that had existed in Chile before the coup. Many of the *poblaciones* had begun as squatter camps at a time when Santiago's newly established industries offered the hope of employment to the country's rural poor. Chile's almost feudal agricultural system, by which a small landowning elite held vast areas of land known as *haciendas*, renting out plots to tenant farmers in return for their labour, survived well into the 20th century: Farming started to modernise only when the landowners' incomes began to fall with the onset of national industrialisation in the 1930s. The collapse in international prices during the world depression of 1929 and the fall in revenue from Chile's main export, copper, prompted a drive towards industrial development, with a series of governments offering protection and incentives to the production of national industrial goods. The slow shift towards commercial farming not only failed to halt the long-term decline in Chilean agriculture, but the break-up of some of the old estates left the tenant farmers with less land and few work opportunities. To the rural poor, the new factories springing up around Santiago offered an escape from landlessness and unemployment. Limited support from governments meant that most rural migrants were left to their own devices to build their homes and communities. Most built their homes themselves, as well as installing basic urban services such as piped water, sewerage, streets, pavements, electricity and rubbish collection. Almost all the social and neighbourhood organisations created to campaign for these basic necessities were linked to political parties and became targets when the military seized power.

Women, usually at home all day looking after the house and children, bore the brunt of the discomfort of poor living conditions and were active in campaigns to improve their homes and community services. Their community participation, however, tended to be restricted to the Church and to Mothers' Centres and they played only a secondary role in the more openly political organisations. The Mothers' Centres were set up in the *poblaciones* in the 1950s by the Church and charity groups. Their original purpose was to provide a place where women from the poor neighbourhoods could learn a craft and earn some extra family income without travelling long distances to work or being restricted to rigid working hours which interfered with their work in the home. Successive governments used the centres to promote their political programmes. Under President Allende, the Centres were recruited to support the government's social policies and to collaborate in health, housing and cultural campaigns. By 1973 some 30,000 centres existed throughout the country.

The Mothers' Centres did little to prepare women for participation in the world of work and politics, worlds from which Chilean women in general and *pobladoras* in particular, had been excluded. Chilean women were less likely than their Argentine or Uruguayan counterparts to work outside the home or enter higher education. Few women figured in leadership positions in political, union and community organisations. None of the political parties, the left included, dealt with issues of women's rights or discrimination. Instead they saw women as mothers and housewives and tried to capture their votes with policies centred on their concerns for housing, and the education and health of their children.

In a typical family in the *poblaciones*, the man was the breadwinner and the meaning of life for a woman was closely linked to her role as a mother. Women were expected to stay with the children and the lack of childcare facilities and work opportunities made it even harder for them to participate in the world outside their homes.

LUZ MARIA: This *población* started in 1969 when a government housing foundation bought and divided up the land. The men came in tents to guard the lots and the factory gave us loans to build a wooden one-roomed house. In the beginning we didn't have bathrooms or kitchens. Lorries brought the water once or twice a week and there was emergency lighting in the street and we used to connect cables to the street lights to get electricity. The streets weren't paved then, and when it rained the mud came up to our knees. We had to go out without shoes, leaning on sticks or the fences of the houses. When the men went to work they went barefoot with their shoes in their hands and their trousers rolled up to their knees.

There were plenty of jobs then. Most of the men in the neighbourhood worked in the textile factory. The women spent their lives searching for the essentials: queueing for water and food, travelling a long way to hospitals when they were pregnant or to take the children when they were ill. Neighbourhood committees were formed to campaign for a health centre, a school, telephones, a chapel. We occupied buildings, organised protests, demonstrated at the council offices — we didn't get anything without a fight. A man donated some wood and we built a sports club and organised lots of activities — artistic things, films, slide-shows and dances. It was a hard life but in those years there was a lot of enthusiasm. No one was afraid. There was a lot of solidarity. When you were queueing for the water, you talked and got to know everyone.

The truth is that at that time I was a 'lady' who didn't understand big things. I used to go to a Mothers' Centre which they set up in the sports club. In retrospect I don't think the Mothers' Centres were much good

— I realise now they weren't educational, as they should have been. They only taught skills like sewing and knitting; nothing to prepare women for work or for participating in organisations. The Mothers' Clubs weren't 'political' so I was never in any danger. I didn't understand anything. When my husband came home late on Saturdays and Sundays after his union meetings I used to complain. I couldn't understand why the meetings went on so long and he used to say they were preparing in case there was a coup and that they had to organise so as not to be taken unawares. But people weren't prepared for the coup, not socially or politically. The community organisations just fought for the basic things. We were all happy and full of enthusiasm and the coup came as a terrible shock. It's only now I ask myself why there was no political preparation. The women could have done more. We couldn't do anything because we didn't understand anything.

OLGA: La Victoria began as a land seizure in October 1957. I came here the first night from La Legua where we were members of a homeless committee. We were *allegados*, lodging in other people's houses. People from homeless committees from all different areas arrived at the same time. I came alone. My husband didn't want to come because he had work in a factory. I told him, 'you can stay if you want, but when I get a house I'm not going to let you live there!' It was a plot of agricultural land and we all brought warm clothes and two poles and a flag. We made up our tents with the flags so at least if they came to evict us they would have to respect the flag. They never tried to kick us out. My husband came later and we built the house. Everyone built their own houses as best they could. There was no water, electricity, nothing. At first we got the water from a nearby *población* and then the council sent lorries and we had to queue at five in the morning with our buckets. We had to fight for everything. This has always been a very organised community. There were many neighbourhood organisations, homeless committees and many good leaders. The women helped too, but women were always too busy with their children and homes to take a big part in the organisations.

The coup had a devastating effect on the lives of the men and women of the *poblaciones*. The massive searches and arrests left entire communities paralysed by fear. The closure of community organisations, including the Mothers' Centres, the imprisonment of community, political and union leaders and the replacement of elected representatives in local councils by military supporters left the pobladores with no political leadership and no voice in the political system. The principal victims of the concentration camps, torture, disappearances, executions and imprisonment were manual workers, mostly men, in part because women had always played what were considered marginal or secondary roles in the targetted organisations. Men were also the main victims of the wave of unemployment which spread through Santiago's industrial centres. Union activists were the first to be sacked but as the 'shock' austerity measures took effect and the opening of the Chilean market to foreign goods squeezed national industry, unemployment became a more widespread problem. The numbers out of work doubled in the first year of military rule and by 1977 the national unemployment rate stood at an estimated 18 per cent; in the *poblaciones*, where the majority of Santiago's industrial workers lived, the rates were much higher than the national average. The 'shock' policies caused a drastic deterioration in the living conditions of the *pobladores*.

While the persecution of unions, political parties and neighbourhood organisations cut the traditional lines of communication between the poor and the state, it failed to break the bonds of solidarity that had existed before the coup. Small, clandestine self-help groups began to appear to deal with the immediate problems of unemployment, poverty and terror which were affecting the *poblaciones*. From the beginning these organisations found support in the Church. Strongly influenced by the new 'liberation theology', which placed an emphasis on promoting social equality and democracy, the Church formed the Vicariate of Solidarity to provide humanitarian support for the victims of poverty and violence. As well as offering protection to the new organisations, local churches helped set up children's canteens, unemployed committees, income-generating workshops and health groups.

Women played the key role in building the first networks of mutual support. Women whose husbands or sons had been murdered or tortured or imprisoned were the first to organise solidarity groups for political prisoners and to publicly condemn the human rights abuses committed by the military regime. Women like Luz María, who had experienced first hand the brutality of the coup, were among the first to respond to the Church's community initiatives. Their minor role in pre-coup political organisations gave them a public 'invisibility' which allowed them to organise without drawing attention to themselves. Women had also traditionally worked with the Church in welfare and humanitarian projects. Flora lives in a *población* in the northern zone of Santiago.

FLORA: I think what helped us a lot was that we had been militants in a Catholic movement for a long time. We had this image of doing church work and so it didn't look suspicious when we got together to talk. We formed the job-training workshop at a meeting in the church. The priest had no idea what we were doing but he knew us and our work with the

church so when I asked him for a place to meet he didn't ask why. We
met there four times to organise the department and then we had to ask
for a bigger room because so many people wanted to come and I had to
explain what we were doing. He almost went running out in a panic,
'why didn't you tell me?, the bishop has to OK this, I can't commit
myself'. Everything was illegal so it was very difficult organising. There
were unionists and people from political parties involved and we had
to do it all secretly, looking both ways as we left the building as there
were spies all over the place.

LUZ MARIA: Committees of unemployed people began to meet through
the Church and they began to give out information about work — if
there was any building work it was shared around. They also analysed
what was happening in Chile. The chapel began to organise communal
canteens for the children and built an oven where they made bread.
Women worked in the canteens, making bread and preparing food and
the men from the unemployed committee worked on the allotments, on
some land that the church owned, and grew vegetables for the children's
dinners.

The priests wanted volunteers to do something for the people who
needed medical treatment. In my youth I'd worked in a hospital and I
knew how to give injections, remove stitches, and other basic nursing
skills. For the first time I began to get involved in the community and I
was very enthusiastic about it. I'm a Catholic but I'd never taken part
in church activities before. In the south the church was so big and the
mass was said in Latin and we looked up at the priest reading his lesson
and he seemed so remote from ordinary people. The new Church which
grew up during the dictatorship was different and something I
understood. At that time the priests were Canadian and they visited
people's houses, they went out to the community on their bicycles, they
helped to make bread in the chapel and to get the food for the children's
canteens. I was born again. I liked singing so I was the one who started
off the singing at mass and after so many years of not reading — women
go to school and then never read again — I began to read biblical texts
in the church and I learnt to read aloud and to speak in public.

There was nowhere for many of the people who needed medical
treatment to go. There was what they called a a rural health post, but
there were many families of disappeared people who were terrified,
people wounded or in hiding, too terrified to go to a public place where
they took your details and asked you questions. They went to the Church
for help. The Catholic and evangelical Churches set up health posts. It
was an attempt to rescue those who were traumatised, those who stayed
inside their houses alone and afraid. There were many men in this
condition. The Church asked for trustworthy people from the

community to refer patients to these health posts. I volunteered and referred people from my community. You had to search them out, ask priest for help when they had no money for the bus, and follow up their cases.

We were mainly women in the health groups and we learnt a lot from them. We had meetings where we analysed the concept of health and what was happening to the health system in Chile under the military government. It was there we began to learn about the struggle of the workers to win what we'd got and how everything was being lost by the day.

Many thought that the new organisations would be temporary, emergency measures and that Chile's economic and political situation would soon return to normality. In 1977 the beginning of Chile's 'economic boom' seemed to confirm this. An enormous inflow of foreign loans and investments signalled the international banking community's approval of the military's economic programme, economic growth rates improved, unemployment fell and real wages began to rise. With unions and community organisations destroyed and their leaders in prison, the regime set about consolidating their political control over the population. New trade union laws were introduced, designed to render the old union organisations ineffective and to formalise the erosion of worker's rights. Some neighbourhood organisations were re-organised under military supervision. Mothers' Centres, for example, were put under the control of General Pinochet's wife and used to promote the military's vision of women as defenders of the family and the nation. All traces of their former social and campaigning roles were removed. Problems of 'extreme poverty' were left to private charitable organisations and to two government employment schemes, the Minimum Employment Programme (PEM) and the Work Programme for Heads of Households (POJH) which paid unemployed men and women $14 and $23 a month respectively for community work, well below what was needed to feed a family.

The benefits of the 'boom' for the poor, however, were limited and ended abruptly with the beginning of the international recession in 1981. By 1983 a third of the labour force was out of work and in some *poblaciones* unemployment was as high as eighty per cent. In the same year it was estimated that thirty per cent of all Chilean families lived in 'extreme' poverty, that is, they depended on income which if spent solely on food would be inadequate to obtain the necessary nutrients and calories to sustain life. In 1982 over one third of the population had no adequate place to live, with as many as a quarter of a million families living as *allegados*, sharing rooms in houses. Poverty, hopelessness and despair struck the neighbourhoods and particularly the men.

LUZ MARIA: With each year that passed the economic situation got worse. The most serious problem was unemployment. The factory closed down and nearly all the men who lived here were left without work. Before, you could always get odd jobs in private houses, cleaning windows or gardening, but in the early 1980s there was nothing. We were all in debt. Many of us had had our electricity cut off and we were connecting to the street lights. This meant you kept your door locked all the time and lived in fear of the electricity man. The neighbourhood development had stopped. The ownership of the land passed to a government agency and they made it clear there would be no more improvements. People lost hope, about getting a job, about having a decent house, about the future.

Instead of improving things, PEM made everything worse. Men who were used to working got a small amount of money every fifteen days for going out to the streets and repairing roads, digging gardens where they weren't needed, covering holes in the main roads and they were sent to the hills to plant trees, stupid things that weren't productive. Women worked for PEM too.

Margarita is a single mother from a *población* in the northern zone of Santiago.

MARGARITA: Women used to leave their babies under the trees and work with the men. We went backwards and forwards with wheelbarrows all day. It was never very clear what we were supposed to be doing. The men began to lose the habit of working and began to buy alcohol. Many men bought wine or beer as soon as they received their money and the alcoholism began. It never used to be as bad before. The government programmes were degrading but we had no choice. I think the government programmes had a tremendous crushing effect on the community.

LUZ MARIA: We felt helpless. There was nowhere we could go for help. I remember one year there were terrible floods in the neighbourhood and many people were left homeless. We went to the Church for help, but then we realised that it wasn't the Church's responsibility and we went to a lawyer with the the the idea of opening the neighbourhood committee building to use as a temporary shelter. The neighbourhood committee had been closed down by the military and the building was locked up. The lawyer came to the church to speak to us and after the meeting we decided to break into the committee building. The following Monday I went with some others to the council to try to get authorisation for the building to be used as a shelter for those made homeless by the floods. When I got back I found my house burnt out. Everything inside was destroyed. We never found out exactly who did it, but that's the kind of thing that happened to you if you tried to do anything.

It was the floods that made us realise the conditions in which the community was living. Some of the roofs of the houses fell in with the rain, and people couldn't hide their poverty any more. You could see that people had no beds, no furniture, that they'd had to sell everything to survive and that many families were living together in two or three rooms.

Normal family life in the *poblaciones* broke down with the strain of the economic crisis. Many women described how their husbands were unable to cope with long-term unemployment and the collapse of their traditional role as the provider. Children were forced to leave school to help support the family, alcoholism and domestic violence increased, families broke up and drug addiction became a problem among the young. In conditions of severe economic hardship, issues which had typically been the responsibility of women — education, children's health and feeding the family, suddenly took on vital importance in the community. Survival had become the main issue for millions of families and it was women, often burdened by demoralised, chronically unemployed husbands, who looked for ways to bridge the gap between the basic needs of their families and their limited resources. Many were forced to find work outside the home as cleaners, street vendors or beggars. They had to spend extra hours in the search for cheap food, on mending and making clothes at home instead of buying them and on caring for the sick and old instead of using expensive medical services.

For many families the individual efforts of women to eke out their resources were no longer enough to guarantee even the most basic family needs, forcing them to devise new, communal strategies in the battle against poverty. They were the driving force behind some 500 'popular economic organisations' which sprang up in the poor districts of Santiago by 1982. The *olla común* was one example of these organisations. Literally meaning 'common saucepan', the *ollas* were not charitable activities like soup kitchens, but communal kitchens, run by the women themselves for the benefit of their own families. Women moved one of the most fundamental of their family responsibilities, the buying, preparing and serving of food, out to the community.

LUZ MARIA: The Church helped us set up the communal kitchens. It donated basic things like beans, oil and flour and we had to find the rest begging in the markets, in shops or through someone who knew someone who sold fish and threw away the heads, things like that. It was always what was left over, what wasn't wanted, which went to the kitchens. Sometimes they gave us sacks of rotten apples and we would cut out the bad parts and salvage maybe a third to give to the children. At the markets no one gave willingly. They got fed up in the end because it wasn't only the kitchens that were asking for food but also groups of unemployed people and individuals. People queued to beg. In the kitchen, we used to take turns, some would cook and the others would go out to beg. We only cooked lunch and what we cooked depended on the luck of the collection. In the end we had about 150 families eating from the kitchen.

Sara lives in Pudahuel, a working class district of 340,000 inhabitants in the western zone of Santiago. She helped set up one of Santiago's first communal kitchens.

SARA: In 1981 I belonged to a women's group connected to the Church. At that time a lot of us were in debt and had our electricity cut off, so we decided we'd go round asking questions to find out the extent of the problems in the *población*. It was only then we saw the hunger. In one of the houses the woman told me that her husband wanted to kill himself because there was nothing to eat. The day we went they had no food at all in the house. So a few of us, members of the Christian community, decided that giving her food would solve nothing because the next day she'd still have the same problems, so we decided to form a communal kitchen. It was difficult to set up because it was one of the first kitchens and the only support we had was from some of the unions. No one wanted to give us a place to cook, they were afraid, or they worried about the rubbish it would make, but the economic problems were so great that when it began they supported it. In the end we had 300 families eating from the kitchen.

Women set up kitchens primarily to feed their families, but in many kitchens, such as the one set up by Olga and other women in La Victoria, they were also seen as a way of publicly condemning the hardship which the *pobladores* were suffering.

OLGA: There were tremendous economic problems because so many people were unemployed. They closed the factories, there was no building work and there were many redundancies. We formed committees of unemployed people to do something about it but we realised that you can't fight when you're hungry, so in 1981 we set up a kitchen. In the beginning it was in the street and the people came to collect the food and took it home to eat it. We never had a canteen. Everybody came with their tin cans — we didn't have saucepans, we'd already sold them. Over the years many people in La Victoria had managed to buy chairs, settees, tables, electric ovens, televisions and so on, but in the crisis we had to sell everything, even the saucepans. So they brought their tins and if there were five people in the family we'd put five big spoonfuls in.

There were more than 200 families involved. People felt ashamed. We were poor but we still had our dignity. They used to cover the tin with something so other people wouldn't see it was food from the kitchen. Then at a meeting we decided this wasn't the point. You should never hide your hunger behind shame. If you're hungry you must do what you have to do. The kitchen had to be visible because it was a form of protest, to show there was hunger in our country, that in our neighbourhood people were unemployed and hungry.

In the beginning we each brought what food we could and we asked for donations from the local shops. Then we went everywhere begging, in the community, in the markets. One day we decided to go to the army barracks. We took pots and tin cans and a letter. I explained that we were from a communal kitchen and that we had a lot of unemployed people and the children were hungry. We asked for paraffin for the fires, blankets and food and clothes for the children. We wanted to go inside to speak to them but they wouldn't let me or any of the other leaders in. They picked out five women and gave them lunch and five pairs of tiny trousers for the children.

The Church helped and — you know that La Victoria became famous all over the world — journalists began to come to see the kitchen. They began to make contacts with Chilean exiles abroad and the exiles raised money for us. We kept the kitchen going with this money. When we had money we would go to the market to buy 200 kilos of pasta and beans to last us two months. It was all very well organised. There were five women in the kitchen leadership. The men helped too. They washed the vegetables and helped with the cooking and sometimes, if the woman had found a job outside, the man came to collect the food, but it was mainly women who did the work.

The kitchen never stopped. During all the protests and the repression we kept the kitchen open.

In May 1983 massive protests broke out on the streets of Santiago as thousands of demonstrators from all sectors of Chilean society defied the authorities and responded to a trade union call for public resistance to military rule. As the protests spread and political parties began to reorganise and take up their positions at the head of the opposition movement, the regime declared a state of siege. It was followed by yet another clampdown in the *poblaciones*.

In the beginning most of the women involved in the kitchens did not consider their activities as political. For the majority of *pobladoras*, politics was what the trade unions and political parties did and by definition, what men did. Organisations such as homeless committees, which carried out more militant actions such as land seizures, or unemployed groups and debtors' clubs which dealt directly with the authorities in attempts to renegotiate rent and public services arrears, were seen as more political and men dominated these organisations, particularly in the leadership. Many women shied away from anything that might be construed as 'political' activity, most explaining their participation in the kitchens as an extension of their domestic work and the need to feed and care for their families.

For the military authorities however, this idea of good mothers and wives was not what they had in mind when they eulogised motherhood and the role of women in the family. Their political programme required the destruction of all organisations outside their control and the simple act of women searching together for solutions to their problems was seen as an act of open defiance. Communal cooking and eating became subversive activities and whatever their original intentions, women found themselves at the centre of the resistance to military rule.

LUZ MARIA: In the beginning we cooked on the patio of the church. People came to collect the food to take to their houses but always with this terrible fear, with their food hidden under their clothes. But it wasn't until we organised the kitchens away from the church that they were raided by the police. Women put tables in their yards and families went to eat there. The kitchen was being watched. Suddenly the police would arrive and kick people about, destroy all the food stores and arrest everyone. Children used to come home from school crying, saying that their friends had said, 'you're in the kitchen and it's against the law'. Some children wouldn't go to the kitchen. Sometimes the neighbours got angry or frightened and told the authorities if there was a kitchen next door. According to the military the people who worked in the kitchens were communists.

SARA: Two years after we set up the kitchen the protests began. As a kitchen we were already known to the police — with 300 people involved it was difficult to hide what was going on. They came and turned the food stores upside down, they made us stop cooking and took all the leaders prisoner. Twenty nine people were detained and some were held for five months. I was detained for seven days. They came many times but we never stopped cooking. People came and went but the kitchen went on.

OLGA: The police came: 'What's going on here?' 'A communal kitchen' 'So why are you doing it if you know it's prohibited?' 'Because we're hungry and the children are hungry' 'Stop the cooking!'. They said it was political. The beans were half-cooked and we had to throw them all away. They walked around and kicked over our collections of food and money. Lots of people from the community began to arrive and went to tell my husband that the police were going to arrest me. They told us to put out the fires and people came with water and threw it hard at the fire so that all the smoke and ashes came up and went all over the police. It was funny, but it was frightening too, because they arrested all the men. My husband came with all the men and the police took them all, all the committee leaders. In the police station they looked in their computers and found that my husband had been detained. Then the next morning he appeared on television! They said he was a terrorist, that he'd been to the Soviet Union and Cuba and that he was a communist militant, paid to spread communist ideology in Chile and to teach people how to seize lands and how to organise communal kitchens. It was all lies. My husband had never been anywhere. He was just a leader in the unemployed committee. They kept the men incommunicado and every day the women went to the police station to ask for them to make sure they were freed and didn't disappear. They released them after five days.

The police came many times but we always managed to keep the kitchen going, one week in one house, the next week in another.

While most of the women involved in the kitchens saw them as a part of their responsibilities as mothers and wives, it was not simply a case of women doing the same work in a different place. Moving an important part of their domestic work to the community not only brought them closer to the world of politics but also became a focus for self-education. Planning fund-raising raffles, food collections and menus, distributing shifts and responsibilities, meant that many women with no previous experience of community activities learnt about organisation, administration and decision-making. The success of the kitchens in providing thousands of families with what was often their main or only meal of the day made women realise they could do more than look after the house and the children.

Women's new-found self confidence combined with a growing awareness of the common problems that women faced in their daily lives. The kitchens were also a place where women could make friends and share their concerns. Issues once considered to belong to the private world of the family, such as domestic violence, were openly discussed. The struggle to keep the kitchens going was often matched by a battle inside the home, as many women had to learn to deal with husbands who objected to their wives spending long periods outside the house. The kitchens in themselves did not challenge the traditional family roles of men and women. Men participated little and the extent of women's involvement was still determined by other family responsibilities. They were, however, often the first step towards questioning the basis of the roles of 'male provider' and 'female housewife'.

OLGA: There were up to ten women cooking at any one time. There were women who'd never taken part in anything in the community before and they all loved it. They met other women and talked about their problems at home, they made new friends and women who'd spent years inside their houses got to know the community for the first time.

We also had regular meetings involving about fifty women, where we talked about the problems in Chile and about women's rights. There were women who arrived with black eyes, who'd lived with violence for a long time and who believed that you had to live all your life with a man however he treated you. I used to read a lot and I read a book once on women's rights which said you're not a slave or a piece of furniture. I'd tell the other women that it was our right to liberate ourselves from men and that we're not just here to sit in a chair and sew or look after the children, which is what the men want us to do. They used to laugh at me and say 'what are you teaching us!'

SARA: Women are so worn out by housework and bringing up children that they don't have time for anything else; they feel isolated and alone. In the kitchens they begin to talk about their problems, while cooking, while they go out begging for food and everyone gets to know everyone else. They develop friendships and don't feel alone any more. Women talk to each other while they're cooking. If one has a black eye, they talk with other women and they begin to find the confidence to deal with their situation. Some men don't let their wives out of the house to work with us but we say to them, can your husband feed you? The husband problem is a battle you win along the way. If their wives find work some men look after the children or they come to the kitchen to help out with the cooking, but they're the minority.

LUZ MARIA: A lot of men felt ashamed and stayed at home waiting for the women to bring them something. Women used to come and say, 'He's at home in bed, he doesn't want me to come to the kitchen, but if I don't come what are we going to eat?' Many didn't like the idea that their wife wasn't cooking the food just for them. There were big fights. It was good for women because they began to learn to stand up for themselves.

There were other problems too. When we went out to ask for food the young girls always did better than the women, the shopkeepers filled their bags. When we asked them why, they said they had to put up with a lot of dirty comments, even with the shopkeepers asking them to sleep with them. The food we were eating tasted bitter after that.

The kitchens were not immune from leadership conflicts and problems over the distribution of work and management of money and resources. Solidarity and co-operation did not come automatically. At a time when the very survival of many families was at stake, those in control of food supplies were in a position of considerable power within their organisations and communities. Deprivation and insecurity in the population was the root of many of the problems. The extreme poverty that many women faced meant that they were not always able to contribute actively to the work of the kitchens. The clandestine nature of the kitchens made difficulties. These conflicts led some women to question the organisational value of the kitchens, both as a form of resistance to military rule and in terms of their educational value for women.

> OLGA: We used to take turns with the cooking, but then the women who spent more time there began to take it over as if it belonged to them. They got selfish with the kitchen and criticised the work of the others. They'd leave the problems to me. They weren't able to sort out problems and I used to say, you have to learn. Sometimes journalists would come and the women would come looking for me and if I wasn't here they'd send the journalists away. I said they had to learn to speak to people, they couldn't leave everything to me, but they never found the confidence to deal with these situations.

> LUZ MARIA: We were always very clear that the objective of the kitchens was to condemn hunger and educate people as well as to feed ourselves. There were lots of arguments over the food or because people got food without helping — 'I saw you buying a drink and if you can buy drink why can't you buy a plate of food?' Some people treated it like a restaurant, they went in, ate and then left. Very few participated in the work and many people became dependent on them. Some didn't help because some were too afraid and others apologised saying they couldn't for some reason or other. We tried to organise a weekly educational meeting on health or human rights and asked that everyone who used the kitchen participate in community organisations like the health groups and the unemployed committees but there wasn't much response.
>
> Things like this meant that the kitchens didn't last long in our neighbourhood. We were one of the first neighbourhoods to close the kitchens. We'd discovered that apart from a plate of food, there were many other things we needed, education, self-esteem and to organise in a more dignified way. If the kitchens didn't work on the organisational level, it was just begging and we didn't see it as dignified.

The role the kitchens should take in the resistance movement and their relationship with political parties was a constant source of tension in the organisations. While the kitchens identified with the resistance movement, for some it conflicted with the need to solve the urgent economic problems of the community. Sylvia worked in a kitchen in the northern zone of Santiago.

> SYLVIA: The kitchens were a response to hunger, but many leaders didn't have an awareness of why there was hunger. In the end it worked in the dictatorship's favour. Instead of going out to the streets to protest, we were all in the church cooking. Many were dependent on the Church, they were isolated and didn't work with other community organisations. There were some very combative ones, like La Victoria and Pudahuel but many others that weren't interested in protesting against the government, or demanding a decent salary. The greater the repression was, the harder it was to develop the educational part of the organisation. If you're hungry that's the most important thing. In some kitchens there were a lot conflicts and it did a lot of damage.

One characteristic of the new economic organisations was their transience, but as some groups disintegrated others evolved to take their place. Some 1,100 organisations existed by 1985 and an estimated twenty per cent of the population in the poor areas of Santiago belonged to one.

As the women became more experienced, they ironed out many of the initial problems in the kitchens. Some adopted more formal procedures, defining more clearly the responsibilities of those involved, establishing rules and regular meetings and formalising democratic procedures. They began to strengthen their independence from political parties and develop closer links with other community organisations. Efforts were made to co-ordinate the huge variety of educational, social, cultural and economic activities of the slum dwellers. Many kitchens began to combine cooking with educational workshops and training courses on social and political issues.

In Sara's district of Pudahuel the kitchen played an important role in attempts to build a united local movement which culminated in the first district-wide strike in 1984. In 1986, after the military regime had begun talks with selected members of right-wing parties, it played a key part in the establishment of a central co-ordinating committee, known as the Command, for all Santiago's kitchens. The Command joined over two hundred grassroots organisations, trade unions and political parties in the Civil Assembly (*Asamblea de la Civilidad*) which organised a two-day national strike in 1986.

SARA: We set up the Command when some leaders of the political parties began talking to the government. It became clear that no one was going to listen to us unless we built a strong united movement. We were all working separately, dispersed all around Santiago. We began to meet with the leaders of other kitchens to set up an organisation that was independent of the political parties.

The objectives aren't confined to eating. Many of the kitchens have begun to organise skills workshops on bread-making, allotments, sewing and knitting. Three or four people are trained who will then pass on that knowledge to the others. Many of the kitchens have also developed educational groups on social and political issues and women's rights. The workshops are designed mainly for women, but men also go, though not in great numbers. We're not only interested in women or in segregating them from men. Some co-ordinators don't want anything to do with men. We respect their decision. Each organisation is autonomous and decides its own rules, but in general we believe women should work alongside men.

In organisations like the Command, educational programmes were primarily designed to encourage women's participation in the opposition movement to military rule. At the same time other groups began to focus on their concerns as women within the opposition. The proportion of organisations composed only of men had fallen sharply and women-only organisations in the *poblaciones* had increased by 1985. Many of these were new and increasingly creative collective efforts by women to find ways of feeding their families, but many also began to combine practical activities with consciousness-raising groups, where issues more specifically related to women, such as childcare, health and sexuality were discussed. They developed links with women's federations which had formed to organise women against the dictatorship and around human rights issues, several of which were influenced by feminist thinking. One of these organisations was MOMUPO, the Movement of Women *Pobladoras*, formed by women from the *poblaciones* to co-ordinate all-women groups.

María first began to take part in her community when the Church set up children's canteens. She worked in a communal kitchen and a women's craft workshop, all supported by the Church. Together with some women from her neighbourhood she also set up a shopping collective.

MARIA: Things got so difficult that it became impossible for some of us to buy a whole bottle of cooking oil or a whole packet of flour, so a group of nine of us got together and formed a shopping collective. The idea was to buy our food together so we could get it at cheaper prices from the wholesalers. We weren't sure how to go about it but we got a contribution from MOMUPO and we began to work it out. We each contribute something and every month we go to buy basic things like flour, pasta, sugar, soap, then we share it out amongst the members. We've been doing this for five years. We began with $20 and now we've got a fund of more than $90. Then we set up another fund by organising raffles and used it to buy presents like saucepans once a year or on birthdays for all the members. We also went to training workshops to learn how to organise ourselves better and to learn about women's rights and health.

When Teresa's communal kitchen closed down she began to attend a church-run sewing workshop.

TERESA: The Church gave a prize to a group of women for their work in our neighbourhood. The prize was the funds for a teacher to come to teach us how to make *arpilleras*. So instead of the kitchen we began to organise sewing workshops.

The *arpilleras* were an education for us and they also helped us to earn money, because the Church bought two or three *arpilleras* a month from each woman to sell in the Vicariate (the Vicariate of Solidarity was set up by the Church in Santiago to provide humanitarian support for the victims of poverty and violence). You collect the scraps of material that are thrown away by workshops and people who make clothes and give them a new life by making an appliqué and little dolls which you stitch on. Each *arpillera* gives a message without words about the life of a neighbourhood. When you learn to make one, the first thing you do is take some paper and a pencil and do a drawing about your life, things like little houses, women in the yard washing clothes and hanging them out, people connecting to the electricity cables. Then you begin to talk about what you've drawn. For example, one woman says, 'I did this because they cut my electricity and I have to connect to the cables', and the other women hear and realise they're not alone with their problems. Someone else does a hospital with long queues and says 'I did this because I had to get up at five in the morning and I waited until midday, when they told us there was no doctor available', and then there's a discussion — why are there no doctors? Do you think it's the same for rich people?, and so on. That's why I say the *arpillera* has a profound educational content. As you get more involved you begin to show what's happened to community life, the communal kitchen, people waiting in queues for doctors, so as well as communicating, you're condemning the situation. Always at the back of the *arpillera* is a little pocket with a written message by the person who made it. As the years went by we specialised in *arpilleras*, making such good ones that our *arpilleras* became famous.

The church had so many groups and it stretched itself so thin that sometimes there were no rooms for us to work in. Sometimes we worked on the church patio or went to someone's house, but always with everything very well hidden. When they raided us the first thing we did was parcel up and bury the *arpillera* under the earth because anyone who made an *arpillera* was considered a revolutionary. Before the Church was involved, the families of the disappeared sent a parcel of *arpilleras* abroad to be sold and the packet was opened and reported to the police. They were shown on television like the most terrible crime, because they exposed the hunger in Chile to foreign countries by showing the communal kitchens and the children's canteens. So from then on the *arpillera* was considered subversive and we made them in fear.

As the years went by, the church became too small and there were difficulties working there. The bad thing was that the church taught 15 women and only these women benefited from the income and they never allowed in new people. I didn't agree with that because I thought everyone should have the chance to learn. I didn't care if I lost out on the money from the Vicariate, I was determined to teach other women. The priests understood and they helped me find a sales outlet in the US.

Many of the organisations outgrew the Church, both in the numbers that could be accommodated on church premises and in their aspirations. The Church encouraged women to participate in the public life of their communities by appealing to their caring natures and their traditional devotion to their families. The point, even for the most progressive sectors of the Church, had not been to 'politicise' women or to question their roles in the family. As women began to take a more active part in the resistance movement, the Church began to distance itself from their organisations.

In 1986, after the general strike and an assassination attempt on Pinochet, the regime imposed another state of siege in an attempt to crush protests in the *poblaciones*. Massive military operations were carried out in the slum areas of Santiago as troops in full combat gear, supported by helicopters and armoured vehicles, fought against protesters armed with stones and home-made weapons.

SUSANA: During the strikes we didn't send the children to school or go out shopping and at night we would bang the saucepans for an hour. You could hear the saucepans banging all over the neighbourhoods and one hour later they would all stop together. It was our way of protesting. In some places the young people made molotovs and barricaded the streets with burning tyres or wood to defend the neighbourhoods against the police. We made the *miguelitos* at home. These were pieces of metal, like nails which were twisted in such a way that when you threw them on the streets there was always a sharp point facing upwards. You threw them at the army trucks and whichever way they landed the tyres would burst.

Luz Maria: During the protests the health groups needed somewhere to treat the youngsters who were shot in the protests, or those who were burnt. When a protest was organised they burnt tyres with all the rubbish in the streets to make a barricade, to close off the streets to the police so they couldn't get in to the neighbourhoods. Sometimes the police arrived shooting and throwing bombs and made the young people put out the fires with their bare feet or their bare bottoms. There were many people wounded by shrapnel. Of course these people couldn't go to the church health post because they'd have had to explain where they'd been. I remember a very big protest, in 1989, one of the last against the dictatorship, when the church didn't let us inside to use the medical supplies and we began to see that we needed a place of our own.

The Church was also being attacked. It was afraid that if they treated the wounded protesters, people would think they were getting too involved in politics. And perhaps we needed to be more independent of the Church, even though it made things more difficult for us. It gave us the chance to organise, grow and develop our potential and we always looked on it as a refuge. It was thanks to the Church we could organise, but there were limits.

In some areas, such as the southern zone of Santiago, the Church opposed programmes specifically designed for women.

Claudia: The church had set up a communal kitchen to give breakfast to the children of a shanty town in the area and the workshops developed out of this. The priest gave a piece of land to the community and they built a big shed where they had courses on sewing and cooking and helped us to sell what we made. But there were limits to the number of people who could go there and it became more difficult to sell what we were making. Women got more interested in educational workshops, where we analysed the situation in Chile. With the triumph of the 'No' in Chile in October 1988 the church wanted these workshops to become more craft-based because it didn't want to be involved in politics. We had to break away to be able to continue.

After the defeat of the military regime in the plebiscite of October 1988, through which Pinochet had sought to maintain himself in power for another ten years, the military regime lost all claims to legitimacy and the way was opened for the transition to constitutional rule. The negotiations that followed were almost exclusively a military-political party affair and the new organisations had little say about the terms of the transition. The aim of the military was to retain the greatest possible political influence over the future government and to a significant degree, it succeeded. When President Aylwin, leader of the Christian Democrats, took power in March 1990, the transition to democracy was far from complete. Important social institutions remained in the hands of supporters of General Pinochet, including the judiciary, the educational system, local councils and most significantly, the armed forces. Pinochet remains Commander in Chief, and the labyrinth of legal instruments he enacted to block any attempt to bring his men to trial, including an amnesty for all crimes committed between 1973-78, means the President has only the feeblest authority over the armed forces and the police.

Unlike other countries of the Southern Cone, Chile's new government did not face the kind of acute economic crisis which made emergency economic programmes necessary. During the late 1980s economic conditions had been slowly improving and unemployment was beginning to fall. Despite an increased budget for social welfare programmes and local and national policies for dealing with poverty, the civilian government has made no significant break with the economic policies of the military regime. The persistence of poverty and the need for 'social democracy' — equal opportunities and wider social participation — are the explanations given by those involved for the continued existence of the popular economic organisations. The organisations continue to grow, doubling every two years and have spread from the metropolitan zone of Santiago to all regions of the country.

The changing circumstances have presented new challenges. Foreign aid is now being channelled through government agencies rather than directly to the organisations, forcing them to become more self-sufficient. Some groups complain that high expectations of the new government have caused apathy among their members.

When President Aylwin took power in March 1990 the communal kitchen in La Victoria closed.

OLGA: It wasn't just because we lost financial support from the Church and from the exiles who had returned to Chile, we'd always said that when we had a bit of democracy we'd have to fight the battle for work for men and women.

Olga, together with other members of the kitchen, has set up a self-employment project for pensioners, 'Old people can't afford to eat properly or buy the medicines they need, so we set up knitting workshops, dressmaking classes and craft courses, and now we're organising a library. About 150 men and women come, but mainly women. The men still haven't got much initiative.'

The number of communal kitchens still continues to grow. The Communal Kitchen Command now co-ordinates 700 kitchens with a total of some 80,000 members. At their first national congress, held in June 1990, five women and two men were elected as the national co-ordinating team. Sara was elected president.

> SARA: The government accepts the kitchens because they recognise the persecution we suffered during the dictatorship and our role in the struggle for democracy, so they can't turn round and say 'no more kitchens'. Due to a lack of funding we can't let any more kitchens into the organisation. The Europeans think that because we've got an elected government we're all eating well, but it isn't true. There are still lay-offs, there's still hunger and repression, although it's not so visible. We can't do away with the kitchens today or in the foreseeable future. We've received help from the Dutch government and now we're trying to get the Chilean government to contribute. We're trying to build up our independence and find our own resources. We're not interested in paternalism. We're finished with this 'give me food and I won't do anything'. What we're saying is 'give us a part and we'll make up the rest'.
>
> We have about 1,500 leaders, almost all women. We have local assemblies of a hundred people. If we hold one-day events they have to be organised by region, because they're so big. So there is massive participation and education for women about social issues, health, politics and women's rights. Many leaders in the neighbourhood organisations come from the kitchens, many of them women. Women are much more politicised now than we were before, because of the kitchens. I've learnt everything I know in the kitchen. The leaders that came out of the kitchens will never be lost.

When the military regime abandoned a wide sector of Chilean society, the responsibility for feeding and caring for the nation's poor families fell largely on women. Not only has their struggle turned work that was previously an 'invisible' family affair into a matter of public debate, but women themselves are taking a more active role in that debate and in demands for the new government to assume responsibility for social welfare. The organisations have placed a huge additional unpaid workload on women's shoulders, but they have also provoked many positive changes in their lives. Women point to the greater public importance they now have in the lives of their communities, the opportunities for new types of relationships with other women and for education and skills training. The organisations continue to grow, even as the economic situation becomes less critical, suggesting that poverty and hardship are no longer the only reasons for women's participation. The issue of women's personal development has become central to a number of organisations being set up by *pobladoras*, often with a more feminist orientation. Two such groups are explored in Chapter Six.

Uruguay
Chronology

1932   Women win the vote.

1973   Military regime seizes power, closes parliament and declares trade unions illegal.

1975   28 per cent of women of working age are in paid work or searching for a job.

1980   Uruguayans vote 'No' in the military's plebiscite on constitutional change.

1981   Legalisation of factory or company-based 'labour associations' to negotiate with employers over wages and conditions of work.

1983   47 labour associations form the Inter-Union Plenary (PIT) and organise the first public celebration of May Day since the coup; 200,000 people demonstrate in the first mass protest against military rule.

1984   Female banking employees set up the first women's commission in a trade union. Working Group on the Situation of Women takes part in negotiations on the transition to constitutional rule. Elections. No women are elected to parliament.

1985   34 per cent of women of working age are in paid work or searching for a job.

1986   The national trade union organisation agrees to the formation of a women's commission. The first police station staffed by women for victims of domestic violence and rape is opened.

1987   The Women's Institute, a government department responsible for promoting women's policies, is created in the Ministry of Education and Culture.

1989   The government ratifies the International Labour Organisation convention on equal pay, introduces equal opportunities legislation and eliminates discrimination from collective bargaining agreements. Six women are elected to parliament in the general elections.

2

Hard Labour

Trade Unionists in Uruguay

CELIA: The union's publications and speeches are thought out from a man's point of view and they're written for men. The language has nothing to do with women and their everyday lives. It's not a bad thing that the political economy is explained in terms of a football game, but how many women understand football? Why not recipes or language related to the family economy?

The Women's Commission of Uruguay's national trade union confederation is unique in the southern cone of Latin America. At the union headquarters in the capital, Montevideo, women factory workers, government employees, domestic workers and teachers have worked for the past six years on campaigns for equal pay, creches, nursery schools, healthcare, abortion, and sex education. On the noticeboards, amongst information on union resolutions and pay awards, there are invitations to workshops on breast cancer and domestic violence. Until recently the country's trade unions have paid little attention to women. It was only when they fought alongside men to rebuild the labour movement, crushed by the military regime which seized power in 1973, that they won a space for themselves in the trade unions.

The unions became a battleground for the women's movement which grew up during the dictatorship partly due to the huge increase in women in paid work that has taken place in Uruguay over the last twenty years. Between the mid 1970s and the mid 1980s the number of women in the workforce rose by a quarter and by 1985 the female rate of economic activity, the proportion of women of working age in paid work or searching for a job, was 34 per cent. This represents one of the highest rates in Latin America and approached the figure for Britain, which in 1984 was 37 per cent.

Until the 1970s Uruguay had always been considered one of the most modern countries of Latin America. Like Chile, most of the population lived in cities and worked in the industrial sector and until 1973 the country had one of the continent's most stable parliamentary democracies. In its standard of living, educational standards, health and welfare services and labour legislation Uruguay surpassed Chile and earned it the description 'the Switzerland of Latin America'. On women's rights, Uruguay was not only more advanced than other Latin American countries, but also ahead of many European ones. The strong and militant women's movement that grew up at the beginning of the 20th century had opened up many areas of political and cultural life to women. Divorce was legalised as early as 1913, in 1932 Uruguay became one of the first Latin American nations to award women the vote and by the 1950s women had won paid maternity leave and equal rights in marriage. After winning the battle for suffrage and equal civil rights, the Uruguayan women's movement began to disintegrate and discrimination against women ceased to be an issue for Uruguayan society in general. Until the 1970s it was popularly believed that discrimination against women did not exist in Uruguay.

Yet the gains women had made did little to change the make-up of the country's political organisations, which continued to be largely a male preserve. Although female participation in the labour force was growing, women played little role in Uruguay's strong and independent trade union movement. Women tended to be concentrated in low paid sectors of the economy and areas which were notoriously difficult to organise. Domestic servants were the largest single group of women in the workforce and had no union organisation. Even in organised sectors where women formed the majority of workers, such as textiles and food processing, most of the union leaders were men. At a factory level, women played a more active role. In the textile industry, for example, women not only took part in industrial action, but led strikes and factory occupations for union recognition and improved pay and conditions. Women textile workers, earning between fifty and sixty per cent of the average wage for men doing similar jobs, first brought the union world's attention to the question of equal pay. After a three month strike and factory occupation in 1960 the textile union became the first to win equal pay for equal work. Concern for women's issues, however, was the exception rather than the rule within the trade unions.

At fifty, and with a long history of trade union militancy, Mabel is one of the Women's Commission's most experienced members. She began her working life in a metallurgical factory at 15, when her father's ill health forced her to leave school to help support her family. Her father was a textile union militant and her mother also worked in a textile factory. In 1960, when she was in her early twenties Mabel, too, found a job as a machinist in the industry. Within a few months she had been elected as a union delegate:

> MABEL: There were a lot of women militants in the union then, perhaps not in the leadership but at the factory level a lot of women took part in industrial action. We never discussed women's issues in the union; we talked about more general issues. After winning equal pay we won the right for women to work sitting down at the machines because standing up all day gave women problems with their spine and varicose veins. Apart from that, women's issues weren't discussed. The big strikes of the late 1960s were over wages and conditions of work and the political repression of the trade union movement. At that time the government was trying to break the union movement by banning strikes and putting militants in prison. The survival of the union movement was the main concern, not women. There was discrimination of course, but we didn't feel discriminated against, not at work, nor in the union.

In general, trade unions saw women as a source of support and solidarity during industrial conflicts, rather than as potential leaders of their organisations. It was in this role that the union movement appealed to women in the growing political crisis of the 1960s. Underlying the crisis was a fundamental weakness in the country's economy: its dependence on foreign demand for the country's agricultural products. As demand began to contract from the 1950s and prices began to decline on international markets, Uruguay's national industry began to falter. Successive governments replaced industrial and welfare-based programmes with policies favouring export agriculture and foreign investment and these were accompanied by a series of 'security' measures, including a ban on strikes by public employees, the prohibition of trade union meetings and the closure of some trade union branches. Uruguay's era of prosperity and political stability was coming to an end. Falling living standards and increasing political repression triggered a reorganisation of the union movement, culminating in the creation of the country's first national trade union confederation, the National Labour Convention (CNT). Together with the student movement, the CNT embarked on a plan of industrial action aimed at forcing a change in the direction of government policy. At that time Moriana was a student in her early twenties, working part-time in the department of social security in its offices in Montevideo. Like her husband, she was a leader of the student union, the Federation of University Students (FEUU).

MORIANA: On the whole the unions weren't interested in discrimination against women at work and there were no union demands specifically designed for women. What little there was appealed to women in their traditional role, the children, the home etc. In 1973 the CNT created a Women's Secretariat, headed by a textile worker. However, it didn't have a feminist focus and its main objective was to get women doing solidarity work during strikes. In 1969 there had been a long bank strike and one of the difficulties which the leadership of the bank union perceived was that the wives of bank employees were pushing their husbands to break the strike, in the traditional role of 'don't get involved, think about the kids' etc. This was, I would say, the first time the union movement saw the need to work with women — but note, seeing women in terms of workers' wives, not as workers themselves.

By the early 1970s massive strikes had thrown Uruguay's economy into chaos. Left-wing political parties had united in a coalition known as the *Frente Amplio* (Broad Front) and support was growing for a small guerrilla movement known as the Tupamaros. The latter served as the pretext for the military seizure of power in June 1973. One of the regime's first measures was to close down trade unions and political parties. All public meetings were banned, the press was censored and education was put under military control. In a last stand against the coup, the CNT called a general strike. The military responded with a wholesale purge of union activists.

MABEL: The military came to the factory, picked out the union leaders, stood us up against a wall and ordered the owner to sack us and kick our heads in. The owner was a decent man but he was forced to sack us. The next day he sacked another 150. Many unionists were being persecuted, leaving the country and going into hiding. Many of the prisoners who were tortured and passed through the 'centre' were union leaders. Soldiers were always stopping you in the street, at the bus stop, on the bus, in the bank, everywhere, asking for your identity card. They said they were looking for union and political activists but it was more a case of intimidating the population than looking for anyone in particular. They completely decapitated the union movement. Until 1978 they wouldn't hire me in any of the big factories because I was on the blacklist and I had to take any job I could get.

Union and political activists were rounded up and tens of thousands were sent to prison and secret torture centres. The former offices of the National Construction Workers Union were seized and turned into a prison and torture centre by the Montevideo Police's Grenadier Corps. Universities and schools were put under military control and student activists were arrested. Moriana went into exile in Mexico. 'The military declared the Federation of University Students illegal. By then I was also working and was a union leader in social security — I was on the wanted list. My husband had also been a student leader and he was in prison. My mother and stepfather were also in prison.

For nine years it was impossible to join a union or to negotiate wages and working conditions. Crushing working-class organisations was essential for the implementation of the military regime's economic programme of expansion through exports and foreign loans. Low wages provided the key to the country's competitive edge in international markets and this meant cracking down on any resistance. Between 1971 and 1979 real wages fell by forty per cent, unemployment and underemployment increased and state services were drastically cut back. By the end of the 1970s, for the first time in Uruguay, there was open evidence of poverty.

Poverty forced many young women and housewives into the work market for the first time and their wages became increasingly important to the survival of their families. In approximately 68 per cent of homes in absolute poverty and forty per cent in poverty, women contributed half the total income. For a growing number of families, women's wages were the only source of income. During the dictatorship one in thirty of the population spent time in prison and hundreds of thousands went into exile. Of the nearly one million Uruguayans living outside the country for both economic and political reasons, the majority were male, a factor which contributed to the rise in the number of female-headed households. In 1986 in Montevideo for every 100 women there were only 87 men and nearly one in five households was headed by a woman.

The relative shortage of males in the population also increased job opportunities for women. Demand for female labour also rose as a result of the military government's economic, and to some extent, political strategy. Key export industries promoted by the regime were to a large degree sectors which had traditionally taken female labour, such as the fish industry, new textile products, leather and shoes. The new export industries were relatively small scale, low cost operations based on short term contracts or out-work, where goods are made up in the home using materials such as leather, wool or cloth supplied by companies or middlemen, offering no social benefits. These small production units increasingly replaced large-scale factory production and served to fragment the working class and to make organisation more difficult.

Low pay and poor conditions characterised the new employment opportunities available to women. Teresita is in her early fifties and works as a cashier in the administrative section of the water industry. Since 1986 she has been an active member of the union, responsible for women's issues. Born in a small rural town, 600 kilometres to the north-west of Montevideo, she came to live in the capital in the 1960s. In 1973, separated with a young child, she started work in a small sock factory.

> TERESITA: We worked inside a shed in permanent water vapour, without any ventilation, because the thread has to be damp otherwise it breaks. Women machinists earned a third less than the men. We were paid by the hour and sometimes worked up to 16 hours a day, but at least it was a secure job and I got paid holidays. There was no union and we never got involved in any union activity. I had a child to bring up, I was alone and when you're in that situation you only think about the child and how you're going to survive economically. Most of us were in the same position, bringing up children alone.

Fish processing was one of the fastest growing industries under military rule. Cheap loans and the chance of a quick profit encouraged a huge expansion in the number of private plants processing fish for export. They were typically low cost affairs, in some cases rapidly converted warehouses, with little investment in modern technology or safety. Labour costs were kept to a minimum by employing women, many with no previous experience of paid work. Isabel started work as a domestic servant at the age of thirteen. At fourteen she was raped and made pregnant by the son of her employer. She had three more children by him, and spent seven years living in the household as a paid servant and as the mother of his children. At 21, she decided to leave. With the help of the social services and the Red Cross she found a room where she lived with her four children. Left with sole responsibility for supporting them, she began work in the fish industry in the early 1970s.

> ISABEL: The fish is filleted, frozen and sent abroad. You stand in water eight hours a day because the fish need water and the taps are running continuously. The fish comes packed in ice so you work in the cold and the wet. You get a lot of pains and headaches. You have to be warmly dressed and wear wellingtons and waterproof overalls otherwise you get rheumatism and arthritis. The conditions are very unhealthy, especially for pregnant women and during menstruation. The men mainly unload the boats and drive the lorries. Cutting fish is a woman's job. It's the women who cut the food in the home so it comes from that I suppose.
>
> When there's no fish they lay everyone off. The filleters, the women, are usually paid by the day or by results and the men who transport the fish are paid monthly, so during the lay-offs it was the women who suffered most. I had four children then and I was separated. Most of the

women in the factory were in the same position. When you've got
responsibility for four children you just have to carry on working.

We secretly formed a union in our plant during the dictatorship. After
a long struggle we got the company to pay for our wellingtons. Unions
were illegal but there were some demands you could make, like the
boots and the overalls. The owners knew the union was operating but
they never found out who the leaders were.

Female labour had a double advantage for the new industrialists.
Not only was it cheap, but with little experience of union organisation,
women were less likely to protest about poor working conditions and
the precarious nature of the employment. In 1977 the fish employers'
lack of concern for industrial safety had tragic consequences.

Carmen was one of the few women in the fish plants with political
experience. She began working in the industry in the late 1970s after
serving seven years as a political prisoner. Her husband was still in
prison and she had a young daughter:

> CARMEN: Our biggest worry was the gas leaks. We were working in
> dangerous conditions because the rooms were kept cold by a pipe system
> that carries ammonia gas and sometimes these leaked because they
> weren't kept in good condition. In 1977 thirteen women died in a fish
> plant when the pipes blew up. Why did women die? Early that morning
> there had been a gas leak, a valve had broken. The managers said the
> problem had been solved and there was a catch of fish waiting to be cut.
> But there was still a strong smell of ammonia in the factory. The men all
> refused to work and told the women to leave and not to risk lives to
> save the fish but the manager began to put pressure the women. He said
> those who left would be sacked. So the women, without experience,
> thinking if they went they'd lose their jobs, stayed and worked. In my
> plant we were always in fear of a leak and there was no union to protect
> us.

Banking and finance also expanded under the military regime. The
shortage of men forced banks, traditionally an almost exclusively male
area of employment, to open their doors to women. The bank union
had been one of the most militant in Uruguay. Pilar is in her early
thirties and has been active in many areas of the women's movement.
Her first job on leaving university in 1980 was with a bank.

> PILAR: The banks have always preferred men and there used to be one
> bank which wouldn't take women at all. During the dictatorship the
> banking sector grew and because so many men were in prison or in exile,
> they began to take on women. They paid women less than the men.
> During the dictatorship you were paid according to how submissive and
> obsequious you were but there was a big difference between men and

women's pay.

You couldn't mention the word 'union' at that time. I remember on May Day 1981 we organised one minute's silence for the bank workers who had been kidnapped and disappeared in Argentina and they began to investigate, to call us in to find out who was behind it and what it was for. No one said a word so they picked out someone and sacked him. They could sack you whenever they felt like it because we had no rights at all.

With the labour movement crushed and the leadership in prison or exile, the military government set about restructuring the trade unions. In 1981 employees were allowed to set up factory or company-based 'labour associations' to negotiate with employers over wages and conditions of work. The associations were strictly controlled to prevent them becoming a political force or the focus for resistance to military rule. They were prohibited from creating national organisations, going on strike or taking up political demands and had little power to defend the interests of the increasingly pauperised working class.

In the absence of a strong union movement, the struggle to solve the immediate problems of poverty moved from the workplace to the community. New organisations began to be set up in the neighbourhoods, many of them by women. From the early 1980s women began creating housewives' associations around the periphery of Montevideo. They organised communal kitchens and canteens and helped set up local clinics and housing groups in an attempt to compensate for the cutbacks in the state provision of basic services. Industrial action in the factories was replaced by women's-style protests. The night-time *apagones*, when entire districts of Montevideo turned off their lights, and the *caceroleos*, the banging of pots and saucepans that could be heard echoing across the neighbourhoods around the capital, were intended as constant reminders to the military authorities that the spirit of resistance had not been broken. Women were also prominent in creating other organisations which were more openly opposed to the dictatorship, in particular human rights groups.

In these new organisations, dominated by women, which developed alongside attempts to rebuild the union movement, a concern for problems specific to women first began to develop. Mabel worked both with women's organisations and in attempts to rebuild the unions.

MABEL: We began to meet in different women's houses to talk about what to do at the neighbourhood level. The central struggle was against the dictatorship but in those meetings we began to talk about the new problems women were facing — the number of women alone, with their husbands in prison, women with unemployed husbands, women in badly paid jobs. There were also a lot of women involved in human rights groups. I worked with Families of Political Prisoners and the Disappeared and organised food parcels for the textile workers in prison.

In 1978 I found a job in a small textiles workshop. There were 15 women working there and the pay and conditions were the worst I'd experienced. Some of the old leaders got together with the new people who were trying to set up unions and we began working secretly to rebuild the textile union and the national organisation. The CNT was functioning outside the country and we were communicating with them through people who were travelling abroad. Women participated, secretly handing out leaflets, getting letters from abroad, visiting prisons and passing on information.

Instead of complying with the military's vision of a new unionism, the labour associations began to rebuild the old union movement and to include political demands for freedom and democracy in their programmes. By 1983 they were openly defying the military regime. In that year 47 associations joined together to form the Inter-Union Plenary (PIT) and called the first public May Day celebration since the coup. Two hundred thousand people demonstrated in what became the first mass protest against military rule and the first step on the road back to democracy.

From the beginning the new women's organisations identified themselves with the movement against the dictatorship. They recognised the central role of the labour organisations and participated in union demonstrations. The struggle for democracy remained paramount, but the nature of the future democracy and its ability to represent women's interests was beginning to be questioned by several of the new women's organisations. Wives of political prisoners who had become responsible for their families, women from all social classes who had gone out to work or joined community organisations for the first time, became conscious of discrimination against women in Uruguayan society. Encouraged by the appearance of academic research groups with a feminist perspective, such as the Study Group on the Position of Women in Uruguay (GRECMU), at least eight women's organisations were formed between 1983 and 84 which included both general and gender issues among their objectives. The Commission of Uruguayan Women (CMU), for example, was a clandestine group formed by wives of building workers, students and working women during the preparations for the May Day demonstration of 1983. It began as a support committee for the effort to rebuild the unions but very quickly came to identify itself as a feminist organisation.

Women in the labour associations, many of whom had contact with these new women's groups, were also no longer prepared to play their traditional supportive role in the trade union struggle. Women in such diverse sectors as banks, journalism and domestic service set about building a new movement that reflected their own interests. Pilar was a member of both the CMU and the labour association at her bank. She helped set up the first women's commission in a trade union.

> PILAR: The association wasn't a place where women felt comfortable — it was a male world and they didn't take much notice of us, so our idea was to work out our own demands and to pressure the men to accept them. We formed the women's commission in 1984. We wanted creches, equal pay and promotion opportunities. A lot of women got involved. We were influenced by the work being done by feminists here and by the returning exiles.

> MABEL: The majority of women who came back from exile came with new ideas and even if it was European feminism, it attracted us. They began to work with the groups here. There was no friction. They'd had their experience from outside and we'd had ours from inside. There were conflicts but we discussed things with a lot of respect. There was a good relationship and we could work together.

With the end of military rule in sight, exiles began to return to Uruguay, some of whom were women who had been active in trade unions in the period before the coup. Although the unions they had known had paid little attention to women's questions, some of these women, influenced by feminist movements abroad, returned with new ideas about the labour movement. They found their ideas coincided with those of the new women activists.

> MORIANA: I had my first contact with feminism in Mexico and only then did I begin to recognise the discrimination women faced in their work and in the unions. I'd always been critical of the small number of women leaders but I hadn't sat down and thought out the whole issue. When we returned we found women here were thinking along the same lines.
> The conflict between the returning exiles and those who'd stayed was more marked among the men. I'm not saying it didn't happen between the women, but I get the impression it was much less. Because women talk more about our lives, there's less confrontation, the atmosphere was different — at least that's what I felt.

Mariela went into exile in Brazil after eight years as a political prisoner. She arrived there at the same time as exiles from Brazil's own military regime were beginning to return.

MARIELA: Brazilian women began to return and brought with them feminist ideas from Europe. It was my first contact with feminism. When I came back to Uruguay several women's groups had been set up. I joined the Commission of Uruguayan Women and got involved in the union movement. It was still something very new and it didn't represent the ideas of the mass of Uruguayan women. It certainly didn't represent the ideas of the men. When the men came out of prison or returned from exile they took up all the spaces, sat down in the same chairs and expected the women to go back to the home.

By 1984 the political parties began to reorganise and, together with the union movement, took the leading role in mobilising opposition to the dictatorship. In December 1983 they called a march for democracy which became the biggest demonstration in the country's history. Half a million people, one in six of Uruguay's population, filled the streets of Montevideo calling for elections. This was followed in January 1984 by the first general strike in eleven years. Mounting popular pressure for their withdrawal combined with a growing economic crisis forced the regime to begin formal negotiations with the political parties for a return to civilian government. The date of the election was set for November 1984.

Once political parties were legalised, political activity returned in its traditional form as men took up the leadership positions in the parties and unions. Women, however, were determined to find a place for themselves in the political process. Various parties had established women's sections, the most notable of which was that of the *Frente Amplio*, which campaigned actively in the neighbourhoods. Shortly before the election it rallied 100,000 women in a demonstration which supported the *Frente Amplio* but also raised gender issues, including the call for 'democracy in the home', in open defiance of the party's electoral committee which had earlier vetoed the demand. Some parties did include policies for women in their manifestos, but this reflected electoral strategy more than a fundamental rethinking of their programmes. Women were absent from the decision-making posts of the party structures and from the lists of candidates.

The example of the CONAPRO perhaps best illustrates the difficulties women faced in getting their demands onto the political agenda. In late 1984 political parties, social organisations, unions and employers came together in what became known as the National Consensus Building Programme (CONAPRO) in an attempt to agree on a common programme for the new democracy. The executive and working parties of the CONAPRO were composed entirely of men. Representatives of the new women's organisations protested, calling for the creation of a working group on women's issues. The

CONAPRO members rejected the demand, so the women set up their own working group outside the official organisation. On 17 November 1984, for the first time in the country's history, more than seventy women from all sectors of society sat down together to assess the situation of women in Uruguay. Twenty days later, in a spectacular about-turn, the CONAPRO agreed to include a working group on women.

> MORIANA: We insisted that if the CONAPRO was going to consider all Uruguay's problems, it had to include the situation of women. Women from political parties, the unions, student and employer organisations sat down together and began to analyse the position of women in general and to design policies for women. This was a great achievement. It's not very common to get women from all social sectors — employers and workers together — to agree on anything. I would say that was the moment when Uruguayan society realised that discrimination against women existed. Before that people claimed, and it's still a common attitude, that in Uruguay there was no *machismo*. 'We're so European it doesn't exist — the girls all go to school and university, the women work, there's divorce. *Machismo* is a problem for other latitudes'. That's what most people thought in Uruguay, myself included.
>
> After the CONAPRO, consciousness of discrimination against women began to grow. Especially after it was proved in the most disgraceful way, when in the first election after the dictatorship, for the first time since 1942, there wasn't one single woman in parliament.

While the growth in women's activities and organisations after the elections ensured that the awareness of women's issues grew in Uruguayan society, the absence of women from parliament reflected the difficulties they still faced in entering the male world of politics. This was as true for the unions as for the political parties. The women unionists who had produced documents on women and work for the CONAPRO may have managed to get the issue discussed within the unions, but they failed to make any impact on union policy. There remained a marked disproportion between their participation in the labour force and in unions, and a particularly marked absence of women from the union leaderships.

In the wake of the CONAPRO, women trade unionists from both white collar and blue collar jobs organised a series of meetings to consider ways of getting more women involved in unions. They outlined three main constraints to women's participation: the sexual division of labour in the family which assigns women the bulk of domestic duties and creates a 'double day' of work inside and outside the home and a double identity, restricting both the time available and the inclination of women to involve themselves in union activity; the segregation in the work market which concentrates them in areas, particularly in home-based work and domestic service, which unionism has little chance of reaching; and sexism in the trade unions.

In the years before the coup María Julia was one of the few woman leaders in the textile industry.

MARIA JULIA: The union is an extra day's work for those involved. This was the problem before and it's still the problem today. And also there's the social cost. The neighbours or your family say, 'you like to be out on the streets' as if it was something terrible. In their hearts husbands are opposed to women's participation and they always opt for their women to stay at home. It's very rare that a husband, however progressive, says, 'I'll stay with the children, you go'. They leave it to another woman, a neighbour or the mother-in-law. There are very few men who take responsibility for the children and at the same time women are taught to identify more strongly with their domestic role. If the most important thing for them is to be a good mother and if the only jobs available are those with the worst pay and conditions, they're not going to feel very positive about their working life.

The other difficulty is that the union policies don't reflect their concerns. The problem of childcare causes women workers great anxiety. There isn't a mother who doesn't ask herself at some point in the day, 'what are the children doing?' Women feel guilty for going out to work, but at the same time they feel guilty because they can't feed their children if they don't work.

Sonia is in her early thirties, married with three children. Both she and her husband work in a rubber factory.

SONIA: I was overburdened with work. I left the factory at five o'clock to go home to all the responsibility for the house and the children. My husband also worked in the factory and was a union militant, so he spent a lot of time outside the house. He got back every night at about ten or eleven, after union meetings. It didn't occur to him that I might want to go out sometimes. I didn't think about it either. I saw myself mainly as a mother and I didn't want him to share in the housework, perhaps because I thought it was the only thing I was really good at. He never did anything at home. He didn't have a clue. When I married him he'd never even made a cup of coffee, his mother did everything for him. I was brought up to think like this too, that women were supposed to be at home and men were supposed to work. When I finished primary school my mother didn't want me to study any more. She wanted me to make clothes at home like her, so that I wouldn't have to go out and meet people or get buses or walk the streets. She thought women should stay inside the house with the children and have no contact with the corrupt world outside. You have to get rid of all that stuff your parents tell you before you can do anything.

The first time I thought about these things was when we had our first women's workshops at the factory. They told us how, as women, we had a right to enjoy our lives and to take part in everything and that we had to educate our husbands, but slowly because confrontation would be counter-productive. So I went home and told my husband everything that happened at the meeting. I told him everything I'd said about him. 'You told them I didn't help with anything in the house?' 'Yes'. 'How embarrassing. Now you've really put me in it!' When I told him that we wanted to start a women's commission he said, 'it sounds wonderful!' I stood there looking at him. I said, 'yes?' He said, 'yes, it's a great idea!' He didn't really know what a women's commission was, but he thought it might get me out of the house. I started to teach him how to cook and clean the house. The floors don't shine like they used to, but none of us have starved to death yet.

The problems start when you don't have a husband who's a militant and who understands what you're doing. Most women have to do everything in the house. They have to run home from work to collect the kids and make the dinner. It's a big problem when your husband is used to you standing around serving him his *mate* [a type of tea]. You need time to participate in meetings and projects. If you have fights before you leave your house and you're fighting to be heard in the union and then more problems when you get back home, you get tired out. You might force yourself to come for a while, against the tide, but then you give up. So in general the women who are active in unions are single, widowed or divorced or they have husbands who are militants, or who are exceptional. Sadly that's the way it is. The other women are interested, they might help you out on the odd day but they don't want to be committed.

The view of the union as a man's world with little relevance to women is reinforced by the practices and style of union life.

Isabel: Union life is arranged for people with no home responsibilities. Meetings are held at times which aren't suitable for women. The meetings are late, you have to find someone to look after the kids, you have to wait a long time for the bus and it's dangerous at night because there's a lot of rapes.

And then when you get to the meeting you find that it's the men who speak all the time — you can't get a word in — and they don't talk about things that are important to women. On top of that they use a kind of language that's difficult for us to understand. There are things you want to say but you don't because you think they'll laugh at you. Women aren't trained to speak in public or to stand up and give reports to men.

You don't feel confident because you haven't got the experience they've got. Women have been educated to be passive and not to answer back. You have to fight against yourself because the experience you get from your life at home is an obstacle.

SONIA: The first time I spoke at a union general assembly was to ask for a union contribution towards a creche. There were 1,500 people and the microphones and my legs froze and I couldn't move. I could only whisper 'I can't speak'. Another woman stepped forward and spoke for one minute and then burst into tears. So one of the leaders, who's got a mouth like a football pitch, took over and explained what we were asking for.

I also remember the first time I spoke in a union leadership meeting. They had some problem about a door and I suggested a solution and no one took any notice of me. Then everyone gave their opinion at great length and after 45 minutes of analysing where to put the door someone said the same thing as I'd said in the beginning and was applauded. I was furious and told them if they weren't going to listen to me I wouldn't bother coming because I had a home and three children and other places to go where people took some notice of me. They said they hadn't understood what I'd said. So I said, 'do I have to give long and boring speeches like you for you to understand me?

Another time the general secretary spoke to me banging his fist on the table so I spoke back banging on the table and everyone looked at me as if I was mad. I told them that no one's stronger than anyone else in union meetings, not even the general secretary, and if he's got the right to bang the table, so have I. In the beginning I had to behave like them to be heard.

Many of the women union leaders found that for women, getting elected depended on more than just a good union work record. When a union was formed in the fish industry in 1982 Carmen was the only woman elected to the national leadership.

CARMEN: In the beginning I thought the natural thing was for people to vote for those they saw taking part in the struggle; that if you worked hard to build the union, were active in all the strikes and participated in all the factory occupations, people would vote for you. But when they put me forward me as a candidate for the union leadership, I saw it didn't work like that. When they gave speeches in favour of the male candidates they said, 'this is so and so, you all know him and his work' but when it came to me, they gave my life history and said so many things that it annoyed me. I asked myself, why in the case of a woman do you have to justify so much; you have to work so much harder to be in the leadership, you have to be in everything for them to recognise

you, whereas a man, with a minimum of union activity automatically
gets elected to the leadership.

The few women who reach positions of leadership do not necessarily
support a separate women's organisation. Some see their own
achievements as testament to the lack of discrimination in union life
and any difficulties they might have faced as purely personal. The
adoption of 'male' attitudes and positions is often the quickest way for
an individual woman to gain access to leadership posts; promoting
women's issues can be the quickest way for a woman to lose her
personal prestige and acceptance by the union.

MORIANA: The unions have always spoken with the voices of men, they've
always had a man's face, been thought out by men's heads. The only
model that exists for how to be a union leader is that of a man. I'd say
that those of us who've got to be union leaders managed it because we've
been very good men, because for a long time we've done what has to
be done and what has to be done is what the men do. The woman part
of ourselves has been very hidden. You don't get up in the middle of a
meeting and say 'I'm going home because the children are alone'. You
hide it. Women aren't always aware of their discrimination and if you
get to the leadership believing you're not discriminated against — 'I'm
a leader, nobody discriminated against me', you can't see the need for
policies aimed specifically at women. And if you're challenged about it,
if someone comes and says that what you're doing, what you've done,
what cost you so much work and so many tears, is wrong, it's very
difficult to accept. I never used to see my problems as problems of
women. I never used to feel I was different from the men. It's only now
that I recognise that I was.

The discussions of the women unionists coincided with wider
concerns being expressed within the movement. Since the end of
military rule the unions had recovered large numbers of members and
re-established themselves as the legitimate representatives of salaried
workers, but the changes in the labour market and the economic crisis
raised doubts about their future role. The new government was
adopting severe austerity measures and there seemed little possibility
that the unions could win wage rises. At the same time the changes
in the make-up of the workforce, in particular the growing numbers
of women in paid work and the large informal sector of self-employed
and casual workers, threatened their ability to maintain their levels of
membership and influence over salaried workers. The unions grew
keen to represent and organise the third of the workforce that were
women.

In the view of women trade unionists, good intentions and determination were not enough to involve more women in union life; the conditions for their participation had to be created. They began to raise the idea of a women-only commission inside the national trade union organisation. The issue of separate organisations for women has produced controversy between men and women in both the unions and political parties. A major objection commonly voiced by men has been that separate organisations divide the workers' movement and detract from what is seen to be the main conflict in society, the class struggle. In 1984 the bank union established the first women's commission. One of the major difficulties faced by the women was in explaining the need for their own space.

> PILAR: When we formed the women's commission at the bank the men were against it — 'why are you meeting separately?' 'You're dividing the movement'. The unions see feminism as divisive and there's always resistance to introducing women's issues. What helped us was the role women played in the struggle against the dictatorship — we were as militant as the men, we handed out leaflets like them, we showed the same commitment as them, so they couldn't turn round and say, 'you don't know what you're talking about'. But it's taking years to be accepted. We've always discussed what we were doing with them but they've never understood.
>
> The women's commission of the bank workers helped set up the PIT-CNT's national commission. With all the problems we were having at the bank union we saw that we needed more women's commissions in other areas to support us. We couldn't do it alone. Together with some women from teaching and the textile industry we called a meeting of women workers for International Women's Day. The PIT-CNT commission was formed after that.

> MORIANA: On Women's Day in 1986 we organised a meeting for women workers. It was the first time in the history of Uruguay that women workers had come together to talk about the problems of working women. From this meeting the demand arose for a women's commission inside the national trade union body.
>
> We went to the PIT-CNT with the proposal. As we have this culture that says there's no *machismo*, the reaction was 'What are women going to meet alone for?' 'What are they going to talk about?' The scandal got much greater when they began to find out what we were talking about...

For the women involved in its formation, the commission was not just a means of increasing union membership. Nor was it going to restrict itself to fighting discrimination at work and in the unions. Many women workers were also mothers and wives, they had a mass of domestic responsibilities which affected their availability for work and their job prospects. If women's home and working lives were so intimately bound up, the commission's concerns would also have to include discrimination in society in general and in personal relationships between women and men. One of the commission's objectives was to support all initiatives which promoted the full participation of women in society. Not only did this question the conventional role of unions by insisting on the need to include aspects other than wages, but women also decided that since their objectives were different, they needed to work in different ways to traditional unions to achieve them. The commission saw itself as part of the women's movement and one of its aims was to promote unity and establish channels of communication with other women's organisations.

The women's commission was created in 1986 as an advisory body within the PIT-CNT. Membership was open to any woman and was to include a female representative from the national executive whose role was to liaise between the union leadership and the commission.

MARIELA: From the beginning the commission wanted to find other ways of working, other forms of expression which had to operate inside the commission itself. We wanted to change the language and all this masculine force and competition and give everyone a chance to speak and to be listened to. To a certain extent we've achieved this. The commission started with about thirty women who were quite representative of women's work in Uruguay. Any woman can come to the meetings. There are political differences but we speak about them openly. We don't shout and bang tables but that doesn't mean the discussions aren't heated. We also give ourselves space in our meetings to talk about problems in our domestic lives which are also a political issue. We wanted the commission to be a space where inhibitions could be broken, where women could learn that their individual worries aren't individual but are common to all of us.

MORIANA: Our first job was to show that discrimination existed. Many of us had believed, me included, that the question of equal pay had already been resolved. There was a big strike in the textile industry for equal pay in the 1960s but in other unions inequality continued and nobody had ever questioned it. Our second job was to make sure that women were aware of their rights and that laws on pay, maternity leave and so on, were enforced.

We wanted to make union life more attractive to women. Everything is formulated for a family where the man works and the woman stays at home looking after the kids, but it isn't like that any more in Uruguay. One of our objectives was to get union policy to take into account women's domestic lives, and to include demands for the socialisation of domestic tasks, for example creches, canteens in factories and companies, washrooms and laundrettes. We also want creches in union offices. We're putting pressure on our male colleagues in a double sense: on the one hand we have to rethink the way the union works, hours etc., on the other hand we've started a discussion with the men unionists on the role they have to play in the home. It's brought us friends and enemies because it's very comfortable to be a union militant and return home and have the food served to you. We tell them this is a contradiction — to fight for social justice, equality etc. but when you return home, to want to be the boss.

The commission wanted to run training courses and maintain a permanent physical presence in the union, discussing the issues. In this we've had a lot of help from women's organisations, both feminist and non-feminist, and we've also taken part in their research projects, so there's a lot of interchange between us. We've done a lot of seminars here in Montevideo and in the interior of the country on a range of issues such as work conditions, the work market, health education and labour legislation. Perhaps one of the themes we've worked on most is the guilt felt by many women workers. If women are guilty about working outside the home, it's also a serious obstacle to their participation in unions.

We needed to prove that discrimination against women existed, which is a long job and we wanted it to be long, because we wanted to get away from declarations of a general nature to show in a concrete way, in each branch, in each factory, how the discrimination was expressed.

The second meeting of women workers on International Women's Day in 1987 decided to promote the formation of women's commissions in all unions. Women still faced a battle with their union leaderships but the commission of PIT-CNT now provided legitimacy and support.

SONIA: A woman in the factory came to me with the idea of setting up a women's commission to campaign for a creche. I'd never wanted to know anything about the union. My husband is a union militant and he spent all his time away from home and for me the union was just something that meant I was left with all the responsibility in the house. But this woman got me interested through the thing about the children. We went to the union and asked for an interview with the executive. There were five of us and it was our first contact with the union. We said we wanted to form a women's commission and they all fell about laughing, 'Yes, we'd been thinking about forming a men's commission'. We were never able to forget this remark because we've heard the same thing everywhere, ever since. 'What do you want a women's commission for?' 'We want a creche.' 'Then why don't you form a creche commission?'. We didn't really know why we wanted a women's commission. We'd heard that in other unions they were forming commissions that were fighting for women but we didn't know how to explain all this.

We began to campaign for a creche and the women's commission of the PIT-CNT found out and invited us to join them. They could see that we knew absolutely nothing about women's issues and that we didn't have the words to confront the men so they recommended we set up a workshop in the union. A women's organisation was brought in to do the workshops, we invited women from the factory and we all sat around talking about our problems. It was the first time we began to realise that as women we were discriminated against. When we'd finished, after two months, we had all the words we needed.

We went to the union to ask for another appointment. The five of us went, trembling, and they were all sitting there waiting. That day they all turned up as if they were expecting to see a circus performance. We explained what we wanted, but this time we were prepared and we went on for ages. They knew there were commissions in other unions but they thought it didn't make sense to have one in our factory. They said when they defend the workers they defend men and women equally. We explained the differences in salaries and promotion and we convinced them there was discrimination. They agreed to the commission.

The principle of equal pay for equal work is enshrined in Uruguayan labour legislation but in reality the average woman's wage is about sixty per cent that of men's. In sectors which employ both men and women, women tend to be concentrated in the lower-paid echelons and find it harder to get promoted. This has little to do with the educational level of women workers, which in Uruguay is generally higher than men in comparable jobs. It is partly the result of open discrimination by both employers and unions. Not only have the unions failed to support women's demands but they have also signed wage agreements that act against women's interests by placing them, together with minors, in separate categories governed by separate rules. Wage agreements have also excluded women from key jobs in the formal sector and limited their access to higher wages. This is particularly true of those which are theoretically designed to 'protect' women and which often derive from notions about women's primary responsibility for the family.

MORIANA: Theoretically there's no salary discrimination in state employment. On paper there's nothing that allows you to say there's discrimination. Everyone gets the same money for the same work. But we began to have suspicions about this very simplistic concept of equality, so we analysed the workforce, the numbers of men and women in each category. We discovered we were 65 per cent of the lowest category and nought per cent of the highest. The educational level of Uruguayan women is higher than that of men, so no one can say it's because women don't know how to do the work. So we began to work on the criteria for selecting staff, which leads us into training, who they train to use new technology etc.

In the electricity industry for example, there was a competition for electricians and in the publicity the word used specified the sex of the electrician as male, which apparently excluded women from applying. One of our battles has been to get employers and unions to change their language and use terms which refer to both male and female workers.

SONIA: Although they had responsible jobs, women in the rubber industry were always paid less than men. Even in sections where they were doing the same work, men were on a higher scale and got paid more. When we pointed this out to the union they fought for equal pay. They managed to get an agreement which gave women a twelve per cent increase in pay. This wasn't complete equality but at least it was a recognition that women are discriminated against.

We've also changed the union statutes so that women can work on the night shift. I was always against this, thinking that women should be at home with the children at night and I thought it was important that they shouldn't have to work at night. But the pay was thirty per cent more and that meant a lot to many women in the factory who were single mothers or heads of families. We discussed it in the commission and decided to call an assembly of women and let them decide. They decided in favour of night work and the union changed the statutes. Now women can work at night but they can't be forced to, and you can't lose your job if you refuse the night shift. Of course now we have the problem that women who work nights get less sleep and their health suffers because they're still the ones responsible for getting the children off to school, collecting them and looking after the babies.

Women's domestic responsibilities often influence male employers considering women for promotion, as do stereotypes they hold about their low job commitment or their willingness to accept low-paid, boring work. Uruguayan law establishes twelve weeks paid maternity leave and two half-hour breaks for breast-feeding. But legislative gains for women can also sometimes have the reverse effect on their promotion chances.

PILAR: The women's commission at the bank won equal pay and full pay during maternity leave. We also got full pay for half a day's work during breastfeeding and days off for children's sickness.

This led us into the area of discrimination against women in recruitment. In theory there's the same chance of promotion for men and women. The banks are always organising training schemes. If they're in working hours, the women go, but if not, they can't. If you don't go you don't get promoted. Women are also less likely to get promoted if they're about to start a family or if they have young children. If the children are sick it's usually the women who take time off, and it goes against them. It's not explicit, but they don't promote you. The commission is now trying to raise these issues with the unions.

Children are a crucial factor in determining when and where women can work. The difficulties of arranging childcare are reflected in the low proportion of married women with young children in paid work. As a result of the women's commissions' campaign for creches in the workplace, the demand has now been adopted by several unions in Uruguay. In the May Day demonstration of 1989 the PIT-CNT included the demand for creches in its platform for the first time. Creches have been installed in a number of industries, though not always in the form requested. In some cases, such as health, education, confectionery and rubber, the unions have set them up. In others, such as the banks, they are financed by contributions from both employers and the workers. In a few cases the company itself provides and finances the creche.

The demand by women for creches also carries the risk of increasing the cost of women's labour and thus diminishing their work opportunities. Conscious of this dilemna, the women's commission began to approach the issue in a different way.

MORIANA: The question of creches is crucial because there are so many women at work and the need is so great. The education system takes children at six years old and the public system has almost nothing for younger children. The prices of private creches are beyond the reach of the average worker.

We managed to get the Department of Social Security to set up a creche for the children of its employees. It involved a lot of arguments. They offered a creche for the children of women workers, which we rejected because this would have the opposite effect on us. Why? Because we would be more expensive labour and also because it reinforces this idea that children are the sole responsibility of women. Now we have a creche functioning which is for the children of men and women workers, so no one can say we're more expensive to employ.

First we demanded it — and look how intelligent we got along the way — as a right of ours, as women. Then we realised this wasn't a right of women but a right of children. It's not just the responsibility of the mothers but of society, but in the beginning we were influenced by the idea that the children were ours alone.

As well as campaigning over health and safety at work, the women's commissions have entered the field of health education, publishing documents on women's health in general and have launched initiatives on cervical and breast cancer. In some unions special clinics have been set up for cancer prevention and free smear testing. They have also campaigned for better public health care provision for women and some have also touched on taboo subjects such as sexuality and abortion. The further women got from conventional work issues, the more conflict they aroused.

GRACIELA: A few women from some of the health unions wanted to present something on women to the Congress of the Uruguayan Health Federation. A law to decriminalise abortion was being introduced in parliament and we felt as health workers who were often being confronted with the issue, that our union should at least discuss abortion. Uruguay has the highest rate of abortion in Latin America, 150,000 a year in a country of three million, and a hundred deaths a year. When we proposed that the Federation discuss the issue, there was uproar, they called for us to be removed, to withdraw the motion, they wouldn't discuss it. But we persisted and explained that the decriminalisation law would only benefit those who could pay for abortions and that this represented class discrimination and that we needed abortion to be legalised so it could be carried out in public hospitals and benefit working-class women. Finally they accepted a motion stating that the Federation would be attentive to issues of women's health going through parliament.

That was the first step. A women's health commission was set up for the second congress, two years later, which presented documents calling for better services for women, particularly in relation to breast and cervical cancer, which are the highest cause of death among Uruguayan women. In the third congress, after a lot of discussion the union accepted the legalisation of abortion as part of its policy. It was the first union to do this. It took nearly six years but it was a great achievement.

SONIA: We've started workshops on violence because we know that a lot of women in the factory are battered by their husbands. We wanted to do some on sexuality, on family planning and sex education but when I suggested it to the leadership they all began to laugh. Some of them offered me free classes. It embarrasses them and they're afraid to take it on in the union. The issue is also difficult with women because it's a very taboo subject so we haven't had much support from them either.

One of the main reasons for the wide difference in pay between men and women is the concentration of women in areas of so-called 'women's work', for which women are assumed to be 'naturally' qualified. These include the 'caring' professions such as health and teaching and those jobs associated with housework, such as cleaning and childcare. They are all low-paid jobs and there are few comparable men's jobs. Paradoxically, perhaps, in many of these areas women have been less successful in establishing commissions. This is partly because discrimination is less apparent when there are fewer men in the workforce and partly because in some women's sectors more women are now reaching positions of leadership in the union, making a women's commission seem less necessary. In teaching and textiles, issues of discrimination in promotion and demands for creches have been taken up by individual women and a group of women teachers is beginning research into the whole area of sexist educational materials and teaching methods. In other areas of women's work the problem has been the irregularity and instability of employment. Carmen helped set up a women's commission in the fish workers' union.

CARMEN: In my factory we organised meetings of women in the half hour rest time so the women didn't have to lose pay or leave the children alone at home. This annoyed many men but all the women participated, which didn't happen in general meetings. Then we organised a women's conference which went over several days. We solved the problem of the children by setting up a creche with videos and we covered the lost wages. A lot of women came, including women from the interior, and we put up pictures and made everything colourful so there was a nice atmosphere. It was a lovely experience. It not only helped us see ourselves in a different way but left the men from the union dumbfounded. We'd invited the union delegates to come and see what we were doing and four or five men came. One worked in the kitchen and the others looked after the children and the general secretary of the union, a man, said to me personally, 'I'm moved, this is something wonderful, we've all got to learn from this'.

In our union the problem is the discontinuity of the work, the lay-offs, so its not easy to get the women together. In terms of tangible achievements perhaps the greatest is that there are now nine women in the union leadership out of a total of twenty. Also it's been accepted that pregnant women shouldn't work in places of risk or have to carry heavy things. In some places we've won creches. We have a lot of projects but in general when we get to the negotiating table all these subjects are treated as secondary; wages and job security come first.

The informal sector has presented the biggest challenge to the women's commissions. With the onset of the world recession in the early 1980s export markets contracted and women were particularly hard hit by unemployment. By 1985 Montevideo had one of the highest rates of unemployment in Latin America and female rates were double that of men's. Women, more than men, have been forced into the informal work market carrying out home-based activities, selling or labouring in sweatshops. Domestic service continues to be the largest single employer of women and like most work in the informal sector, is not covered by labour regulations on pay, hours and conditions and has no health or disability insurance, maternity cover or pension system. A domestic workers' union formed in 1983 has had to struggle to organise a workforce which is dispersed and isolated, characteristics of the informal sector in general.

MABEL: It's very difficult to reach women in the informal sector which is a very serious obstacle, because whatever gains we make in labour law are of little use to a sector where they're impossible to enforce. We've tried to reach women in the small textile workshops but if they unionise, they're thrown onto the streets by their employers. If there's only twelve or fifteen of them they don't have enough strength to defend themselves and their main concern is to keep their jobs.

One of the main conflicts all the women's commissions face is the lack of agreement between them and the union authorities about their real purpose. Unions have endorsed the commissions and included some gender demands in union policy largely to maintain membership. Their support has little to do with longer term goals such as improving women's access to top jobs in the unions or at work. If unions cannot hope to win pay rises for their membership, they may take on new activities related to workers' families such as providing creches and educational and recreational workshops but this does not mean they recognise discrimination. Implicit in this is the danger that they will approach the family and domestic issues in a conservative way, reinforcing female stereotypes. The reaction of the male leadership to sexuality workshops or discussion of abortion shows the limits of men's tolerance to activities which threaten to undermine their roles, both at home and at work.

Because the commissions are advisory bodies they have little independence or decision-making powers and the attitude of the union executive is crucial in determining what they can hope to achieve. The central women's commission of PIT-CNT has no role in selecting the union executive's representative and the success or failure of its projects can depend on her understanding of the commission's aims.

Perceptions also differ over the way in which the commission's achievements are measured. Some union authorities have been looking for fast results in terms of increased female membership, a task made more difficult by the country's deteriorating economic situation and the increasing work load being placed on women, as well as by the general lack of confidence in the unions' ability to influence the government's economic policy.

MARIELA: First a natural exhaustion sets in. You're not only confronting a union movement which is very backward on these issues but also, and this is linked to the absence of a strong women's movement outside the unions, you can be up against a woman leader who is very negative. Many people have got fed up, above all the politically independent women who used to be the majority. We have lost many feminists and independents from the commission.

PILAR: During the dictatorship women participated a lot and got the union to adopt a lot of women's demands. Yet with each success, women participated less. Some were just worn out. It's very uncomfortable working alongside men who are against the women's commission and know you're in it. You can have ideas and initiative but it's always difficult, because you're working with men who can't accept that you can be right or do something well. It's disillusioned many women.

You're not in a position where you can take decisions so you depend on the leadership. You can do things but you always need their acceptance and agreement. The commission has had various representatives from the union executive. She may be a woman but have nothing to do with feminism and no interest in women's issues. Now we're asking for the power to choose the representative.

MABEL: At one time the commission played an important role, organising demonstrations for human rights or against the rise in the cost of living but recently participation has fallen, partly because of the general climate. People don't have much confidence in the unions any more. It's as if the unions aren't doing what people want them to do. At the assemblies people say they don't organise strikes for the right reasons, that there's too much dialogue with the government, that the grassroots isn't consulted enough. There's apathy and a lack of credibility in the union movement and it affects women too. The recession has fallen hardest on women's shoulders so it's even more difficult for them to participate. It's a general problem which is also affecting the political parties.

The future of the unions is related to their ability to democratise their structures and practices and rethink their policies and objectives. The women's commission of the PIT-CNT is suggesting a way forward.

The degree to which the unions will take on board the commission's ideas depends to a large extent on wider social, political and economic circumstances. In particular, the existence of a strong women's movement outside the trade unions is essential for a wider social awareness of the issues associated with the subordination of women. In this respect, the outlook looks a little more promising than it did in 1984. In the 1989 elections six women were elected to parliament. Among them was Carmen, the fish workers union delegate, who is responsible for women in the coalition of left political parties, the *Frente Amplio*.

The women's commission has achieved a great deal. They have enabled men and women in the unions to develop awareness of discrimination and managed to get some of their demands taken up as union policy. Notable successes include the passing of equal opportunities legislation in 1989, the elimination of discrimination from labour agreements and the ratification of the International Labour Organisation's convention on equal pay, also in 1989. There has also been an increase in the numbers of women in the leaderships with gender awareness. The commission has also worked to diminish some of the risks associated with women-only commissions, which sometimes end up isolated or relegated to a secondary position inside male-dominated organisations, by developing links with women's organisations, both feminist and non feminist, supporting and taking part in a wide range of women's initiatives.

MORIANA: Our greatest achievement is making the union movement aware that the issue of women is an issue. We managed to make people understand that equal pay for equal work didn't exist. I'd say that today, except for a few small exceptions, we have won equal pay for equal work. Now we're into something else which is equal pay for work of equal value — why women's skills are categorised in a different way to men's skills.

Another achievement is the increase in women with gender awareness as a result of our courses. We've found some new ways to motivate women. For example, the federation of oil workers set up a series of art and music workshops for the workers' children. Then we realised — it wasn't the result of a plan, but we discovered it almost by accident — that women workers went to the workshops to take the children and that this was a moment when we could organise workshops with the mothers. There are many things we've discovered along the way because what we're doing is something new for Uruguay and there's nothing written down to help us. It's very difficult to quantify this in terms of numbers of participants and numbers of commissions, but if you follow the women involved in commissions in their everyday lives, in what they say, what they do with other women in the workplace — there may not be the formality of coming, sitting down around a table and discussing a project — but they're influencing other women.

When we started, feminism was a bad word. Now it's less so. I remember at the beginning they asked me if I was a feminist and I used to say 'no — if feminism means confrontations with men and that men are bad, but if feminism is to fight for equality, equal salaries, then yes'. In one way or another we all answered like this, partly because it was a tactic and partly because we weren't as feminist as we are today.

The creches are a partial victory because we've only won them in a few branches, although we've still got the childcare project going through parliament. There's still a lot to do. Now we're planning a national daycare law. A discussion has already begun on the issue of school hours, because in public education it's four hours a day until twelve years old. In some sectors we've won canteens and washrooms but in fewer cases than creches. They've begun to put creches in some unions, although not as fast as we wanted. We've also made big advances in healthcare, which isn't just a victory for women workers but for the women's movement as a whole.

We've also influenced other areas of union life. The traditional union protest is all marches, banners, flags, clenched fists and shouting. It's not an accident that the first union in this country which has found another way is the health union, where eighty per cent of the members are women. They invented — for Uruguay — what's been called the health chain, which linked the country's main hospitals to parliament with a chain of linked hands, singing, dancing, protesting about the lack of a decent health budget.

I'm particularly optimistic. Perhaps because I've seen the development of the process from the beginning to where we are now. What you have to remember is that what we're doing is something very new for Uruguay.

Paraguay
Chronology

1954   General Stroessner seizes power in a military coup.

1961   Women's suffrage granted.

1975-6 Fifty peasant leaders killed, 5,000 arrested and hundreds flee
        into exile after the military crush the Peasant Leagues, a
        church-backed peasant co-operative movement.

1980   The formation of the Paraguayan Peasants' Movement (MCP)
        to fight for land reform and democracy.

1981   The agrarian census reveals that eighty per cent of national
        territory is owned by one per cent of landowners and only one
        seventh of the total land suitable for farming is being cultivated.

1982   Beginning of large-scale, organised land occupations by
        landless peasants.

1985   5,000 landless peasants from the MCP organise the first mass
        public demonstration since the 1950s. A thousand peasant
        women take part in a demonstration to mark the formation of
        the Women's Commission of the MCP. By the mid 1980s half
        the population is estimated to be living in poverty and 350,000
        peasants have no land.

1986   Government ratifies the United Nations Convention on the
        Elimination of Discrimination against Women. Street protests
        against military rule rock Paraguay's capital, Asunción.

1989   Fall of General Stroessner in a palace coup led by the second
        in command of the armed forces, General Rodríguez. In
        elections three months later, Rodríguez becomes president.
        First police station staffed by women set up in the capital for
        the victims of domestic violence and rape.

1991   Proposal for a government Women's Department approved
        by the Chamber of Deputies.

3

Breaking the Rock

Peasant Women in Paraguay

'They appeared suddenly in the heat of a Sunday afternoon, coming from all directions. They arrived on foot, in carts, in lorries, carrying their children and accompanied by a few men, protected from the sun by parasols, shawls and pirí hats. They gathered on the patio of the church in Caaguazú. Almost a thousand peasant women demanding land, an end to persecution and the freedom to organise.'

The Paraguayan press report in November 1985 was recording an unprecedented event. Not only did the demonstration in the small rural town of Caaguazú mark the formation of Paraguay's first women's peasant organisation but it was also the largest gathering of women in the country's history. A year later, government lorries took 1,200 landless peasants to 1,250 hectares of land near Paraguay's eastern border with Brazil. The area of dense, sub-tropical forest, close to the River Paraná, was the first victory of the men and women of the Paraguayan Peasants' Movement in their struggle for land. With almost no help from state agencies and few resources of their own, they began to clear patches of forest to build houses and wells and plant crops to feed themselves. They dreamt of creating a model Paraguayan peasant community, based on co-operative farming, mutual solidarity and democracy. Moreover, in a society where peasant women rarely go anywhere on their own and are commonly called 'my servant' by their husbands, it was to be a community where men and women had equal rights. Remarkably, these events took place under a military regime for which these ideals were tantamount to political subversion. Paraguay was in the grip of Latin America's longest surviving dictatorship, a dictatorship which for 35 years ferociously suppressed all forms of popular organisation, shrouding the country in a culture of fear.

From 1954, when he seized power in a military coup, until 1989, Paraguay was ruled by General Alfredo Stroessner and during that time little information about the landlocked country in the central southern area of Latin America reached the outside world. For 35 years Stroessner and his supporters dominated almost every aspect of Paraguayan society. He used the organisational apparatus of a traditional political party, the Colorados, to extend his influence to every neighbourhood and village in Paraguay. By making affiliation to the party obligatory for all public employees, the legal profession and officers in the armed forces, Stroessner kept control of all the country's main institutions. A token opposition allowed him to present to the outside world a façade of parliamentary democracy, but censorship, fraud and persecution of any genuine opposition ensured his power over parliament and seven successive victories in the five-yearly presidential elections. In the 1978 elections, for example, Stroessner received ninety per cent of the vote and in several large towns not a single vote was registered for the opposition.

The system was held together by a combination of corruption and brutality. Stroessner built up the economic power of the state, distributing the profits from smuggling and corruption to his main supporters, the large landowners and the 'neo-Colorados', a civilian and military clique who invested their new fortunes in land. To crush any opposition the army, police and security forces adopted a strategy of 'preventive repression', the systematic use of arbitrary arrest, detention without trial, torture and murder, a strategy which extinguished any signs of protest so efficiently that there was never a significant public threat to his 35 year rule. Until the 1980s Paraguay was the only country in Latin America without an independent peasant movement. When Stroessner was removed from power on 3 February 1989 it was not through a mass uprising, but after seven hours of combat with the military forces loyal to his son-in-law, General Andrés Rodríguez.

The distribution of the country's most valuable resource, its land, among a small group of Stroessner supporters has left Paraguay with the most inequitable pattern of land distribution in Latin America and condemned the majority of the country's three and a half million inhabitants to extreme poverty. Unlike Argentina, Uruguay or Chile, Paraguay is a predominantly agricultural country. In 1982 nearly sixty per cent of the country's population was classified as rural, the majority *mestizos*, of mixed Indian and Spanish blood. There is an indigenous population of some 100,000 Guaraní Indians and both Spanish and Guaraní are the official languages. A tiny minority of landowners, just one per cent, own eighty per cent of the national territory. The majority of farmers are peasants who eke out a living on small, eroded plots of land of less than twenty hectares. Since the 1970s many have combined subsistence agriculture, (growing food for their families) with cash crops, mainly soya and cotton. Sixty per cent of all Paraguayans live in houses classified as unfit for human habitation and one in five homes have more than eight people per room. Only seven per cent of the population have access to safe clean water. By some estimates as many as 57 in every hundred of the rural population are illiterate.

While poverty and poor living conditions affect both men and women, women have to confront most directly the problems of malnutrition, disease and inadequate or non-existent health and educational services. Women's lives in Paraguay are also conditioned by a particularly harsh version of *machismo*, the product of the country's peculiar and tragic history. Its origin lies in the years of wars and repression that devastated the male population and which both increased the economic importance of women and, paradoxically, undermined their role in the country's political and social life. During the 19th century War of the Triple Alliance, when Paraguay fought its British-backed neighbours, Uruguay, Argentina and Brazil, half the country's population was wiped out and of those who survived, eighty per cent were female. The work of rebuilding the devastated country, as well as farming and bringing up the new generation, fell to women. Subsequent foreign and civil wars, political repression and economic hardship have combined to reinforce the crucial role of women on the land.

This has sometimes led commentators to speak of a matriarchal society in Paraguay, a myth reinforced by the Church, official media and educational system with their exaltation of the heroic Paraguayan mother and wife. However, women's important role in production has not brought them political power. At the same time as women were being encouraged to produce (and reproduce), they were excluded from any role in the government of the country. Instead, the culture of *machismo* was strengthened and led to an exaggerated over-valuing of men and boys. The birth of a baby boy is considered a blessing on the family, whereas girls are seen as a burden. Boys are guaranteed access to resources and power in society. Girls are much less likely to be educated than boys and public life is the almost exclusive domain of men. If the succession of authoritarian regimes has limited political participation for most sectors of Paraguayan society, this has been doubly so for women who had no formal civil rights until the mid 1950s and were the last women in Latin America to win the vote, in 1961. Civil and criminal laws still contain many extreme examples of discrimination against women, most notably the law which gives control of matrimonial property to the husband and requires women to obtain their husbands' consent before starting paid work.

Machismo combines with poverty to deprive peasant women of the most basic human needs. Even by Latin American standards, the status of Paraguayan peasant women is low. Until very recently the voices of Paraguayan peasant women have not been heard at all.

Magui lives with her husband and two children in Caaguazú, in the central southern area of Paraguay, in a slum district which grew up on the fringes of the town, beyond the end of the paved roads. The family farm a plot they squatted some years ago in the surrounding fields and she works as a street vendor, selling *empanadas* (meat pasties) and *chipas* (maize bread flavoured with cheese) to the passengers of passing coaches. Magui is also the leader of Paraguay's first peasant women's organisation. In her house, a ramshackle collection of wooden huts between avocado and mango trees, peasant women from all over the region first began to talk about the discrimination they faced in Paraguayan rural society.

MAGUI: It starts at birth. When a baby girl is born people say that she's going to be a burden on the family, that she's not going to contribute anything, but it's completely untrue because women have always worked more than men. It starts from the age of four or five when we have to help our mothers with the housework and the younger children. Peasant children begin to work at five years old, looking after the animals or collecting the crops or helping in the home, but whereas the little boys can find time to play, the girls never do. I had five brothers and five sisters and we were always very poor. I was the oldest so when I was seven I had to help in the fields; there wasn't time for going to school, let alone playing.

The men have this idea that a woman isn't trustworthy. When we're ten years old the father says 'now you're grown up I can't trust you any more'. After that girls can't go out alone so they can't go to school. They say 'girls only pretend to study but really they're going off with men'. They say girls don't need to study to get married and have children. The only thing we are taught is that we're inferior to boys. I was often top of the class but I couldn't continue studying. There was no way out, except to go to the cities, to find work in the houses of rich people.

A girl has to submit herself to her father or brother or husband because they say she can't look after herself and she needs someone to tell her what to do. There's a lot of violence in the homes but it's hidden. The women don't want to talk about it. Women are beaten or raped by their husbands or older brothers or fathers. They can't speak out or defend themselves because they're women.

We never have a social life. City women can go out, even if it's only once a month to do some shopping or take the children somewhere, but it's different for peasant women. Peasant girls go to five or six parties in their life, then they get married and their home becomes their world. Women in the city can go out but in the country you're despised if you go out alone. 'So and so is going out by herself, where's she going? What for?' It can't be for a good reason. Women have to take the children trailing behind them, that makes them respectable. Where do women go? To church, to baptise a child or to take the children out on special occasions, two or three times a year. That's their only social contact. They're completely isolated.

Discrimination against girls in education is reflected in the literacy statistics. While primary education has been extended to many rural areas in recent years, in 1982 32 per cent of peasant women were illiterate, while the figure for men was 26 per cent. Rosita left school illiterate in both Spanish and Guaraní. At twenty she is one of the tiny minority of young peasant women who has been offered a chance to continue her education, at a small college run by a non-governmental organisation known as the Centre for Peasant Education, Training and Technology (CECTEC). Parents have allowed their daughters to attend CECTEC only on the condition that the women's courses run for one week per month and that during that time no males, including the school's director, are on the premises.

Rosita: Most of the girls I know want to study but their fathers won't let them. They don't want them to study in the same place as boys. They don't like boys and girls to be together. They don't trust them.

I didn't finish primary school until I was 14. It wasn't much use. They taught us about the history of other countries and the classes were in Spanish so I couldn't understand everything. It's no use to peasants. A peasant needs to study other things. They never taught us about our bodies or about boys. Girls get married when they're 14 or 15 and they have babies straight away. They don't know anything about relationships or sex. My mother never talked to me about sex. I learnt from girls who'd been to the city. Those girls wake up very quickly. Some girls fight with their parents to go out or to go to the city. My father let me go to the city to work as a domestic. In the city the housework isn't so hard because you've got things like running water in the kitchen, but the woman gave me a lot to do and treated me very badly. I worked until ten every night and I only had Sunday afternoons free. I felt alone in the city without anyone and I earned very little. What could I do with the money?, I asked myself. I sent most of it to my mother. I stayed two months and then I came back.

Families of eight to ten children are not uncommon in rural Paraguay. Six out of ten of all births take place outside hospitals. Most rural communities have only rudimentary health posts and most women visit a hospital only once, if at all, during their pregnancies. The country has Latin America's third highest rate of maternal mortality after Haiti and Bolivia.

Eulogia lives in a three-roomed wooden house on the family's small farm, in a community of 300 peasants in central southern Paraguay. A massive rock sits in the middle of the cotton and soya fields of forty of the families. The families have paid for their land but they have no legal title to it because the landowner wants to ensure the rock, a valuable source of building material, remains in his hands.

EULOGIA: It's a lot of work because I've got 15 children. I got married when I was 13 and in 25 years I've had 15 children. The eleventh time I was pregnant with twins and I went to the priest and told him that we couldn't support any more children. He told me it was wicked to think of stopping pregnancies and that we would be punished, so I never went back to him and I went on having children.

I delivered nine by myself, alone in the house. Our health post is very basic so we have the children at home. If there's a problem we can get the bus to the town but because we're poor we can't pay the fares and you have to pay to have a baby there. Some women die because they haemorrhage or sometimes the placenta doesn't come out. I'm an untrained midwife so I help with some of the births. We use herbs when we're sick and if the herbs don't work, we die, because we've got nothing else.

We've got twenty hectares including the rock, but the rock takes up most of it, so we've only got six hectares to cultivate. It's not enough. We sell cotton, cassava and sweet potatoes but we earn very little from them. When the men tried to break up the rock to sell the stone, the police came and hit them and kicked them and threw them off. They don't want us to touch it.

I've got a big house. All the boys are in one room and all the girls in another and we've got our own room. We get our water from a well. We haven't got electricity. I do everything in the house; I get up at four to go to the fields to bring in the cassava, the beans and the wood for the fire. Then I put the cassava on to boil for breakfast and take it to the men in the fields. I have to cook for everyone and wash all the clothes, help in the fields, look after the animals, clean the cotton. I finish work at ten at night. We have no social life. The men go out to work at six in the morning and come back at four or five. Then they have a bath and eat and sit around drinking *tereré* (a cold Paraguayan tea) or *caña* (an alcoholic drink made from sugar cane), because the work outside is hard too. But the women work harder. There's not one day we don't work. My husband doesn't understand this. Sometimes he says I'm like one of the pigs. He treats me like a pig and that hurts. The men call us *'che serviha'* which is Guaraní for 'my servant'. They don't help the women with their work. Our mothers were *machista* too. They gave the men these bad ideas. In the countryside they only value men. That's what's so hard for us.

Peasant women are brought up to believe in their own natural inferiority and their inability to deal with the world outside their homes. While women do sixty per cent of the work in the poorer peasant households, only the tasks that men carry out are considered 'real' work. Men take the decisions about what to plant, how much of the crop to sell and men handle the dealings with government agencies, the selling and buying of agricultural products and the family income. Even in women-headed households, or families where husbands spend long periods away from home doing seasonal work, women need men or boys to mediate with the outside world. Their lack of education, their heavy workload and their confinement to the home means women have very little chance of a social life or of participating in community organisations and until recently women have played little part in peasant movements. Peasant organisations generally involved women only at grassroots levels and paid little attention to their needs. Since their work was generally considered unproductive and their subjugation to men natural, women were not considered subjects for social and political action.

For most peasant women the only access to a life outside the home was via the Church. The Church was one of the few institutions with a degree of independence during the Stroessner years and from the late 1960s it began to take a more public stance on social issues and human rights. In a country where newspapers and radio stations were routinely closed down for even mild criticisms of the regime and where foreign press agencies were controlled by key government personnel, church libraries were often the only source of real information about what was happening in Paraguay and the world outside. A church bimonthly magazine was the only one to report and condemn the brutalities being committed by the regime.

In the 1960s the Church supported a Christian-based peasant co-operative movement known as the Peasant Leagues. The Leagues, the first significant popular opposition to emerge during the Stroessner years, were a reaction to the growing hardship caused by increasing inequalities in land distribution. As military and civil supporters of the Stroessner regime bought up huge tracts of the best farmland, the peasants were left to scratch out a living on small, infertile plots or to leave Paraguay altogether to find work in neighbouring countries. By the early 1970s an estimated one million Paraguayan men and women were living outside the country, the majority in Argentina.

By the early 1970s the Leagues and their youth section, Catholic Agrarian Youth, had an estimated membership of 20,000. By 1975 they had become the object of official persecution and harassment and in 1976, on the pretext that they were communist-inspired, the regime launched a bloody attack on the peasant movement. Magui was one of the movements' few women militants.

> MAGUI: I didn't have the typical life of a peasant girl. When I was 18 an uncle who was a Jesuit priest gave me a job as a parish secretary in another province and I began to work with Catholic Agrarian Youth. After two months I became finance secretary of the region and a militant in the organisation. I didn't have any experience, only what I learnt from my mother. She was a lay preacher and became a leader in the local church and because it was the church, my father couldn't object. She went to work with the children in her arms. She was a good speaker.
>
> The Peasant Leagues used to organise what they called 'courses for ladies' and always gave women the trivial jobs, like organising raffles, parties, or beauty contests. Catholic Agrarian Youth were more interested in organising women. They gave me a lot of support and I learnt a lot in their courses. It was a very important experience for me.
>
> The repression of the peasant organisations began in 1975 and I learnt through this as well. They began to break up our meetings and take prisoners. One day I heard on the radio that they'd shot some of our friends. It was a big shock to me. In 1976 it got worse. Many peasants were killed, thousands were taken prisoner, many disappeared and many more went into exile. We weren't prepared and they completely destroyed the movement. I got married in 1974 and had my first child. My husband was a leader in the organisation and we began to get death threats. In 1975 we had to leave Paraguay.
>
> We came back secretly in 1977 and together with some of the old peasant leaders we formed a national committee to reorganise the peasantry. We wanted to set up an independent peasant organisation — totally independent of the Church, political parties and the government. From the beginning I was involved in the new movement, not very actively at first because my husband was still based outside the country and I was responsible for the children. It's always difficult when the man is a militant because generally the woman is left to look after the family.

In 1980 Regina's husband was murdered by the military, leaving her with sole responsibility for their five children. They live in a one-room shack in the slums outside Caaguazú and survive with the money she earns selling bread to her neighbours. Her husband, Blas Rodas, was a peasant leader in the 1970s. He escaped the repression of the Peasant Leagues, which between 1975 and 1976 claimed the lives of at least fifty peasant militants, left thousands in prison and forced hundreds into exile, but he became the first victim of the regime's attempts to wipe out the new peasant organisation.

REGINA: We were typical landless peasants. There were twelve in his family and because my husband was one of the youngest sons he was left without land. We fled to Argentina during the repression of the 1970s but we couldn't find work so we came back and my husband got involved in the committee of peasant reorganisation. In 1980 the police tried to evict a community of peasants who were legally occupying a piece of land near Caaguazú. When the peasants defended themselves a thousand troops arrived, they closed off the area and began rounding up the leaders and killing them. On the 6 April 1980 my husband was on his way back from visiting his parents. He was seized and stabbed nine times and his body was thrown on the roadside.

Despite such attacks, the new organisation survived and in 1980, after a series of meetings between peasant leaders from across the country, the Paraguayan Peasants Movement (MCP) was formed. It was the first independent peasant organisation to be established during the Stroessner years and its leaders faced the constant risk of arrest, torture and death. Operating in secret from Magui's home in Caaguazú, the MCP programme demanded land redistribution, government assistance to peasants, freedom to organise and respect for human rights. Like all peasant organisations before it, the MCP saw no need to develop any special programme for women. With the exception of Magui, the leaders were all men.

MAGUI: By 1981 we realised that women weren't taking part in the movement. I was the only woman in the MCP leadership. Regina and I began to set up women-only meetings to encourage them to take part in the organisation. When there are men around the women don't speak, so we wanted to make a space of our own where women could talk about their problems. These meetings were very small, few women came, but it was a very important first step for us. The biggest problem we faced was that men wouldn't let their wives out of the house.

This meant we had to deal with the men. When men are involved in a popular struggle it doesn't mean that they lose their *machismo*. We pressed for the participation of women to be included on the agenda of the national meetings of the MCP and we attacked the men in the movement. We told them that they had to support us, that they had to let their wives and daughters out to come to our courses. We had some very heated arguments. They wouldn't accept what we were saying. When we proposed meetings of women at a national level the men said they didn't want to stay with the children for two or three days — because we need one day to travel there, one day for the meeting and one day to travel back, three days away from home. But we kept up the pressure and we didn't let one opportunity go by without raising the issue of women's participation, without asking why nothing had changed. There were a few men in the organisation who supported us and tried to convince the others. Some thought it would be good if the women helped in the fight for land and others thought it might stop their wives complaining every time they went out to meetings, but almost none of them understood that women had a *right* to participate. In 1982 we won our first battle; the MCP incorporated equal rights for women into its programme.

By the early 1980s the land situation had become critical. Ever since Stroessner had come to power he had tried to attract foreigners to settle or invest in what he called his 'haven of peace and security', but until the 1970s, despite generous tax incentives, few foreign companies had shown interest in Paraguay. Only when work started on the Itaipú dam in 1973, did large-scale foreign investment begin to arrive. Itaipú, at the time the world's largest hydro-electric project, generated economic growth and fuelled a speculative land boom, particularly in the fertile eastern region of the country, on the border with Brazil. The principal beneficiaries of the boom were military and Colorado party officials who obtained the land at cheap prices from the government's Rural Welfare Institute (IBR) and resold it to foreign, mainly Brazilian land companies at huge profits. By the mid 1980s a large part of the region was owned by Brazilians, many of them financial speculators. For the peasant population the 'boom' not only reduced the amount of land available to them, but led to the eviction of peasants with provisional titles to farms in the area to make way for the land speculators. The 1981 agrarian census revealed the full extent of the problem: only one seventh of the total land suitable for farming was actually being cultivated and eighty per cent of the national territory was owned by one per cent of landowners, the most unequal pattern of land distribution in Latin America.

The crisis erupted with the onset of the world economic recession in 1981 and the completion of the Itaipú dam. As soya and cotton prices fell on the international markets and the prices of inputs like seeds and fertilisers, as well as essential household items like kerosene, cooking oil and rice, increased, peasants could no longer survive on their tiny plots. When the Itaipú dam was completed in 1983, thousands were left without work and with little possibility of finding a job on the new mechanised farms or in the stagnant industrial sector. Moreover, the economic crisis in Argentina closed off the traditional source of alternative employment for many Paraguayan peasants. By the mid 1980s half the population were estimated to be living in poverty, over a third of families in the eastern border region were suffering from malnutrition and there were an estimated 350,000 peasants without land.

For many peasant women, the crisis broke down their traditional way of life and with it, their traditional isolation. Impoverished landless peasant families drifted to small rural towns and women began to take on paid work, mainly in home-based activities such as cooking and selling food. By 1984 there were some 7,000 landless families in Caaguazú, the home of the new peasants movement. As women came into contact with others like themselves and became aware of the dimensions of the land crisis facing peasant families, more women began joining the clandestine national and local meetings for the wives of MCP members.

When the peasants began to organise land takeovers women began to create a new role for themselves in the peasant movement. With no money and no jobs, thousands of Paraguayans turned to occupying unused land in a desperate attempt to grow the food they needed. In 19 months between 1983 and 1984, 37 cases were documented, involving nearly 10,000 families. Isolated cases of peasant land occupations had been common in Paraguay, but from the early 1980s for the first time they took on a mass, organised character, claiming their actions were justified by Article 83 of the constitution, according to which all peasant families have the right to own land. The regime responded by declaring war on the squatters.

In 1985 the MCP brought together 5,000 landless peasants in the first mass public demonstration since the 1950s and the Permanent Assembly of Landless Peasants (APCT) was formed. Some of the landless women, like Geraldina, who lived with her husband and six children in Caaguazú, began to recognise that without their support the authorities would succeed in stamping out the struggle for land.

GERALDINA: Some of the men from Caaguazú had got together to fight for a piece of land in the department of Guairá. They squatted the fields and the police came and blockaded the camps, burnt out the tents and arrested them all. They were evicted and taken prisoner three times and it seemed as if there was no way we could win. When the men left prison for the third time they set up the Assembly. From then on the women joined the struggle for land in a more active way. We started to go with them to the government offices to demand land. The women went with their children to occupy government offices. We wanted to work out ways to continue the fight when all the men were taken prisoner and other women in the MCP began to help us.

When the men began to fight for land we saw that we could be important to the struggle. We also saw that if women were going to keep the campaign going we had to find ways to get more of them involved. We began to see that we needed our own organisation.

MAGUI: By 1984 more women were taking part in the movement and we proposed the creation of a women's commission inside the MCP. In the beginning we didn't dare ask for anything too divisive because the men would have opposed it and we wouldn't have achieved anything. Our tactic was to convince the men that women had to organise to support the general struggle and that our first priority was to organise the women without land. There was a lot of resistance but they finally accepted it.

On 17 November 1985, the Peasant Women's Commission (CMC) was formed and a thousand peasant women from 48 rural communities came to Caaguazú to celebrate its foundation.

By 1985 urban women were also beginning to organise. In that year women's commissions were established in the new banking and commerce unions and women's groups were emerging inside political parties to fight for democracy and human rights. Church-promoted housewives' committees were forming in some of the poorer neighbourhoods. In addition, for the first time Paraguay witnessed the appearance of feminist groups. It was too early, however, to speak of the birth of a women's movement in Paraguay. These women were a tiny minority and by the end of the year many of the groups had disbanded or become the victims of official harassment.

The CMC's early programme therefore, was developed in the absence of a wider campaign for women's rights. At first the CMC's demands simply reiterated those of the MCP and their public activities were primarily related to the fight for land. Women began taking a more visible role in this struggle, not only going to MCP demonstrations but also organising their own protests. Public demonstrations were still illegal and the sight of peasant women in the streets defying the authorities took the police by surprise.

In 1986 police shot dead two young MCP members during the eviction of hundreds of families from a land occupation in Alto Paraná, in the forested eastern region of Paraguay. All the men were taken prisoner and all food supplies, torches and tools were confiscated. The women and children were left alone in the forest. Three days later the CMC gathered together 800 women for a protest march in the small square in Caaguazú.

GERALDINA: The police closed off all the streets and wanted all our names. As there were a lot of us we got brave and refused to leave. We got together in the middle of the square and began to sing the national anthem in homage to the dead boys. The police didn't even take their hats off like they're supposed to. We shouted at the police that they weren't Paraguayans, that they were traitors and murderers, that they were in the service of the gringos. It was tremendous. The police just stood there and listened to us all. There were some men around who'd brought some of the women who'd come from faraway places. The police arrested them all and the women said, 'how are we going to get home?' so we all decided to march to the police station to demand their release. When the police realised what we were doing they blocked off the street and tried to arrest Magui and Regina, but we all joined together and said, 'we all go or no one goes and then you'll have to feed all 800 of us in prison!' They left us and we waited. Then one by one they released the men.

These actions were very important to us. They helped us conquer our fear of speaking out and of the police, and they strengthened our organisation.

The CMC's objectives, however, were not just limited to organising women in the peasants' struggle for land. Their programme came to incorporate women's concerns and to condemn their double oppression, both as peasants and as women. It addresses itself not only to the state but to peasant organisations and their communities.

MAGUI: Our objective is equality of opportunity for women in all areas of society, politics and the economy and we also demand respect for the rights of children. As women and as peasants we are doubly exploited. It's clear to us that our objectives can't be achieved in the context of an unjust capitalist system. We belong to a peasant movement and the concerns of the men are also our concerns. The struggle for land and justice is also our struggle. We recognise that we have specific problems as women which means we have to demand our right to participate, not only from the government and society as a whole, but also from peasant men. The CMC works for the full and active participation of women in the fight for socialism. We don't believe that one day socialism will arrive and eradicate all women's problems. They may introduce new laws that benefit women but laws don't change everything. We also need to change the mentality of men and of women and we have to begin inside our own organisation and in our communities.

In 1986 some of the CMC women had an unusual opportunity to turn the gains made at an organisational and policy level into the practices of a new community. After a long battle with the authorities

120 landless families from Caaguazú, all members of the Peasant Movement, won provisional title to 1,254 hectares of land in Limoy, in the eastern border region of Paraguay. By the mid 1980s the bulk of the farmland in this area was Brazilian-owned, either by huge land companies or by landless Brazilian peasants who had flooded into the region in search of a farm. The IBR, ostensibly the government agency responsible for colonisation programmes, had provided both the new companies and the Brazilian settlers with access to credit and technical schemes. To Paraguayan settlers it gave only transport to the site, a machete, an axe and a hoe for each family. The IBR offered no technical, credit or marketing services nor provided basic infrastructure such as roads, water, schools or health clinics. The survival of a community was left to the determination and creativity of its members.

The colony of Limoy is situated in the middle of extensive forests, isolated from the outside world by poor communications. The village is a four-hour bus ride from Ciudad del Este, once Ciudad Stroessner (Stroessner City), on Paraguay's southern border with Argentina and Brazil. The small local bus is always packed full with men, women and children and their sacks of rice, drums of cooking oil and kerosene. The bus driver accepts Brazilian currency and the conversations are in Portuguese, German and Guaraní. The roads are paved until the massive Itaipú dam and the small town of Hernandarias, where the dam construction workers once lived. Hernandarias is now almost deserted, its houses are up for sale and many of its shops have closed down. After Hernandarias the road turns to gravel. The journey is usually made after the rains which fall about once a month in the dry season between May and October, to avoid the choking clouds of dry red dust thrown up by passing lorries.

The journey ends outside the village of Limoy and from there, it is an 18 kilometre walk, or one-and-a-half-hour tractor ride, along rough tracks to the colony. For the first hour there are only the straight ploughed fields of soya and cotton of a Brazilian-owned plantation. Then the track passes through a forested region, still home to flocks of parakeets, deadly snakes and wild pumas, the native inhabitants of the semi-tropical forests that once covered the entire area and which are now only visible on the outer limits of the farmland. The colony of Limoy stands on the other side of the woods, its landscape a dramatic contrast to the Brazilian plantation. The rows of cotton and soya are broken by huge tree stumps and tall palms. 'The government helped us get the tractor but without a machine to break up the stumps it's not much use.' (Magui) There are fields of young saplings, 'We're reforesting some areas because this whole region could become an ecological disaster'. Every 300 metres along the track there are small wooden shacks, each with a well outside and a covered patio with

tables. 'We allocated each family the same amount of wood to build
their houses but many families were so poor they had to sell some of
the wood, so now a few houses are bigger than others.' (Magui) The
track leads to a shady square, the community's meeting place, named
after the two young boys shot dead in the land occupation in Alto
Paraná. About two hundred men, women and children are taking part
in a meeting with government officials about the village school. When
the discussions finish, the men drift off with the children, leaving about
twenty women to their own meeting. Their ages range from seventeen
to sixty and the majority speak little Spanish.

Geraldina's family was one of those which won provisional title to
the land in Limoy.

> GERALDINA: On 11 October 1986 the IBR brought us to Limoy in
> government lorries. There were 1,200 of us. They gave us 200 aspirins,
> forty litres of alcohol for dressing wounds and a few tents and
> abandoned us in the forest with the wild animals. It was all forest, there
> were no tracks and the landowners around here wouldn't let us walk
> through their property. The children were hungry and we had no food
> or water. We ate the fruit of the big palm trees and killed birds and wild
> animals for food. We got our water from the river. At first it was a battle
> for survival and not just against nature. We were constantly threatened
> by groups of gunmen; they stole our tools and when they called the
> police to evict us, the police would come and arrest us.
>
> We worked together to clear the forest for planting. We allocated each
> family twenty hectares. We lived in tents for a year while we worked
> together to build houses and wells for each family.

Fidelina was one of those to suffer the first setback to befall the new
community.

> FIDELINA: Soon after we came we were hit by leismaniasis. The disease
> comes from the bite of an insect which leaves a worm that eats into the
> body. The sores got everyone, the young people, the old. More than 400
> people got the disease. It was a calamity for the community. People with
> the sores can't eat heavy food, they can't work because they're too weak.
> When I worked my arms swelled up. The cure is very expensive and it
> takes four or six months of treatment. If you don't use the medicine the
> sores grow. There's only two places where you can get the medicine,
> from Wellcome in England or from France. The Ministry of Public Health
> didn't have the medicine and weren't interested in getting it for us. We
> went to the Irish priest in the village and he helped us get it from
> England.
>
> You need 160 injections, even for children, before you're cured. When
> your body is weak and ill-fed it doesn't react to the drug. When we took

the medicine for the sores we lost our milk so we couldn't feed the babies. There were many miscarriages and stillbirths. There are children who are mentally or physically affected by the mother taking the drug, because if you're pregnant you still have to take the drug, otherwise you die.

The dictatorship thought that by leaving us here in the middle of the forest we would give up and leave the land. But their plan didn't work because we organised ourselves. Our idea was to create a model community of Paraguayan peasants but at that time it seemed like an impossible dream.

The women of Limoy formed a regional branch of the CMC in 1987 with the aim of involving more women in the life of the community. The region was divided into four blocks of about 35 families and in each the women choose five representatives. From these women, ten are elected to the regional team. The MCP's formal acceptance of the need to promote women's participation in the organisation proved an effective weapon in silencing any public objections from the men about the time women spent away from home.

GERALDINA: Because organising women is part of the programme of the MCP, the men can't stop us going out, they can't be against it, although many would still like to be against it. There aren't any women in Limoy who can't come to a meeting because of their children. The men know they have to look after them when we're out. The men here must respect women — it's written into our community rules. In the beginning we had a case of rape and the community expelled him. We put all his belongings outside the colony and told him to leave.

The women saw one of their first tasks as building women's confidence and esteem through self-education and training.

GERALDINA: At our meetings we discuss our projects and organise training. In the courses we speak first about national history, the land and economic problems. We try to teach about the role of women in history but the problem is that history doesn't talk about women. We talk about *machismo*, the inequalities between men and women and all the ways in which we're discriminated against in our everyday lives. The point is to show women that we haven't always been downtrodden, to make ourselves proud of being women and to fight against discrimination.

A major problem is that the majority of us here can't read or write in Spanish or Guaraní and most of us don't speak Spanish well. I went to primary school for four years, but there are many women here who didn't go at all. Those of us who can read and write help the others. We go to courses and copy it all down from the blackboard and then we come back and teach it here. The meetings are for women only but we explain what we've discussed to our husbands and children, so that they understand and support us.

An important part of the women's work has been to convince their husbands and children that a new model community also means a new model for the family. At mixed regional meetings and in the home women are working to change the culture and traditions of the peasant way of life.

PASTORA: We are struggling to make the men understand that it's an injustice for girls to do all the work in the home. We're teaching the boys to work in the house and look after the children as well, so the girls have the same chances to go to school and to play. My husband is changing, but it's a slow process, for men and for women too. It was difficult at first for us to leave the children but if we don't leave them we're never going to change anything. Older people like us can't change one hundred per cent. The system's already eaten into our minds, although we try to change. We're very authoritarian ourselves, because of the education we've received. Women live under a dictatorship with their husbands and they apply this dictatorship to their children in a military style. But we're changing that. Now we say you mustn't hit the children, or abuse them psychologically. You have to explain and discuss things with them.

The school building is a large one-room wooden hut. The government provided no funds for a school and pays less than than half the wages of the teachers. The rest of the money comes from obligatory contributions from all community members, including families with no school-age children.

PASTORA: In the beginning it was just a little shack with a roof of palm leaves and a single mother from the community was the teacher. She taught more than a hundred children for two years under this roof without receiving a penny and with a lot of personal hardship. We cooked, made bread, organised football matches and sold drinks to get the money to buy wood for tables and benches and a building. We built the school ourselves two years ago, the men and women together. We haven't got books or maps or tables or chairs, only these rickety benches. The teachers have to be magicians to carry out the Ministry programme because they don't give us any materials.

The official primary school programmes of the Stroessner regime are largely irrelevant to the needs of peasants. The programmes are taught in Spanish, they discuss the history and culture of foreign countries more than that of Paraguay, focus on life and work in the cities and present submissive and passive images of women which contradict everything the women are trying to do in Limoy. The women responded by creating their own children's organisation.

> PASTORA: The official programmes from the Ministry are in Spanish and they ignore our culture and language so we formed an organisation for the children, between the ages of seven and thirteen, who are too young to join the MCP's Youth section. The aim is to recover our lost traditions, which have been repressed for so many years. We want to sow again the seeds of our native culture — our theatre, dance, music and our own language — so we're starting with the children. We organise games for them, teach them how to play, how to help and compete with each other, and we organise little shows where the children dance or act or sing. We give classes on Paraguayan history and the history of its peasants. The Ministry stops children from learning their own history, because in the government books the history of Paraguay doesn't appear. The books are machista too, so we teach the children about *machismo*, about the roles of men and women and the injustice of women's oppression.

The community's health needs were dramatically highlighted by the leismaniasis epidemic and the lack of medical provision is still a serious problem in Limoy. The community has only one member, a man, with any health training and the health post is little more than a first aid centre.

> PETRONILA: The government doesn't give us any medicines. We have to ask doctors, hospitals or churches to donate them. Every six months or so a doctor comes from the Ministry to give vaccinations but they only stay for an hour and can't see everyone. The hospital is four hours away, so you could be dead by the time you get there.
>
> We have to manage by ourselves. At government schools they don't teach you about health so we do the best we can. We use the CMC reports and bulletins which teach us about nutrition, health and sanitation. We haven't got a midwife but we help each other, with what we learnt from our mothers and from experience. Women have children here without any medical attention. Twenty one babies have already died here through lack of medical care and some women have died in childbirth.

Birth control is a taboo issue for many peasant women and only just beginning to be tackled by the CMC. Less than a third of women in rural areas use contraception and of those that do, the vast majority use herbal remedies. The lack of basic health services means that most rural women have no access to safe modern contraceptive methods nor to the medical supervision their use requires.

Women's attitudes to contraception are affected by the opposition of the Catholic Church to artificial methods of birth control and by that of their husbands who commonly see large families as proof of their virility. Some peasants also see contraception as part of a foreign-inspired campaign to wipe out the poor, a belief supported by reports which have reached Paraguay of the forced sterilisations carried out on women by foreign institutions in neighbouring Bolivia. Traditionally, large families have been seen as a form of social insurance. Children are needed to work the land and to care for their parents in their old age. In addition, peasant women see a large number of children as necessary since they can expect at least two out of ten of their children to die before they reach the age of five.

> MAGUI: 'We don't give priority to family planning or sexuality. It's a need, but not the most serious one. Women don't know their own bodies or how to look after themselves. Nor do the men. Lots of children are born that aren't wanted. If you speak in private to a woman she might say she doesn't want eight, ten or fourteen children because she's worried about her health. She's pregnant again without recovering from the last birth, she has to breast-feed when she's hungry. But she wouldn't say this in front of her husband. He'll say she doesn't want more children because she wants to find other men. Women are born to have children! In some of our meetings this issue comes up, and in the future we hope to have courses so that parents need only have children when they want them and women have a choice.

The years of repression of peasant communities and their culture have not only isolated women from community life but have also meant that much of their traditional knowledge about natural medicines, food preparation and farming skills has been lost. The staple diet of a peasant family is *reviro*, a heavy pancake made of maize flour and water and fried in oil, which has very little nutritional value.

Petronila, the currently CMC's regional representative, is in her early thirties and lives with her husband and five young children.

> PETRONILA: After the leismaniasis we began to realise that we needed to improve our diets. Before, a long time ago, we used to eat better. Now the children get a lot of diarrhoea. We'd never had any education on nutrition so we didn't know anything about vitamins or how to cook. We used to give the vegetables to the pigs. Then we found out that vegetables helped cure the children's sores quicker. Leismaniasis is a very delicate disease in relation to food — you can't eat beans or maize because it makes it worse, so it was more difficult to cure the disease because there was nothing else to eat.
> We started the communal allotments and we began to teach the others

about the importance of eating vegetables. We collect our pesos together
to buy seeds and distribute them to each block. There's about ten women
working on each allotment and two or three allotments per block.

Paraguay has little tradition of co-operative or communal farming
organisation; as the fate of the Peasant Leagues showed, co-operatives
have been considered subversive activities and are liable to become
the targets for military repression. The people of Limoy are
experimenting with many forms of communal activity. The tools,
tractor and lorry are all owned by the community co-operative which
also buys the seeds and sells the soya and cotton harvests. The plots
are owned by individual families but are farmed collectively and no
one works alone in their fields. The women have also begun to organise
their traditional work, shopping, the care of domestic animals and
family allotments in a collective way and have set up new
income-generating projects which have given them some financial
independence.

GERALDINA: We have six communal shops run collectively by the women
where we sell all the products that people need to buy from outside like
oil, rice, pasta and soap. We bring it in the lorry and distribute it to the
shops. We also have communal strips of land in each block where we
plant cotton and maize and soya, which we collect and clean together
and then sell. We sell the crops and use this money to keep our projects
going. The communal work helps the women to get close, to talk. We're
also preparing a chicken run, we've all taken our chickens and we take
turns in feeding them. It's an experiment. We want to see if we can
make it work.

Most of the work in the fields is still carried out by men and the
bulk of domestic tasks still fall on women, although they say that now
their work is considered 'real' work and they no longer feel like
servants in their own homes. The nature of work in the home is
determined by poverty. Petronila's house is typical. There is one large
room lit by paraffin lamps with an earth floor, where she sleeps with
her husband and six children. The cooking is done on the ground in a
wooden lean-to and the family eat in a covered patio at the side of the
house. In the yard there is a well, a toilet, which is a pit covered with
wooden planks and a wooden hut with two buckets which serves as
the bathroom. In such conditions cooking, washing clothes and
keeping the children clean are major undertakings. To make breakfast
of *reviro* and cassava, each family has to collect wood from the fields
and charcoal from the kiln, build fires, draw water from the well and
dig up the cassava. Petronila's day begins at 5.30am and ends at
midnight.

PETRONILA: We know very well how we should live and all the things we need. We live here like animals in our huts, not in homes or houses. First we need adequate housing and sanitation. We need a health centre and a secondary school, because we've got children who should be at secondary school but can't go. We need courses for illiterate women — they all want to learn. We also need a place to meet. All our achievements in Limoy have come through the sacrifice of members of the community. We've had almost nothing from the government. The big foreign companies get assistance from the Paraguayan government, but we, the Paraguayans, get nothing. We need a government that supports the peasants.

The street protests which rocked Paraguay's capital city, Asunción, in 1986 marked a turning point in civil resistance. Peasants, workers, students and women began openly to question the legitimacy of the Stroessner regime. The organised popular movement remained small and was easily crushed, but other signs of discontent were harder to contain. Business sectors expressed their concern at what they saw as Stroessner's anti-industrialist stance, their exclusion from the decision-making process and the prevalence of corruption and smuggling. At the same time the US began distancing itself from the regime and supporting democratisation processes in the Southern Cone. The fall of military regimes in Brazil, Argentina and Uruguay left Paraguay isolated from the international community and from plans for regional economic integration.

The ageing Stroessner's handling of the issue of his successor precipitated his downfall. In order to clear the way for the dictator's son, Colonel Gustavo Stroessner, hard liners staged an internal coup inside the Colorado Party. They attempted to restructure the armed forces by reorganising a number of military commands and forcing several generals into retirement. The coup took place on the day Stroessner ordered the number two in the military command, General Andrés Rodríguez, to relinquish his post. That night Rodríguez rolled out his tanks and the battle ended seven hours later with Stroessner's surrender and his immediate deportation to Brazil.

After the coup, events moved quickly and took the nation by surprise. Rodríguez lifted all restrictions on the press, freedom of speech and assembly, released some political prisoners, allowed prominent exiles to return, recognised the main political parties, with the exception of the Communist Party, and called for immediate elections.

Impressions of an abrupt break with the past however, were soon placed in doubt by Rodríguez' determination to control the transition to parliamentary democracy. He used Stroessner's constitutional and electoral laws, refused to negotiate with the opposition on the terms of the transition and put himself forward as presidential candidate. After years of persecution, the opposition — weak, poorly organised and penniless — had no time to register its voters and was forbidden to form coalitions. Social movements and peasant organisations had no voice in the electoral process. Campaigning on a platform of democracy, human rights and modernisation, Rodríguez won a landslide victory.

The reforms he subsequently made in civil liberties and labour rights benefited the peasant and worker organisations, but for them the real test of the new government's commitment to democracy was its willingness to redistribute the country's wealth. For the peasants that meant land. By 1989, according to the government's own statistics, 42 per cent of rural households were completely or practically landless.

REGINA: There are better conditions for organisation and free expression but nothing has changed for the poor in the economic or social sense. On the contrary, it's got worse because there's been a big increase in the cost of living in the two years of this government and the peasants are still getting low prices for their crops. It's not much use having the freedom to organise if you can't afford the bus fare to get to a meeting. New political organisations are being created in the name of the workers and peasants, which say they're from the left, and they're all talking about change and socialism, but in practice they are confusing everyone because we don't have a tradition of democracy here. The speeches of the political parties are full of reform but none have actually presented a programme and in practice no one is redistributing the land.

It's difficult to talk about democracy in a country with the Stroessner legacy of 5,000 murdered and 200 disappeared and where impunity reigns. Immediately after the coup several torturers were detained but Stroessner's laws still stand and those found guilty of crimes committed in the 1960s and 70s are released after a few months. We've presented more recent cases to the courts but we're not hopeful because we're dealing with the same people, the same legal system and the same laws.

There are no political prisoners now but there are hundreds of peasants being detained in land evictions. This government set up a committee to study agrarian reform, which invited peasant organisations to take part, but at the same time it created the Joint Task Forces, a police-military force to evict rural squatters. The Task Forces have since been disbanded, but now we are witnessing a new development — the appearance of armed civilian groups who put threatening statements in the newspapers, announcing that they will defend their property against occupiers. There's complicity between the judges and the landowners, and peasants are still being evicted, even after they have won legal title to the land.

In 1989, 200 families won legal title to 1,400 hectares of land they were occupying next to the colony of Limoy.

GERALDINA: They were living in tents and surviving thanks to our community. We gave them cassava, beans and corn because they had nothing. We helped them with the paperwork to get title for the land. The Special Operations Police arrived with 25 lorries and ambulances to evict them. They burnt down the shacks and destroyed the crops and the women from Limoy were the first to go to help. We stood in front of the police to try to stop them. They took 27 men prisoner and left the colony destroyed.

There's another piece of land nearby which is also in conflict. Hundreds of people have been living in tents for more than nine months, also surviving with our help.

The new government has no programme for the peasants. Now, before we've had time to establish ourselves properly in Limoy, they're putting pressure on us to pay for the land.

New civic freedoms have encouraged the formation of other women's organisations and offered the CMC the opportunity to build alliances with women from other social sectors. Only five women were elected to the new parliament and just one was appointed a minister in the government, but in trade unions, professional associations, political parties and in higher education women are making their presence much more widely felt. The main focus of women's energies has been removing discrimination from Paraguay's legal codes, but many of the new organisations have also expressed concern about the situation of peasant women. The most tangible assistance given to women peasants has been via non-governmental agencies, several of which, notably the Paraguayan Co-operativist Centre, the Peasants' Promotion Centre of the Cordillera and the Centre for Peasant Education, Training and Technology have promoted both women's education and training and the formation of women's organisations. They are small-scale projects however, and can have only a limited impact.

The CMC remains sceptical about the contributions outsiders can make to their organisation. Alone in their early attempts to organise women, and forced to work underground, the women invented their own brand of 'peasant feminism'. They have no contacts with the new feminist groups, whom they view as middle-class and unconcerned with the problems of poor women and concentrate instead on strengthening their position within the peasant movement. They are suspicious of urban women in general who, they feel, treat them as inferiors.

REGINA: We differentiate between women from the city and peasant women. We do this because we don't know their world and they don't know ours. It seems to us that people in the city look down on peasant women and we react against this and reject them. Because of this there's a distance between women who work in the city and us. But we can see that women workers are also exploited. We want to create an organisation which includes both sectors so that we can work together to change the situation.

The CMC has organised several meetings with women from the trade unions but, unusually for a rural organisation which has to deal with the problems of poor communications and the isolation of its members, has found itself much more advanced in its discussions of women's issues. Women have found it more difficult to establish themselves as a separate interest group within the trade unions. The CMC is the oldest of Paraguay's women's organisations and is the only one that can claim a mass membership.

Despite this, little is known about the CMC and the women complain that the press in general have paid them little attention. They have often missed opportunities to meet representatives of foreign organisations merely through the lack of a telephone. Although they have occasionally been invited to international events they have never been able to raise the fare to send a representative. They have no financial support and their many achievements have been the results of their own efforts and hard work.

Twelve out of 48 of the members of the MCP's national leadership are now women, and the Women's Commission is present in seven of the thirteen departments in which the MCP is organised. The women have not only succeeded in building a place for themselves in the peasant movement but they have also begun to break out of their isolation, to open up more choices for themselves and exercise more control over their lives.

GERALDINA: We work all the time, more now than ever before, but we've also changed the way we work. We're experimenting with communal work to see if it gives us more time for other things. It also gives us a chance to share our experiences and worries. This is a very different way of living for us. Before we didn't even know our neighbours.

We still do nearly all the housework. The men are starting to work in the house. When we have meetings, they do the cooking and cleaning, they look after the children. But there's still many who won't accept it.

It's taking a long time for the men to understand that they won't change anything without women.

PASTORA: Women still work more than men, that hasn't changed. Women still have to work in the house and look after the children and on top of that there's the organisation and the communal work, so there's an extraordinary effort being made in this community, by men and women but especially by women. But at least our work is recognised and valued and the children are learning a different way. Before, they used to say that women weren't useful for anything, not even for the darkness. Now women speak at meetings, they put forward ideas and the men listen to us. We got braver when we understood the struggle of women, that men and women are equal and that the only way we can get the government we want is if women fight alongside men.

I want to say that one of the most important changes for us is that now we're not afraid. Before we were afraid of everything, of noises, of people, of the police, of repression. If women are afraid, over half the country is sleeping. When the 25 lorries came here, full of police, the women were the first to confront them. We're beginning to recover the strength of the indigenous women. Through organisation, being together, we've recovered our self esteem and our sense of value.

In Eulogia's community the men have begun breaking the rock again. The peasants went to the MCP for support and have begun the battle to win legal title to both the land they have paid for and the rock. Eulogia and Josefina, one of her neighbours, are on the local neighbourhood commission and are now CMC members.

EULOGIA: We're not afraid now. We've got a neighbourhood rock commission of ten people and Josefina and I are the only women. We go to the city, to the IBR and we even went to speak in parliament and they listened to us. We weren't afraid because it's our legitimate right. We weren't telling anyone lies.

JOSEFINA: This land has already been paid for so we're demanding our title to it and the title to the stone so we can break it and sell it. The men respect us...well, more or less — some drink too much *caña* — but the women can go out to meetings. Because of the organisation the men understand, but there's still some men who don't want their wives to go out. It's disgusting. The men here are hard-headed, they're too *macho*.

EULOGIA: We're fighting *machismo*. That's what we've learnt — that women don't have to be downtrodden. I've been married for 25 years and I left my house for the first time one year ago. Now we have to go to speak to people in the town. They listen to us, but not very much because the Stroessner dictatorship taught people who work in the offices to behave very badly. While we're away the children do our work. Now that we're organised we tell the boys they have to wash their clothes and their plates. They don't like it, but they keep their mouths shut.

The men say we're very hard. We want things for the community, for our children. The men want the money in their pockets. They want other women, to dance and to drink. Paraguayan men have got big eyes and see little. It's a hard battle against the men. But now we're struggling to get out of the prison! We're trying to change the men.

Being in the organisation has changed us. We don't go to church any more. There's too much *machismo*, they go around with their eyes closed. After 15 children, I said that's it! The factory's closed!

Faced with one of Latin America's most brutal dictatorships, isolation and poverty, the deeply embedded *machismo* of Paraguayan peasant men and the lack of self esteem among peasant women, the very survival of the women's commission has been a major achievement. In just a few years women once generally considered submissive, humble, ignorant and unable to deal with the world outside their homes have shown enormous strength and courage in the battle against poverty and oppression. The organisation continues to grow, as do the challenges they face. The MCP now has seven new colonies, some legal and others land occupations awaiting the decision of the Ministry of Agriculture, where women like those of Limoy are trying to create a place for themselves in running their communities. As the promised land reform has yet to appear and the new government follows in the path of other southern cone countries, embracing IMF-backed austerity measures, the peasants' movement will need all the strength and courage of its women in the struggle for social and economic justice in Paraguay.

Argentina
Chronology

1976 Nine months after a military coup topples the government of President Isabel Perón, an Amnesty International mission to Argentina finds evidence of serious human rights violations, including illegal detention, summary execution, torture and disappearance.

1977 In the first public protest against military rule, the Mothers and Grandmothers of the Plaza de Mayo begin their search for missing relatives.

1979 The Grandmothers of the Plaza de Mayo locate the first disappeared grandchildren in Chile.

1982 Argentina loses Falklands/Malvinas war. The regime calls elections and passes a self-amnesty law, clearing military personnel of responsibility for the crimes committed in the 'dirty war'.

1983 End of dictatorship. The new president, Raúl Alfonsín, repeals the military's self-amnesty law and appoints the National Commission on Disappeared People to investigate the crimes of the 'dirty war'.

1984 The Commission uncovers 340 secret torture centres and estimates that at least 9,000 people 'disappeared' under military rule. Human rights organisations put the true figure at 30,000. A judge orders a 'disappeared' grandchild to be restored to her real family after the Grandmothers bring their first case before the courts.

1985 Five of the nine members of the first three military juntas are sent to prison in the first-ever trial of a defeated military regime by an elected civilian government.

1986 The Law of *Punto Final* (Full Stop) places a sixty-day time limit on new prosecutions of military officers accused of violations of human rights. Military rebellion by middle-ranking officers demanding an immediate end to the trials.

1987 The law of Due Obedience clears all military personnel except the high command of responsibility for 'dirty war' crimes. The first disappeared child born in a concentration camp is located and restored to her family by the courts.

1989 At least 43 officers charged with human rights violations are pardoned in an amnesty decree signed by newly-elected President Carlos Menem.

1990 21 dead and fifty injured after a military rebellion is crushed. Members of the military juntas are freed in the second wave of amnesties. Fiftieth 'disappeared' grandchild restored to his family.

4

'Where are our Children?'

Mothers and Grandmothers of the Disappeared in Argentina

MARÍA DEL ROSARIO: When I went to the military headquarters the day after they kidnapped my son, I met a woman whose daughter had been missing for two months. I thought, how can she still be standing here? I'd die — I couldn't bear two months not knowing where he was. And then I stood for two months, three months and fourteen years. And in that fourteen years I learnt a lot.

At 3.30pm every Thursday afternoon a group of women gather in the Plaza de Mayo (May Square) in the centre of Buenos Aires. Fastening the white headscarves embroidered with the words, 'Aparición con Vida', 'Return our Children Alive', they begin to walk in a circle around the monument to independence. The silent vigil has taken place almost every Thursday since 1977. In that year the presidential palace and the ministries that overlook Plaza de Mayo were occupied by generals and admirals, the country's principal cathedral, on the square's northern side, closed its doors to the women fleeing the tear gas attacks of the police, and the Argentine population, silenced by the terror of state-organised death squads, kidnappings and murder, knew little of the struggle of the mothers of the 'disappeared'. Since then, the generals have fallen from power and new constitutional governments have imprisoned, then released them. The men who kidnapped and murdered an estimated 30,000 young people, children and babies now walk the streets freely. Support for the Mothers has dwindled since the early years of the new government when they led massive demonstrations calling for the prosecution of the military and their weekly march drew almost a thousand followers, instead of the two hundred or so of today. The foreign journalists and film crews are still there, as they were in the beginning, when no national newspaper dared publish the story of the women's struggle to find their missing relatives. 'Where are our children?' remains an unanswered question, and a constant reminder to those who would prefer to forget the darkest chapter of Argentine history.

The movement which became known as the Mothers of the Plaza de Mayo began in April 1977, one year after a military junta seized power in Argentina, when 14 women gathered in the square to demand information about their missing children. Within months they had been joined by dozens of others, the majority of them housewives, unaware that the search for their children would uncover a secret and barbaric system of detention, torture and murder. Not only did they become the first public challenge to one of the most brutal military dictatorships Latin America has ever witnessed, but they also became a major force in the struggle for democracy and a key influence on the civilian government elected after the fall of military rule in 1983. Outside Argentina, their courageous struggle became a symbol for the human rights movement in Latin America and a source of inspiration for women throughout the continent in the fight for democracy.

The military junta which overthrew the elected government of Isabel Perón (see Chapter Five) on 24 March 1976 promised to restore 'order' to an economy crippled by hyperinflation, debt and industrial unrest and a political system torn apart by violence. A small guerrilla movement had provided the military with the pretext for its 'dirty war'. Under the military's 'Process of National Reorganisation', (*el Proceso*, as it became known) constitutional rights were suspended, political parties and trade unions were closed down, public meetings were banned, the press was censored and any opposition was rounded up and imprisoned. But in Argentina such draconian measures were only the public face of the repression; there would be no political prisoners on a mass scale as in Uruguay and no evidence of mass slaughter as in Chile, with none of the international outcry it provoked. Opposition would be simply wiped off the face of the earth. 'Disappearance', the kidnapping, illegal detention, torture and execution of real or imagined opponents to military rule was the centrepiece of the military's plan of repression.

In an interview with English journalists in 1978 General Videla declared that 'a terrorist isn't just someone with a gun or a bomb, but whoever spreads ideas which are contrary to western and Christian civilisation'. General Iberico Saint-Jean, governor of the province of Buenos Aires was more explicit. 'First we will kill all the subversives, then we'll kill their collaborators, then... their sympathisers, then... those who remained indifferent and, finally, we will kill the weak.'

The generals set up a network of over 340 secret concentration camps throughout the country. Some 30,000 people passed through these camps, never to be seen again. The victims, kidnapped from their homes, schools and places of work, came from all sectors of society, ranging from trade union militants, students and intellectuals to secondary school children and babies. Over thirty per cent were women and of those three per cent were pregnant at the time of their kidnapping. Since Argentina's *'desaparecidos'* , the 'disappeared', did not officially exist, they could be held without time limit or without any constraints on the methods used against them.

The 'dirty war' was not only designed to eliminate all opposition, but also to spread a sense of terror in the population that would extinguish all protest. With a few notable exceptions, the press was silent about the kidnappings, together with the majority of leading political and church figures. Lawyers were reluctant to take up cases of disappearance and normal legal protections against arbitrary arrest and persecution, such as habeas corpus, became meaningless. Those who dared to defy the authorities were persecuted or disappeared themselves; at least 109 lawyers, one hundred journalists and thirty priests and nuns are known to have disappeared under military rule. In this climate of fear the families of victims found themselves alone in their search for their missing relatives. It was usually the women who refused to give up hope, persisting with their endless round of visits to police stations, military barracks and government offices only to be met with obstructions, intimidation and threats. On the trail of cruel deceptions laid by the authorities the women began meeting each other. Realising that only by working together would they have any chance of recovering their children, they arranged to meet in the Plaza de Mayo to draw up a joint letter to the authorities.

María del Rosario's son was kidnapped from her home in May 1976.

MARIA DEL ROSARIO: It's very difficult to explain how you feel when they take a child from you and you don't know what's happened to that child. It's like a terrible emptiness, like something's been wrenched away from inside of you and there's nothing you can do about it. No one would help us. At the police stations and the barracks we stood in queues for hours and they turned us away, they played games with us, they laughed at us. They insulted us or called us the 'mothers of terrorists'. As we began to recognise in the faces of other women the same despair and desperation we felt, we began to realise that we weren't alone, that there were hundreds of mothers like us, searching for their children.

A few of us thought that if we all signed a letter together — which is how we started — we might make more progress. Then we found that if we all went to the courts they paid more attention to us. Then we all stood in lines outside the Ministry of Interior or an army barracks to drive the military mad. Working together was a very important step for us. At first we cried a lot, but together we began to find the strength to fight.

Every Thursday afternoon women began to gather silently in Plaza de Mayo. They sat on benches, identifying each other by a leaf pinned to their lapels or a flower in their hands, secretly passing each other messages. The penalty for illicit association was up to 25 years in prison and the Plaza de Mayo, opposite the presidential palace and historically the site of political and trade union demonstrations, was one of the most heavily guarded areas in Buenos Aires.

By meeting in the square they were ignoring the advice of human rights organisations already in existence which discouraged illegal forms of action. They also ignored the government officials who warned that joining the women in the square would cost them all hope of ever seeing their children again. As mothers, they felt a special responsibility for finding their children and a desperation that they believed only other mothers could understand.

Porota spent part of her childhood in Spain during the civil war where her father, a trade unionist, was shot and killed by General Franco's soldiers. Although she was never politically involved herself, she had experienced life under fascism and dictatorship. When her only daughter was kidnapped from the flat in Buenos Aires where she lived with her three children, Porota was convinced that there was no hope of finding her alive. After initial attempts came to nothing, paralysed with despair, she did nothing more to find her daughter. Six months later, her husband found out about the Mothers.

POROTA: The first time I went to the square I met another woman on the underground. I said, 'You must be going to the same place as me'. She said, 'Where are you going?' I said, 'To the Plaza de Mayo. My daughter's disappeared.' And then I began to tell her everything all at once — how she disappeared, how they'd taken her and left her three children and stolen everything from her house. The woman looked at me as if I was crazy. It was very dangerous to talk about those things in public at that time. It shows you what a state I was in. I was desperate. When I got to the square I went to walk with them. I cried all the time and the other women came to comfort me. We were all mothers together, all mothers whose children had been taken away, and we understood each other's pain. It was a tremendous relief and for the first time since my daughter had disappeared I felt I could do something.

Hebe de Bonafini is in her early sixties. She was brought up in a working-class district of La Plata, a town 56 kilometres to the south-east of Buenos Aires. With only a primary school education, she was forced to leave school to help support her family. After she married she continued working at home as a seamstress and her life centred around her husband and her two sons and daughter. She joined the women in the square after Jorge, a student, the first of her sons to disappear, was kidnapped in 1977.

> HEBE: In the other organisations we didn't feel close to each other, there was always a desk in between us, it was always something more bureaucratic. In the square we all felt equal — What happened? How did it happen? — They'd taken children from all of us so we all felt the same. We were afraid, but as mothers we felt our children needed us more than ever, that we had to do everything possible to find them.
>
> When the police saw there were a lot of us in the square, sixty or seventy sitting on the benches, they said 'you can't sit here, there's a state of siege, this is a meeting; you'll have to move on' and they began to hit us with their hands and with sticks. So we began walking. It was the police that forced us to march around the monument.

The majority of the women were housewives, between the ages of forty and sixty. They came from varied social backgrounds but they all shared a lack of experience of the world of politics and little understanding of the situation they had found themselves in.

> MARIA DEL ROSARIO: Most of us were uneducated women, all with the same upbringing — you mustn't get involved in politics, you mustn't talk about politics, that was what the men did. We might have had discussions inside the house, but outside, never. We only cared about our children and our families, not about the world outside. Few of us even worked outside the home.
>
> We were women who understood nothing. I didn't understand about 'disappearances' and concentration camps. Like all the Mothers, I thought the military were bad — no one was in favour of the military — but we thought in a month or twenty days, our children would be back. For almost a year I left all his clothes ready, kept the light on at nights, his favourite food in the fridge, expecting him to come back any day. No one realised that they'd never come back, that they were going to put them in concentration camps. It never crossed our minds.
>
> HEBE: We had to educate ourselves. The majority of us had hardly been to school. This is a *macho* country; we were used to talking about dress patterns and cooking, while the men discussed politics and football in another room. Women like us lived in an isolated world which finished at the front doors of our houses. We were taught to iron, wash and cook and look after the children and that politics was for the men. I'd never been anywhere except to Buenos Aires and that was always a special

occasion. Apart from that, my longest journey was twice round the four blocks of my neighbourhood every Sunday. When you live like this, you don't know what rights you've got, you don't know there's a United Nations, an Amnesty International, a habeas corpus, you don't understand anything, that is all from another world. We began to read and we began to collect information to help us understand what was going on.

The women learnt quickly how to organise themselves in a world where meetings of more than two or three people risked attracting the suspicion of the police. The women's sewing clubs, fashion shows and birthday parties became the cover for the first organised challenge to military rule.

Clara is 73. She was widowed at twenty eight, when her son was just six months old, and began working to support him. A religious woman, with no time for politics, she dedicated herself to her only child. After 12 April 1977 when he was kidnapped by security forces together with his wife, who was three months pregnant, she devoted her life to finding them. Her search quickly led her to the women in the square who were looking not only for their missing children, but also for their grandchildren. These women formed their own group within the Mothers and became known as the Grandmothers of the Plaza de Mayo.

CLARA: It was difficult communicating with each other. The telephones were tapped. We used to meet in someone's house but we had to be very careful coming and going to avoid suspicion, or we'd meet in a cafe and so that no one would realise what was going on, we took paper and pretended we were copying dress patterns and someone would say that on a certain date at a certain time we'd have a fashion show. Or we'd pretend we were celebrating a birthday. Really we were arranging visits to orphanages or to the courts. There were many of us who, like me, were looking for children without a name, without knowing their sex, and often without knowing if they'd been born or not.

HEBE: 'As we were always being followed and always under pressure, we had to be creative and find new ways of doing things. For example, we'd write on banknotes, especially high denomination ones, 'we have a missing child who's name is so and so'. We went to the market with scribbled notes and handed them out. They circulated fast because it was dangerous to be found with anything which criticised the regime and no one wanted to hold onto them. We left messages on buses or we'd put information about our missing children inside the pages of the prayer books.

Our first demand was 'we want our children back'. When I was reading our old letters recently I nearly had a fit. We were so supplicant, practically begging for our children — begging to mass murderers. We didn't begin to shout until much later, and only then because a group of doctors who were attending an international conference asked us why we said nothing. We explained that it was a silent march. But they said that we should at least shout something, so we did, we shouted, 'Where are our children?', which was both a difficult, and a very important step for us.

Towards the end of 1977, at the popular annual pilgrimage to the shrine of the Virgin of Luján, the Mothers and Grandmothers first used the white headscarves which were to become the symbol of their struggle throughout the world. As they grew more defiant so the attitude of the military towards them began to change. One of the reasons that women had taken up the search for their children was because it was considered more dangerous for their male relatives to do so. The activities of women, who had traditionally played little part in organisations like political parties and trade unions, were less likely to be considered as 'politically' motivated. The Mothers reinforced this idea of themselves, wording their pleas in terms of motherhood and the defence of their children. This presented the regime with a dilemma. Much of its claim to moral legitimacy was based on its defence of the Christian values of family and motherhood in the face of a godless communist threat from the left; the first public challenge to their rule, however, came not from the unions or political parties, but from a group of women who were appealing to those same values.

The authorities also fell victim to their own prejudices about women: a group of middle-aged housewives could offer no serious threat to a seemingly invulnerable system of repression which had silenced the country's organised opposition movement. In the face of the unlikely challenge of the Mothers of the Plaza de Mayo, the regime vacillated. They dismissed the Mothers as 'mad women' and gave them the breathing space needed to organise themselves.

In October 1977 the Mothers, together with other human rights organisations, published a half-page advertisement in a national newspaper demanding information about the disappearances. This was followed by a petition signed by 25,000 people demanding the release of those in illegal detention. Police broke up the march which accompanied the presentation of the petition to the regime and some 300 people were arrested.

When the military's scare tactics failed to frighten the Mothers off, the 'mad women' became the 'mothers of terrorists' and in December 1977 the military struck. The Mothers and other human rights organisations had begun collecting for their second advertisement. María del Rosario was at the Santa Cruz church where final signatures were being collected: 'As I was leaving a group of men seized the two Mothers I was walking with. They said it was a drugs raid.' In all 13 people were taken that night and in the following days two French nuns, one of whom had been working with the Mothers, and the leader of the Mothers, Azucena de Villaflor, were kidnapped. None of them were seen again. Much later the Mothers discovered that their organisation had been infiltrated by an officer posing as the relative of a disappeared person. The officer, for whom the Mothers had felt pity and offered their sympathy and support, was Lieutenant Alfredo Astiz, later known as 'the Blond Angel of Death' for his role in disappearances, torture and murder.

The kidnappings, however, failed to break the Mothers' determination to discover the truth.

MARIA DEL ROSARIO: The kidnapping of the Mothers was a great blow to our organisation but it only made us more determined to find out what was really going on. Of course there was a lot of fear. Everyone felt it. My family said 'be careful, something might happen to you', but I said to them, 'what can be worse than them taking my child?'

It was only gradually that the women became aware that they were confronting not the excesses of a few military officers, but a systematic plan of repression that extended across the whole country. As some detainees were released the women began to learn of the existence of concentration camps, they began to hear the same chilling testimonies of horror, identical descriptions of torture methods and they discovered the truth behind the 'transfers', the military's euphemism for extermination.

Some women began to receive information about the fate of their own children.

HEBE: In 1977 a man called and told me he had been in prison with one of my sons. He said that Jorge had been badly beaten and tortured and left for days without food. The man gave me little hope that he could have survived. Jorge had asked this man to let me know where he was. He was at the same police station where I'd already been to ask for information about him. I went there and screamed at them to let me in. I shouted at them that they were murderers. They hit me and threw me out into the street. There was nothing I could do.

Some of the Mothers and Grandmothers themselves had first-hand experience of the horror. When the military seized power Leonor was a university lecturer aged 53, with seven grown-up chidren. The husband of one of her daughters, María, had disappeared in June 1976.

Both María, who had two young daughters and was seven months pregnant, and Leonor were kidnapped from their homes on the same day in September 1976.

> LEONOR: After five days they told me they'd made a mistake and that I was an excellent person and that they were going to free me. They said they would keep my daughter for further questioning and they warned me not speak to anyone about what had happened otherwise they'd kill her.
>
> They used the *picana* to give me electric shocks. They tied me to a table and my body jerked up and down until I thought my back was going to break. Then they gave me two mock executions. Sometimes they tortured us together. They tortured my daughter more than me. She couldn't eat because she felt like she'd swallowed her tongue. They tortured her so badly that I thought the baby could never have survived.

However, the Grandmothers soon began to receive information which suggested that their grandchildren were being born inside the concentration camps and were being disposed of as the spoils of war. They discovered the names of gynaecologists and doctors who co-operated with the military, taking away newly-born babies hours after their mothers had been 'transferred'. Clara was told by ex-detainees that her son and daughter-in-law had been held in a torture centre in an army garrison in the province of Buenos Aires. Estela de Carlotto, whose daughter's dead body had been returned to the family one year after her kidnapping with the explanation that she had been killed a few days earlier in an armed confrontation, discovered that her daughter had been detained in a concentration camp and had given birth to a boy. Enriqueta was told by a couple released from a secret detention centre that her kidnapped daughter, María, had given birth to a girl: 'Straight after giving birth she was made to clean up everything. The chief of police took the baby away. She had five hours with her daughter and then she was "transferred".'

If the women had lost their fear of the military, they trembled with anger and frustration at the indifference of the courts, the Church, the political parties and the trade unions. Many of the women were practising Catholics and had believed that the Church would use its powerful influence to condemn and stop the disappearances. The hundreds of letters they sent to the influential Episcopal Conference asking for help were never answered. Instead they were confronted by priests who warned them not to get involved and that making a fuss could threaten the lives of their children and grandchildren. They were advised to pray. Clara visited the chaplain of the Armed Forces who appeared sympathetic to her plight and told her that he, personally, was going to concern himself with the case.

CLARA: I returned a few days later. He said, 'Have you got enough money for a taxi?' I asked him why. 'Because your children are waiting for you at home'. I went rushing home, ecstatic. There was no one. Later I received a letter from him saying that despite his efforts he hadn't been able to find out anything, and that I should put my faith in God. I went to a church school, I grew up fearing God, respecting the priests and the Church. What did they do? They went to the concentration camps and blessed the tortured youngsters and then they told us they knew nothing. I feel deceived. Now I don't know if God exists.

Only much later did the Grandmothers and Mothers discover that armed forces' chaplains who had promised to help them were frequent visitors to the concentration camps. Pío Laghi, the Pope's representative in Argentina, received some of the Mothers and offered them his sympathy. Evidence given later to the constitutional government's report on the disappearances showed that he was one of several priests who had witnessed the torture and execution of detainees.

The Grandmothers began to discover that some of the judges who had denied knowledge of their missing grandchildren had themselves handed over children to orphanages as NNs (names unknown) or for 'adoption', in spite of knowing their names and their origins. Some of them were less secretive about their activities, endorsing wholeheartedly the view of the military, made clear by General Ramón Camps, 'Subversive parents educate their children for subversion. This has to be stopped'. One judge responsible for juvenile cases, Delia Pons, said to the Grandmothers of their disappeared children, '(terrorists) don't have the right to bring up children. Nor am I going to let them be returned to you. It's not right to disturb children now in the hands of decent families who know how to educate them, as your children didn't. Only over my dead body are you going to get the children'.

The women expected support from the leaders of the banned political parties, but received only warnings about the evils of subversion. Clara went to Italo Luder, a lawyer and leader of the Peronist Party, whose reaction was typical of the majority of politicians to whom they appealed for help.

CLARA: He said he felt very sorry for me. But he took advantage of the situation to add that if it hadn't been for subversion none of this would have happened. He finished by recommending that I didn't join the other mothers or families of victims because this would damage my chances of getting my grandchild back.

Nor did the Mothers find any support for their cause in the media which made almost no mention of the disappearances. Censorship and persecution guaranteed the acquiescence of the national press and made it an accomplice in the military's whitewash of history. The Argentine public knew nothing of the mothers of the disappeared.

The foreign media were more difficult to manipulate. In the beginning the clandestine nature of repression had ensured that the Argentine military takeover never received the international condemnation of the Chilean coup. As early as 1976, however, international human rights organisations, including Amnesty International, had published disturbing reports of what was happening inside the country. The World Cup, which was held in Argentina in 1978, offered the military the opportunity to counter these reports and project an image of respectability to the world. Any challenge to the military version of events was brutally repressed. An estimated 367 people disappeared during the preparations for the event and at least 46 during the competition itself. Several women, such as Elsa Pavón de Aguilar, whose daughter, son-in-law and 23-month-old granddaughter, Paula, were kidnapped just before the tournament started, were told that when the World Cup was over, their children would be freed. Elsa never saw her daughter and son-in-law again. Porota's daughter was also kidnapped by the security forces in 1978.

POROTA: The World Cup was a very painful experience for us. We suffered the repression and the indifference of our people who told us it was unpatriotic to speak against our country when the eyes of the world were on Argentina. But we also saw that the foreign journalists were interested in us and that the Dutch team, instead of being at the opening ceremony of the football, came to be with us in the square. Dutch television sent out pictures of the Mothers. We discovered that outside Argentina there were people prepared to listen to us. That was the year the support groups began.

Encouraged by their contact with foreign journalists, the Mothers and Grandmothers began organising collections to send women abroad in search of international support. Showing a complete disregard for protocol and red tape they managed to get an interview with representatives of the US State Department, spoke at the United Nations and visited the Pope in the Vatican. However, they were left disillusioned after their meetings with the rich and powerful. 'We thought they would intervene to stop the disappearances. It wasn't until much later that we understood about the 'Doctrine of National

Security' and realised that governments were more interested in trade and politics than the fate of the *desaparecidos*'. (Hebe)

Although they received little concrete help from foreign governments, they won world attention for their cause and in Europe a number of support groups began to spring up. International publicity offered the women and their organisations a measure of protection, but it did not prevent the military from intensifying their efforts to break the human rights movement. By the time the International Commission on Human Rights of the Organisation of American States finally arrived in Argentina in late 1979, police repression had become so fierce that the Mothers were forced to abandon their weekly meetings and resort to 'lightning' demonstrations in the square.

MARIA DEL ROSARIO: They filled the square with mounted police in riot gear. We ran to the churches for refuge and the priests turned off the lights and threw us out. They took us prisoner. They hit us. They put dogs in the square and we carried rolled up newspapers to beat them off. They threw tear gas at us. We learned to take bicarbonate of soda and a bottle of water — grown women, who'd never left the kitchen, were learning what so many young people had learnt so much earlier.

In 1979, amid growing concerns that the tactics of the police would succeed in breaking up the movement, the Mothers held elections and registered '*Las Madres de Plaza de Mayo*' as a legal association. It was formally decided that the Mothers would be an all-women's organisation, membership being confined only to mothers of disappeared children. A commission of twenty mothers drew up a statement in which they called for information on their children, respect for human rights, freedom and democracy.

HEBE: Working in the streets and churches had the effect of dispersing us; setting ourselves up as an association meant that if they kidnapped us there'd be proof of our existence.

The next big step was getting the office in 1980. Before that we'd had our meetings in our homes and the police were always turning up and breaking them up. Besides, working in someone's house wasn't effective as there was always a great waste of time, what with cakes and tea being served. I lived a long way from the capital, so I couldn't waste my time. Not that it's changed an awful lot. Personal things always creep into meetings, fortunately. I say this because being more personal lets us be more human and feeling.

A group of Dutch women sent us some money and with our one typewriter we opened an office.

By 1980 cracks were beginning to appear in the armour of military rule, yet it was not human rights, but the collapse of the military's economic programme which led to the first mass demonstrations against the regime. The newly reconstituted, but still outlawed, political parties and trade unions began organising protests against unemployment, inflation and falling living standards and to demand an end to military rule.

In 1981 the Mothers organised their first 24 hour 'March of Resistance' in the Plaza de Mayo. The march coincided with the fall of the regime of General Viola and his replacement as president by General Galtieri. With military rule crumbling, General Galtieri seized on the popular nationalist cause of the Malvinas (Falklands) islands as a last-ditch attempt to bolster support for the regime.

> POROTA: We were in solidarity with the mothers of the soldiers in the war but we didn't believe in the war, it was another World Cup — a trick to deceive the people. They accused us of being unpatriotic. People asked how we could go to the square when there was a war on. We told them 'the Malvinas are Argentina's and so are the *desaparecidos*'. We even had to fight with our children, our brothers and sisters, who didn't want to believe what the military were really like.

Defeat in the war made the military's fall inevitable. To protect themselves from prosecution by a future constitutional government, the military passed the Law of National Pacification, exonerating all members of the armed forces from any criminal responsibility for actions carried out in the 'war against subversion'. They also took the precaution of destroying evidence of the clandestine network of concentration camps and any written reference to their existence.

The Mothers and the Grandmothers, however, were determined to turn human rights into the central issue of the election, which ended military rule. Experience had left them sceptical about the promises of political leaders. Many of those standing for the new parliament were the same politicians who had ignored their pleas for help during the dictatorship. Their greatest fear was that the political leaders would strike a deal with the military over the issue of the disappearances.

No longer the pleading, weeping mothers of the early days, they began an active campaign to press all the political parties to include in their election manifestos their two principal demands, the return alive of the disappeared and the prosecution of all those responsible for the disappearances.

> HEBE: The first time the political parties met we all went and they said 'Have you asked for an interview?' 'No'. We opened the door and eighty of us walked in and said 'Hello, here we are'. They couldn't believe that we'd got inside. They were horrified! We'd taken our document on the disappearances and we said, 'you've all been in cold storage for five

years and now you've come out, we want to give each of you a document'. Every time they met, we were there, going in through the back door, with or without an invitation.

We said to each of the parties, don't accept the legacy of 30,000 *desaparecidos*. We talked to the leaders, trying to convince them that it was their duty to bring those responsible to justice. It was exhausting work, trying to persuade politicians who didn't want to listen, partly because they were responsible for the disappearance of our children. The Radicals were the party who worked most for the dictatorship, the largest number of councils were run by Radicals. And the Peronist candidate, Luder, was the one who signed the extermination decree in 1975*.

That was why they didn't want to help us.

They all talked a lot about human rights. All the political parties tried to get a Mother by their side at demonstrations or meetings, they all made a lot of vague promises, but none of them would tell us exactly what they were going to do about it.

The new president, Raúl Alfonsín, was inaugurated on a wave of euphoria, as Argentines took to the streets to celebrate the end of the dictatorship. Despite doubts about the extent of the government's commitment to their cause, the Mothers were encouraged by the popular support they had received at mass demonstrations in the final months of the dictatorship. Like the other human rights organisations, their hopes centred on their demand for *aparición con vida*, the return alive of their children. The Mothers were granted an audience with the president soon after he took office.

HEBE: He was very sympathetic and we left feeling optimistic. He told us he thought there were *desaparecidos* alive, which is what we also thought. He told us he was going to search for them.

The human rights organisations had demanded that all *desaparecidos* be freed within the first 48 hours of constitutional rule. Some Mothers and Grandmothers had clung to the hope that their children were still alive. There were rumours that *desaparecidos* were being held in rehabilitation camps in the interior of the country or in Paraguay, still under the military dictatorship of General Stroessner. Their hopes were raised when several families received letters and telephone calls

---

*Footnote: In 1975 the government of Isabel Perón, of which Italo Luder was a member, signed a decree which gave the army a virtual free hand to deal with a small guerrilla organisation operating in the north-western province of Tucumán. The site of the first secret detention centre, Tucumán was the testing ground for the kidnappings, torture and disappearances used after the coup

which suggested that some of the disappeared were still alive. Cecilia Viñas, who disappeared in 1976, telephoned her family seven times between December 1983 and April 1984. After a recording of the conversations was made public by the Ministry of the Interior all communication ceased.

In the country's graveyards, however, the evidence pointed overwhelmingly to the fact that the *desaparecidos* were dead. The new government called in US forensic experts to ascertain the cause of death and identify bodies buried in hundreds of unnamed graves in prohibited zones which had appeared in cemeteries throughout the country during military rule. The Mothers, who had once pleaded with the authorities for the bodies of their children so they could mourn at their graves, opposed the exhumations.

> MARIA DEL ROSARIO: They began digging up bodies and called in a team of US anthropologists to examine the bones. We said, no, we don't want to know how many shots killed them, we want to know where the murderers are, who took them, who ordered the torture and execution and we want them put in prison. They wanted to give us the bodies without telling us anything. Our dead children are no use to us — we don't want a tomb to cry at; we want to know who was responsible and we want them in prison.

Aparición con vida was less about the expectation of seeing their loved ones alive, and more about the trial and punishment of those responsible for the disappearances. If their children were not going to return it was the government's responsibility to explain what had happened to them and to prosecute all those responsible. *Aparición con vida* was intended as a radical challenge to the new government.

The government's human rights policy however, was formulated almost exclusively by the president and his advisers, with little reference to the views of parliament or those most affected by the disappearances. Whether the armed forces had a role in drawing up this policy has never been clarified. The human rights organisations demanded a bicameral parliamentary commission to investigate the disappearances with powers to subpoena military officers and initiate prosecutions. Instead, the government set up a presidential commission, known as the National Commission on the Disappearances (CONADEP), whose objectives were restricted to enquiring into the events relating to the disappearances and investigating the fate of the *desaparecidos*. CONADEP's brief did not extend to finding those responsible for human rights abuses and bringing them to trial.

The exhumations, carried out at the commission's request, were seen by some of the Mothers as a way of paralysing their struggle for justice.

By proclaiming their children dead, the whole issue of the *desaparecidos* would be erased from history.

> HEBE: They weren't telling us anything we didn't already know. Everybody knew about the mass executions, that they burnt bodies in huge incinerators and about the secret night flights when planes emptied bodies into the sea. They began to send some of us telegrams saying that our children were buried in such and such a cemetery. They sent some of us boxes with bones saying they were the remains of our children. We decided to reject the exhumations because if we accepted their deaths without anyone telling us who killed them, who kidnapped them, it would be as if we were killing them again. It's not an easy decision for a mother to make. There were many meetings, many arguments.

The search for bodies also threatened to break the unity of the human rights organisations whose strength was based in the collective demand for the return of all the disappeared. The Mothers argued that treating the disappearances as a series of individual cases only diverted attention from the organised and systematic nature of the repression.

> POROTA: We had grown as an organisation from looking for our own individual children to looking for all the children and the commission was a way of sending us back to the beginning again, to the individual struggle with everyone involved in their own individual case. We don't want our struggle to be reduced to a list of separate cases. Our struggle is not about one child, but against a system which crushes all opposition.
>
> The commission was something created by Alfonsín to waste time. How many times had we already done this? We'd explained our own cases to the courts, to foreign organisations, to international commissions. They already had all this information.

Since the presidential commission was not concerned with determining responsibility for human rights abuses and had no powers of subpoena, there was little prospect that it would uncover the truth about a system which had been specifically designed to protect the impunity of those involved.

> MARIA DEL ROSARIO: They found the concentration camps, they visited them and they got together a list of some 1,500 people responsible for human rights violations and it was all given to the President. What did the President do with it? He gave it to a General who was one of those named on the list. They published the report but not the list, which eventually came to light when it was leaked to a newspaper. The report said that the disappearances were a result of a battle between 'two evils'

— the military and the guerrillas. We couldn't accept that. If there had been a guerrilla force of 30,000 people, the military would have been defeated. The military themselves admitted in secret documents that the guerrillas had been destroyed before the coup took place.

The rationale underlying the second arm of the government's human rights policy, the prosecution of the military for human rights abuses, directly conflicted with the demands of the Mothers. 'They had called for the prosecution of all those implicated in the disappearances; the government wanted to limit the trials to a few military chiefs and to avoid a confrontation with the armed forces in general. Three days after the new government took power, President Alfonsín signed two decrees, one ordering the arrest and trial of the members of the three juntas and the second calling for the prosecution of former guerrilla leaders. The latter was meant to prove that the government was not engaged in an anti-military campaign. The view of the government was that the military coup and subsequent repression was a response to the actions of the armed left and that the 'two evils' should be treated equally. To the dismay of the human rights organisations the president chose a court martial rather than a civilian trial for the juntas. The goverment hoped that the armed forces would purge itself, but had taken the precaution of including a provision that civilian courts should take over the cases in the event of unjustified delay by the military court.

The Supreme Council of the Armed Forces was given six months to reach conclusions about the accusations against the members of the three military juntas. Nine months later it had produced no report and claimed that it was not possible to hold the commanders responsible for acts committed in the 'war against subversion'. The civilian courts duly took over the case and the trial of the juntas began in April 1985. The nine military officers were charged with 711 offences ranging from organised robbery, rape and illegal detention to murder. The world's press gathered in Buenos Aires to cover an event dubbed 'the trial of the century'; it was the first time an elected civilian government in Latin America had dared to put its former military rulers in the dock.

ESTELA: The trial was very positive in some ways. Many people came from abroad and within Argentina, many who had refused to believe what we'd been saying about the military had to face up to the truth. But we weren't happy with the way the trial was carried out. It didn't deal with the systematic kidnapping of young children and babies. They talked about 'errors' and 'excesses' when it was clear that the disappearances, torture and murder were part of a systematic plan, which involved written orders from the highest military officers.

The truth revealed at the trial was of unimaginable horror. The first victim of the concentration camps to give evidence was a young university teacher who had been kidnapped, six and a half months pregnant, by ten armed men in 1977. Two months later, blindfolded and with her hands tied behind her back, she gave birth to her baby in the back of the car taking her from one camp to another. The baby fell to the floor, still attached by the umbilical cord and her pleas for help were ignored. The woman and her baby were released some months later. She had spent most of her detention in the Fifth Police Commissary and told of the torture of a fellow detainee, '...they tortured him for three days and left him thrown in the passageway from where we heard his agony... they began to torture him again, this time they didn't want information, they were enjoying themselves... the only object of this torture which lasted hours and hours was that he should say, 'I'm a queer and my mother is a son of a bitch'. They spent hours torturing him, trying to make him say it. He never did.

The witness was referring to Jorge Bonafini, Hebe's eldest son.

> HEBE: We don't want revenge; we want justice, justice for all the *desaparecidos*. The pain is still with us, of course. We used to imagine how they died and how much they suffered and we will never forget, but the point is to fight so that it never happens again. The trial of the juntas never had that purpose. It was the complicity of many people that allowed the military to do what they did — the complicity of the trade unionists, the politicians, the Church and the judges themselves, who covered the tracks of murderers or remained silent. Instead of prosecuting them, the president began promoting them. They chose a certain number of testimonies which didn't touch the multinationals, which didn't mention the complicity of the multinationals, the factories that helped the military pick out victims or who had concentration camps on their premises.

The Mothers' demand for the prosecution of all those responsible for the disappearances extended to non-military collaborators in the repression. The military itelf claimed its actions were blessed by the Church and endorsed by members of the political parties. The Church never accepted publicly that, either through omission or outright collaboration, it had a share of responsibility for the crimes committed by the military regime. Ninety per cent of the judges under military rule, all of whom had been forced to take an oath of allegiance to the *Proceso*, had been confirmed in their posts by the constitutional government. While the trial of the juntas was under way the president asked Congress to approve the promotion of members of the military and the judiciary, among whom were officers and judges who were named in the files of the human rights organisations as accomplices in the disappearances. Several major national and foreign companies in Argentina had furnished the regime with the cars used in the kidnapping operations, names of union activists and even with detention facilities for potential suspects. Many doctors, politicians and trade union leaders co-operated with the military, either through their silence or their quiet approval.

The verdict was delivered in December 1985.

> HEBE: When the judge read out the first acquittal I walked out of the court. I left alone. I had expected that the other human rights organisations would leave too.

General Videla and Admiral Massera of the first junta received life sentences and its third member was sentenced to four and a half years in prison. From the second junta, General Viola was sentenced to 18 years and Admiral Lambruschini to eight. Its third member, together with all the members of the third junta, was acquitted. The human rights organisations were unanimous in their condemnations of the verdicts. Hebe called it a 'terrible and tragic fraud perpetrated on the Argentine people'.

> HEBE: In 1985 we asked for a meeting with Alfonsín about the acquittals. He gave us an interview and Mothers travelled from the interior to meet him. When we arrived we were told that Alfonsín couldn't see us because he was at the opera. We decided to wait and we occupied Government House for twenty hours. We took mattresses and tea and blankets and we slept there. We wanted to show that we wouldn't accept the sentences handed out by the courts and that we would continue our fight for true justice.

The government sought to turn the end of the trial into the concluding chapter of the human rights question and called on Argentines to look to the future. The demands of the Mothers and other human rights organisations, with their slogan 'we will not forget and we will not forgive' were seen as an obstacle to national reconciliation. In terms reminiscent of the attacks made against the Mothers during the dictatorship, Alfonsín criticised the Mothers' first March of Resistance under the new government, saying the 'political interests' of the demonstration did not 'coincide with the national interest'. While on an official visit to Germany he replied to journalists' questions about the Mothers of Plaza de Mayo saying, 'We have serious discrepancies with the position of the Mothers... which I believe are political positions. I believe that it is highly negative for democracy to think about the defence of those who caused all the terrible bloodshed in the country.' The Mothers replied with a statement on the meaning of the national interest and democracy for them: education, jobs, decent wages, independent judges and a military and police force under the control of and working for the people.

The Mothers were the obvious target for the government's exasperation with the demands of the human rights movement. Starting with the exhumations, their response to CONADEP and the trial, the Mothers proved the most outspoken of the critics of official policy. Their newspaper, founded in 1984, became a focus of opposition to the government and its journalists relentlessly investigated the role of both military officers and civilians in the disappearances. With their uncompromising style the Mothers also found themselves at odds with other human rights organisations. They had been the only group not to join the march which accompanied the presentation of the presidential commission's report on disappearances to the government. Even though the other human rights organisations also condemned the government's handling of the human rights issue, some saw the Mothers' style as too abrasive for an elected government, which could not be treated in the same way as a military regime. Some felt the Mothers were not facing up to political realities and were naive in their expectations, and others that their attacks on the political system were too extreme and confrontational.

Within the Mothers themselves there were also differences. In January 1986, after elections which confirmed Hebe as president, ten of the original twenty Mothers who had formed the Association in 1978 left the organisation to form a small breakaway group, known as *Las Madres de Plaza de Mayo, Linea Fundadora* (Founding Line). It was a difficult and painful experience for all the women, the result of growing differences over leadership style and over the position the Mothers should take on government human rights policies. Members of the *Linea Fundadora* had grown increasingly uneasy about the Mothers' continued insistence on *aparición con vida*. In their view, some government initiatives offered ways of discovering the fate of individuals that did not weaken the principle of the collective struggle, nor the demand for the trial and punishment of all those responsible for the disappearances.

Renee Epelbaum is a member of *Linea Fundadora*. Her three children all disappeared within the space of four months in 1976.

RENEE: In the dictatorship we had a clear enemy and we had to fight it head on. When the democratic government came, the situation changed for the better. Democracy in Argentina is fragile and we had to be careful. We had to change our style. The enemy was no longer in Government

House. The constitutional government isn't our enemy. It may not be the government we wanted, it hasn't done what we asked for, but this government didn't kidnap, torture and murder our children. If the government provides us with ways of getting evidence of what happened to our children, we won't turn this down. We opposed the early exhumations, because they were an attempt to prove that our children were dead, but we don't oppose exhumations which are carried out by experts in order to provide us with evidence to prove that a crime took place. As an organisation we don't say *aparición con vida*, but nor do we accept their deaths without an explanation and the trial of those responsible.

MARIA DEL ROSARIO: There were differences among the Mothers when Alfonsín came to power. That's why a group of Mothers left. They said the government was doing something, that we had to give them time. It was a political difference because we wanted to go on being firm and critical. The others said no, we're in a different era, we're in a democracy. We can't put pressure on the government, now we have civil rights and there's no more violence, things have to be different. But we thought it was all a lie, that this wasn't democracy. The military wasn't in government but they were behind it. The proof was that the government did everything the military wanted.

Throughout 1985 and 1986 military unrest over the continued trials of officers accused of human rights abuses had erupted in a series of military uprisings. If the government had wanted an end to the human rights question, the judiciary had other ideas. The judgement made at the trial of the juntas had left the way open for further prosecutions of middle-ranking officers and by 1986 an estimated 1,700 prosecutions had been initiated against some 700 officers and civilians for crimes committed during the period of military rule. In December 1986, after presidential instructions which would have effectively put a stop to the prosecutions failed to take effect, Alfonsín presented a law to parliament which became known as the *punto final*. The *punto final* (literally 'full stop') set a time limit on the new prosecutions of military officers. Within sixty days lawyers had to present all outstanding cases and the courts had to decide if there was sufficient evidence to prosecute individuals, otherwise all charges would be dropped. Even if new evidence were found after this time-limit, cases could not be reopened. The courts reacted by trying to rush through hundreds of cases before the deadline expired in April 1987. Middle-ranking officers facing trial responded by staging rebellions in military headquarters across the country. Confronted with the refusal of other army units to move against the rebel officers, the government acceded to their main demand; an end to the prosecution of officers on active service. Trials of twenty naval officers accused of illegal detention and torture were immediately suspended. Within weeks Congress sanctioned the law of Due Obedience, which formally limited responsibility to the top generals except in the cases of rape and abduction of young children, by exempting from prosecution all those who had committed abuses at the order of a superior officer.

The law of Due Obedience freed from legal proceedings the immense majority of those accused of human rights violations and those who were already serving prison sentences after being found guilty of human rights abuses. One of those to benefit was Astiz, the infiltrator responsible for the disappearance of the Mothers' first president. Charged with illegal detention and torture, he was one of the naval officers whose trial was suspended. He was then exonerated of all charges under the law of Due Obedience.

> ESTELA: The government was influenced by the armed forces but we must still separate the times of the dictatorship and the times of democracy. Even though this is no democracy, it's still a constitutional government, elected by popular vote. If it's true to say they don't comply with popular wishes, we still can't equate them with the dictatorship. If it hadn't been for the constitutional government we wouldn't have found the children we've found. As soon as the dictatorship was over we submitted our cases to the courts. We had, of course, previously tried to do the same. We tried to present writs of habeas corpus, we reported the disappearances of a hundred or so children to the courts and they ignored us. But we knew that this was because the judiciary were in the hands of the military. If this government gives us the chance to find a child then we'll use it. We will not close the doors on these opportunities.

Constitutional rule offered the Grandmothers the chance to recover their grandchildren through the courts and they wasted no time in testing the legal system. The day after the new government took power they presented the case of a child thought to be Paula Logares, Elsa's granddaughter. By 1983 the Grandmothers had already located five missing grandchildren. In the main, these early successes had been cases of families who had 'adopted' the children in good faith and had no connection with the military regime. Some of these families had themselves contacted the Grandmothers and the children had either been returned to their legitimate families without legal action being taken, or had remained with their adoptive families, in close contact with their natural family. As they began to come across people associated with the military regime who knew the origins of the child in their care, the Grandmothers' task became more difficult. These families, who had knowingly falsified the origins of the child, refused to co-operate, moved house or ran away. The Grandmothers had to become detectives in order to find their grandchildren.

The investigations begin with the arrival of a piece of information, usually given anonymously by telephone or letter and often relating to a family in which the wife was never seen pregnant, but who has a child who was first seen during the dictatorship. The Grandmothers compare the information with the details in their files on missing children or, in the case of a child born in a concentration camp, with the possible date of birth. In the case of Paula, investigations began in 1980, when the Grandmothers received a photograph of a young girl and an address in Buenos Aires which had been sent anonymously to a Brazilian human rights organisation. The child, thought to be the daughter of *desaparecidos*, was registered as the daughter of a policeman and his wife.

The Grandmothers began to keep watch on the address, trying to catch a glimpse of the child. Following up information such as this has involved the women in painstaking detective work, which has even involved them using disguises, admitting themselves to mental hospitals or working as domestics in the household under suspicion. The need for secrecy is imperative, not only to avoid alerting the family with the child but also to avoid creating anxiety in the children. The Grandmothers have always been concerned that their work should not alarm children that have been legally adopted.

When Elsa finally caught a glimpse of the child she was convinced it was her granddaughter, but when she returned to the address a 'to let' sign was outside the flat; the couple had moved. It was not until 1983, when the military regime was on the brink of collapse, that the Grandmothers received further information about Paula. By this time it was possible to publicise their campaign in the newspapers and a photograph of the baby Paula was seen by a couple living in the same block of flats. Elsa and other Grandmothers kept watch on the building until one day she saw Paula getting off a school bus. Paula, kidnapped when she was eighteen months old, was now seven.

> ELSA: I was shocked. The child was identical to her mother and it was like seeing my own daughter when she was a child, standing there on the pavement. At the same time I felt confused. Paula was seven years old. What was she doing going to infants school? She should have been in the second year of primary school. Later I realised that the police couple had registered her as born at the moment of her kidnapping. She was a seven year old living the life of a five year old.

Tracing the child was only the first stage in the struggle to recover their grandchildren; to bring the cases to court the women required conclusive proof of their identity. As early as 1979 the Grandmothers had realised that as time passed photographs, details of birth marks, hobbies and tastes were becoming less relevant. In that year they read a magazine article about genetic markers in blood. The Grandmothers became scientists.

> ESTELA: At that time we became aware of scientific things. There were characteristics which were passed on to the children, such as features, gestures and aptitudes. We enlarged the photos and began asking if a congenital mark persisted over time, if scars disappeared, how long a vaccination scar remained. We found out that teeth and hair could give evidence of a child's relationship to a particular family and about X-rays which could determine their true age. In 1982 we did a tour of twelve countries and visited hospitals to ask about the possibility of blood analyses which could prove the biological connection between grandparents and their grandchildren. They said they would investigate. In November 1982 the Society for the Advancement of Science in Washington told us that doctors had researched the subject and that the tests we needed to prove the connection between grandparents and grandchildren were possible. Our enquiries had led to a scientific discovery.

The basis of the analysis is the inherited genetic material carried in the blood of family members. The inherited pattern is easily identified by reliable scientific methods, it does not change over time and each individual pattern has an extremely low incidence in the population in general, making it almost impossible for a couple pretending to be the real parents of a child to have the same genetic make-up as the natural family. The test can prove the biological relationship between a grandparent and grandchild to a degree of certainty of 99.9 per cent.

Blood analyses, used for the first time in August 1984 in Paula's case, provided the conclusive evidence that the child was Elsa's granddaughter. Six months later Elsa and her husband were called to court to take custody of Paula; for the first time the courts in Argentina had restored the child of a disappeared couple to her legitimate family.

Paula knew nothing. The family had told her only that a mad woman thought she was her grandmother.

> ELSA: I went in to speak to her with my husband. She was crying a lot, she was very angry and she asked me who I was. I told her I was the mother of her mother. 'Lies!' she shouted, 'My mother is Raquel and my father is Ruben.' (the names of the couple she had been living with) 'That's what they say', I told her, 'I say something else.' She began to scream, saying that the only thing I wanted was to destroy her family. I replied that the only thing I wanted was her, because she was my granddaughter. 'I don't believe you.' 'I've brought you some photos so

you can see what you think, see if you remember your parents.' I'd
made enlargements of photos of her parents with Paula in their arms.
She looked at them and threw them on the desk. 'It's not true', she said,
' the photos look too new.' I explained that I'd made enlargements so
she could see the faces of her parents better and that the originals were
at home. She looked at one photo of herself and said, 'yes, that's like one
in my house'. The kidnappers must have stolen one of the last photos
taken of her before she disappeared. She stood looking at the photo of
her mother and said nothing. She looked at the photograph of her father
and cried and cried, we couldn't stop her. So I said to her, 'Do you know
what you used to call your father?' 'No', she said. 'You used to call him
Calio.' When I said it she just looked at me and she repeated it, in just
the same way as she used to when she was little. Then she began to shout
and scream.

Paula adapted quickly to life with her real family. As was to happen
in later cases of grandchildren kidnapped when they were babies,
Paula appeared to recognise her grandparents' house and the relatives
she had known in the early months of her life. The family who had
brought up Paula were found guilty — not of kidnapping or hiding
the identity of the child, but of falsifying legal documents. It was not
until March 1988 that Paula received her new identity papers. For Elsa
it was a moment of great happiness: 'It meant more than just the legal
recognition of Paula's identity, it also affirmed the existence of my
daughter and son-in-law. They were still alive in their child. The
military had tried to erase them from history and failed.'

The Grandmothers had hoped that the new government would
investigate the hundreds of cases on the Grandmothers' files.
However, with the exception of three children located in 1985, the
government has played no direct role in the search for the
grandchildren. Only indirectly did government initiatives, such as the
exhumations, sometimes uncover their fate. Among the corpses
exhumed in the first months after the new government took power
were those of two children aged five and six who disappeared in 1976
with their parents. In a third grave, where it was expected to find the
body of their six month old sister, only an empty bundle of blankets
with a pink bear and a dummy were found. The child, like 213 others,
is among those being sought by the Grandmothers. Estela had the
body of her daughter Laura exhumed to ascertain the cause of death
and to determine whether or not she had been killed in a gun battle,
as the police had claimed when they returned her body to her family.
The investigation proved that Laura had been shot at close range and
the bones of the pelvis contained fissures that only appear in women
who have given birth. Estela now had irrefutable evidence that her

grandchild had been born, although she still had no clues as to her whereabouts.

Only a government commission to identify those responsible for human rights abuses could have helped the Grandmothers discover the whereabouts of their grandchildren. The presidential commission set up by Alfonsín did not have this objective and subsequent government policy offered little hope of new government initiatives. Although in theory the restrictions placed on prosecutions by the *punto final* and the law of Due Obedience did not cover those implicated in the disappearance of young children, many of those involved in child abductions benefited from the laws. The Naval Hospital gynaecologist responsible for the list of marines who were willing to adopt children of *desaparecidos*, the officer responsible for pregnant detainees and the disposal of their babies and the doctor who attended the births were all beneficiaries of the law of Due Obedience.

In the absence of government action, finding the children was left to the Grandmothers. They began to call on lawyers, psychologists and researchers, financed entirely by foreign donations, to assist them in a task which was becoming more difficult as time passed. For grandchildren presumed to have been born in concentration camps, such as those of Leonor, Enriqueta, Clara and Estela, where there were no photographs, no idea what the child looked like and often no certainty of the date of birth or the sex of the child, the blood analyses provided the only evidence of the children's true identity. It was here that the government offered most assistance.

In 1987 the Argentine Congress passed a law which created the National Bank of Genetic Data, a store of the genetic information contained in the blood of relatives of disappeared children. The Bank has made it possible to trace a child's background even after their grandparents have died. Taking into account current life expectancy figures, the Grandmothers have calculated that the Bank should continue in operation at least until the year 2050. The project, developed by the Grandmothers together with national and local government agencies and the immunology department of a Buenos Aires hospital, won support from President Alfonsín and Congress. As well as regulating the procedures for blood testing and guaranteeing the preservation of blood samples from each family, it obliges judges to refer to the Bank in the case of any child whose family background is in doubt.

> ESTELA: If there was one really positive thing that came out of the Alfonsín
> government it was the creation, at our request, of the Genetic Bank.
> Thanks to this we now have a register of all the blood test results so that
> in the future, when we're no longer here, anyone who is suspicious about

their background can go to the hospital and with a small blood test can check with the register and verify whether or not he or she is the child of a *desaparecido*.

1987 was also the year that the first child born in a concentration camp was returned to its legitimate family. In 1981 a young woman had approached the Grandmothers with information about a police officer suspected of living with the daughter of a disappeared couple. The Grandmothers began their investigations and by 1986 they had discovered the name given to the child and that the wife of the police officer was unable to have children of her own. They also obtained a copy of the false birth certificate which said the baby was born at home, not in a hospital, strengthening their conviction that she was the daughter of *desaparecidos*. The Grandmothers started legal proceedings on behalf of a number of possible grandparents whose blood was to be compared with that of the child. When the police officer was ordered by the courts to submit to blood tests, the suspicions of the Grandmothers and their legal team grew; unlike other police or military families, the couple co-operated willingly with the courts. The lawyers began to suspect that the police officer knew the child's real identity and that she was not the grandchild of any of the named grandparents.

At the last minute Leonor's name was added to the list. Her blood analyses matched those of the child in question and on 21 April 1987 the ten-year-old girl, known as Viviana Nancy, was reunited with her family. The judge explained to the child that her real parents had been kidnapped.

LEONOR: She didn't cry but asked two questions, 'Did the policeman know my real identity?' and, 'What happened to my mother and father?' She said to me, 'Thank you for looking for me grandma but I was going to find you anyway'. She asked what name her parents were going to give her. I said, 'If you were a girl, Elena, after your other grandmother'. One of my other children couldn't help crying when he called by phone that day and asked who was speaking and she replied, 'Elena'.

The second child born in captivity to be returned to her grandparents was the granddaughter of Enriqueta. Enriqueta had received information in 1979 from a couple released from a secret detention centre that her daughter had given birth to a baby girl. She heard nothing more until the mid 1980s, when an anonymous telephone caller gave information about a girl living with the brother of a police officer who was suspected of being the child of *desaparecidos*. Blood tests proved the girl, María Victoria Moyano Artigas, was Enriqueta's granddaughter. María was returned to her family in 1987.

ENRIQUETA: At first it was very painful for her, but she adapted very quickly. She knew she was adopted. She'd always had the sensation she was not the child of this couple and when she asked them, she was told she was adopted. She asked who her mother and father were and the woman said her mother had died in childbirth and that the father had abandoned her. Now she knows it wasn't like that. The question she asked most insistently, like all the other grandchildren, is what happened to her mother and father. Now she knows the truth about her parents.

The Grandmothers work with a team of psychologists to help the children in the difficult period of adjustment to life with their families and to support them as they come to terms with the truth about their parents. Not one of the psychologists consulted by either the Grandmothers or the courts has questioned the principle that a child has an inalienable right to know the truth about his or her background. On the contrary, it is generally accepted that hiding the truth is likely to cause severe psychological damage; if a child is being brought up by a family involved in the death of their natural parents, the results are likely to be catastrophic.

The views of child psychologists, have not always been shared by the general public, as was was shown in the case of 'Juliana', which was also the Grandmothers' first major setback. In 1988 the Grandmothers had traced a young girl whom they believed to be the daughter of *desaparecidos*, a belief which was backed up by statements made by the family with which the child was living. Blood tests appeared to indicate that she was the granddaughter of one of the Grandmothers of the Plaza de Mayo who was given temporary custody of the child. The 'Juliana case' attracted a barrage of media attention and generated a public debate about the rights and wrongs of taking children that are now young teenagers, from the family which had brought them up. With the glare of publicity focussed on the Grandmothers' work, it was discovered that a mistake had been made in the blood analyses and 'Juliana' was not, in fact, the granddaughter of the Grandmother.

CLARA: The problem was that during the tests someone made a mistake. The blood tests were accepted by the court and she was given temporarily to the family it was thought she belonged to. Then another judge reversed the decision and returned her to the family who had brought her up. Then this family had their own tests done and it was discovered that the girl wasn't the grandchild of the Grandmother of the Plaza de Mayo. But the child spent only a short time with them so the situation wasn't so serious. However, she is the child of a disappeared couple and the Grandmothers are still looking for her real family.

The mistake made in the 'Juliana' case stemmed from human error and was not related to the reliability of the scientific method used in the blood tests, but the controversy aroused by the case gave fuel to the opponents of the human rights movement. Public sympathy, so essential for the success of the Grandmothers' work, threatened to turn against them.

ESTELA: We think it's sad that people don't remember the traumas suffered by a child separated from his or her real parents. They live in a situation where the terrible secret filters through in hundreds of ways, through all the gaps in their histories, the stories that don't match up. The relationship between the imposter and the child is not one of love, it's one of perversion. If the child's true history and origins are hidden and he or she finds out at a later stage, the trauma is much greater. Perhaps the strongest evidence to prove that what we are doing is right comes from the children themselves. None of the children we've restored to their families have ever said they want to go back to the family that brought them up.

Some judges have also seemed unconvinced that psychological damage could be caused by children remaining in the hands of people who had falsified their history. The Grandmothers have accused judges of dragging their feet. A quick response by the courts became crucial to the winning of the cases; by 1987 some families with disappeared grandchildren had begun to flee the country.

ESTELA: It can take years of work before reaching the stage of the blood tests. We've got cases of abductors taking the children abroad when the judge finally issues a summons for them to take blood tests. And then, even when the judge has the conclusive blood evidence, he doesn't always hand over the children. We've been asking the courts why put up so many hurdles? There have been cases where it's taken four years before the child is returned, even when the identity of the child is perfectly well known.

We have the example of the twins in Paraguay. Blood tests have proved they belong to the Reggiardo Tolosa family. The family have been demanding the children from the courts for two years and the courts have refused. There are always excuses, even after the blood tests.

In 1987 the Grandmothers located in Paraguay an ex-police officer and his wife living with children suspected of being the twins of *desaparecidos*. The officer had worked in concentration camps and was well known by survivors as a torturer. The couple were finally extradited to Argentina to face charges and admitted that the twins were not their natural children and that they had falsified their birth certificates. In October 1989 blood tests proved the twins to be those born in a concentration camp in 1977 to the disappeared couple, Juan Reggiardo and María Tolosa. In spite of the falsification of the birth certificates and their involvement in the repression which possibly included a connection with the murder of the children's real parents, two and a half years later the former police officer and his wife still had custody of the children.

Even for grandchildren now living with their legitimate families, the legal battle is still not finished. After four years the identity documents of Leonor's grandchild, Elena, still bear the name given to her by the police officer and his wife. Enriqueta's granddaughter is in a similar state of legal uncertainty and the battle to obtain legal recognition of both children's true identity continues.

In 1989 the human rights organisations suffered two major setbacks. The first was the decision by the newly elected government of Carlos Menem to grant an amnesty to 277 officers and civilians convicted of human rights abuses. Menem was sworn in as Argentina's new president in July 1989, in the first handover of power from one elected president to another in more than half a century. Although he himself spent five years in prison under the military regime, in his election campaign Menem had not ruled out granting an amnesty for those convicted and imprisoned for crimes commited during the 'dirty war'. The first batch of amnesties came in October 1989, leaving only the junta members, guerrilla leaders and a few senior officers in prison.

The second setback related more directly to the Grandmothers' search for their grandchildren. In 1989 the Grandmothers presented before the courts the case of Ximena, who had been left in an orphanage in 1977 after the kidnapping of her parents, when she was just nine months old. Although Ximena was eventually returned to her natural family, the judge, invoking a provision in the Custody Law, ruled that in future only the parents or guardians could initiate legal proceedings on behalf of a child, even in cases where both parents are *desaparecidos*. According to this decision, grandparents are not legitimate custodians of minors and the Grandmothers can no longer appoint a family lawyer to represent their grandchildren. Children in disputed custody cases must now be represented by court-appointed lawyers. The Grandmothers are contesting the ruling and at the time of writing the Chamber of Deputies has agreed to prepare a draft bill to amend the Custody Law. So far, the decision has not prevented the women from continuing their work.

ESTELA: At the moment there are seven cases going through the courts which are at an advanced stage. We've got information on forty other cases which our research team is following up. It seems to me that there are orders from above for the cases to be slowed down. We're struggling against the obstacles put up by the legal system, but we have to work with the system we've got. There's no other way.

The Grandmothers have not only worked closely with the courts in their battle to win back their grandchildren. They have also worked with other human rights organisations, including the breakaway Mothers' group, *Linea Fundadora*, to present various proposals to parliament aimed at changing the law for the benefit of the dependents of *desaparecidos*. In the closing stages of the dictatorship, the military, claiming that all *desaparecidos* were dead, offered welfare benefits to affected families only if they registered the deaths of their disappeared relatives. The human rights organisations have all consistently refused to do this and instead have fought for legal recognition of the term '*desaparecidos*'. A recent project which would have exempted from military service the sons and brothers of *desaparecidos* was recently approved by parliament, but was then vetoed by President Menem and then amended so that only relatives of those 'presumed dead' would be exempt. The organisations have, however, scored one major legal victory. Under Alfonsín's government, the word '*desaparecidos*' entered the statute books for the first time when pensions and monetary compensation were introduced for their dependents, with the proviso that these would be withdrawn if the *desaparecido* returned. The families were not forced to accept the death of their relatives.

The human rights struggle of the Mothers, in contrast, has taken a very different path from that of the Grandmothers and the *Linea Fundadora*, which has increasingly distanced them from the other organisations. The Mothers have rejected the legal concessions won by the other human rights groups. Rather than working within the system, the focus of their work has become condemning its injustices and they have remained steadfast in their refusal to negotiate with governments which they believe have protected the murderers and torturers of the disappeared.

HEBE: Someone had this idea of a monument to the *desaparecidos* and we were furious. 'This has to be left for history' What history? For history the murderers have got to be in prison. Are we all going to go to a monument to cry while the murderers are walking the streets free? We reject the posthumous homages because we feel this is another way of closing the chapter on the disappearances. It's not important to us that people remember the *desaparecidos* or love the Mothers. What interests us is that they support us and the struggle of the those that disappeared.

Then they began to talk about compensation. It was very difficult for us to oppose it, but how can we accept money from the same government that is pardoning the murderers? Nor do we want privileges for our children. The Mothers believe that military service should be abolished and that no young people in Argentina should be forced to do it.

We're struggling against the system, we don't accept the laws the governments have imposed because they are the laws of corrupt politicians and judges, the same people who were traitors during the dictatorship. They shouldn't be occupying positions of power. We're struggling so that the murderers be condemned for the terrible horror they brought on Argentina. We don't want them to forget, not because we want them to remember our children, but so that we can say there is justice in Argentina.

The people of Argentina can't solve their problems in the courts. We can only do it by participating and fighting.

Only recently have the Mothers recognised their own struggle and that of their disappeared children as 'political'. During the dictatorship, when 'politics' was outlawed, such an assertion would have endangered their own lives as well as their chances of recovering their disappeared children. Moreover, for the Mothers, politics was what the political parties did, and many believed human rights were essentially ethical matters which transcended party interests. While still remaining independent of all political parties — most Mothers do not vote in elections, although they sometimes publicly support independent candidates who share their beliefs — the Mothers see themselves as transforming 'politics', by introducing new, ethical values based on non-violence, participation and solidarity into their struggle for social justice, a struggle inspired by the ideals of their children.

POROTA: We got together to fight for our children. At first to find them, then to demand their return alive and then to recognise how right they were and to be proud of what they did. We learnt this as we fought.

HEBE: Our organisation grew a lot when we began to understand what our children had been fighting for, instead of saying they'd done nothing. At first we used to deny they were politically involved. 'Politics' was a dirty word for us. Some Mothers said, 'my son didn't do anything, he only defended convicts, my son was a lawyer', others said 'she was a poet, a writer', but they weren't taken away because they wrote pretty poems. Nor were they taken, as the military says, because they were all terrorists. If there had been an army of 30,000 guerrillas, the military would have been defeated. They were taken because they made a stand against the military and against injustice, whether it was in their factories, schools or universities. We began to realise that 'politics' meant more than just the political parties. When we began to understand our children's real histories, their concern for social change, we began to make the same demands. Every day when we wake up, we think of the day of work that our children call us to, those children that are in the square, who are in each and every one of us, those children which gave birth to us and to this awareness and to this work that we do.

Now politics means more to us than political parties. The parties ask for little so that many will join them. We have always asked for everything, even though few will join us. Now when people say 'your children were involved in something', we say, 'yes, luckily'. Moreover we say it's a beautiful thing — if only everyone did it, then they would realise what rights they have. We're political, but our politics are moral, ethical and with love. We believe in non-violence, but we're armed with guts, determination and the truth.

Their efforts to disassociate themselves from party politics have not stopped either of the main political parties accusing them of belonging to the other and their increasingly radical stance has led some to link them to left-wing groups. As a focus for popular opposition, the Mothers are often called upon, or volunteer their support for, grassroots movements protesting against privatisations, unemployment and the increasing poverty caused by government austerity measures. As the Mothers have moved further from the image of 'the weeping mother', so the public support that was based on the powerful emotional appeal of their campaign has slipped away.

A strong and continuing source of support for the human rights movement comes from women's organisations, both feminist and non-feminist, the majority of which not only support their campaigns, but also acknowledge the enormous contribution the Mothers have made to the women's movement in general. They have challenged the traditional image of mothers as passive and apolitical, concerned only with their own children and families, and instead made motherhood the basis of an ethical condemnation of society and its values. Their struggle against state repression has inspired the women's movement's campaign against domestic violence. However, the Mothers do not consider their organisation as feminist. Their only contact with feminism has been through the annual National Women's Meetings, a forum for women from political parties, trade unions, human rights organisations and feminist groups.

MARIA DEL ROSARIO: We see it as a moral struggle, in defence of men and women. We don't want men or women in concentration camps. But nor do we want men to hit women or women to be paid less. We believe that in Argentina women don't have the respect they have in other countries. There is discrimination of course — this is a *machista* country. We've taken to the streets to fight like no other group of women has.

The feminists take us as an example but we're fighting for the rights of both women and men.

HEBE: Of course we've suffered from discrimination against women and we still do. We've won our place by years of huge efforts. We've banged our heads against the wall a hundred times. This society is very *machista*. But our priorities lie with human rights issues. It's not that we don't see divorce or other women's issues as part of the struggle for human rights. If women come along with a divorce petition, of course we sign it. But we don't go out campaigning for divorce. There are other people doing that.

The Mothers aren't feminists; we believe in equality between men and women. Feminists here are very radical. They want men out of the way and we don't agree with that. If we are going to become free we have to do it together. Feminists here are more middle class, more concerned with gender demands, which isn't the most important thing. But we've challenged many ideas about women. We socialised motherhood by making a social issue out of what we were doing. It was a very difficult process. As our movement grew we realised it was very hard not to pursue one's own individual interest. The headscarves are an example: first we embroidered the names of our children on them and hung a photo around our necks. But one day we tried to do something more revolutionary, and each person picked up any photo. That was an important step, which not all the Mothers could take — it's not easy. In 1990 we stopped carrying the photos altogether. It was a contradiction. We said we were looking for all the missing children, yet we were carrying a photo of our own sons or daughters on our chest.

We've also changed the traditional image of the mother, an image which the Church is largely responsible for. We've fought to get rid of the picture of the weeping mother who lays a flower at her child's grave and instead to build the image of mothers who fight for all the country's children. We've learned that there are more important things than washing, cooking and ironing.

People still think of us as exceptional women. Others think they can't do what we've done, so we have to work a lot with women on this, even inside the organisation. It used to be thought that there were Mothers to give speeches and others to clean. All Mothers can do everything and I know this from my own experience. In the Mothers' House we all cook and in the streets we all take the microphone. When we go abroad we always send different Mothers and we try to make sure that everyone gets a chance to speak on the radio. All women are capable. We have to demystify the story of the Mothers of the Plaza de Mayo.

In December 1990 President Carlos Menem faced his first military uprising, which left 16 officers and five civilians dead. Of the 277 men who had benefited from the amnesty in 1989, 174 took part in the rebellion. Less than three weeks later the president announced the second round of amnesties which included absolution for the junta members. Polls showed eighty per cent of Argentines opposed the amnesty.

As human rights becomes a side issue in mainstream Argentine politics and public attention turns to more immediate economic problems, the Mothers and Grandmothers, in their different ways, continue to try to keep the issue alive.

> MARIA DEL ROSARIO: The square is our citadel. We'll only stop going to the square the day we're all dead, and not even then, because now Mothers are dying and they ask for their ashes to be scattered there. Of course there's fewer Mothers now and many of us have problems. Some have got parents who are ill. I couldn't come for two years because my parents are very old and they needed my attention. Some are looking after their grandchildren or they're ill themselves. We're all getting old. The youngest of us are now sixty something.
>
> We don't work for the future. We're working for today. We're sowing the idea of honest politics, politics for the common good. We hope that the young people who work with us continue our work. At least we can leave behind an example of struggle.

> HEBE: Our struggle is forever. In Argentina torturers and murderers walk the streets freely. I've met two of the torturers of my younger son, Raúl. I know where they are. But they know we are fighting so that one day we'll have a government that will condemn all those who have forced us to live through such horror for all these years.

The Mothers' struggle has inspired human rights organisations across Latin America. There are streets in Spain, squares in Holland and schools in France named after them. They have won international prizes for their commitment to freedom and justice; they have support groups in Europe, North America and Australia and their newspaper is now translated into several languages and sold in a number of countries.

The Grandmothers have also been acclaimed for their struggle to find their grandchildren and for their work in the field of children's rights. In 1990 they located their fiftieth grandchild, kidnapped in 1980 at the age of four, together with his parents and younger sister, and once a detainee in the torture centre at the Higher Engineering School (ESMA). There are still an estimated 213 disappeared children, of whom 26 are children and babies who were kidnapped together with their parents and the remainder are children assumed to have been born in captivity. The Grandmothers still receive anonymous telephone calls and information that might relate to their grandchildren. Clara received information about her grandchild two years ago and her case is one of the forty currently being followed up by the research team. So far, Estela has received no further news about her grandson, Guido, born in a concentration camp in 1977.

Argentina
Chronology

1947 Women win the vote.

1976 Military junta led by General Videla seizes power.

1980-2 Military's economic programme collapses. One and a half million workers take part in the general strike of 1981.

1982 Argentina loses Falklands/Malvinas war. National Housewives' Movement formed.

1983 End of dictatorship. Raúl Alfonsín elected president. National Women's Committee created in the government department of Human Development and the Family.

1984 The world's first Housewives' Trade Union (SACRA) is formed and demands pensions and wages for housewives. Women from political parties, trade unions, housewives' and human rights organisations create the Women's Multisectorial, whose demands include pensions for housewives, equal pay and the creation of a state department for women.

1985 Ratification of UN Convention on the Elimination of Discrimination against Women. Legislation amended to give women equal rights over children. Economic crisis. Government implements IMF-backed austerity measures.

1986 Government department for women created. Nationwide health insurance system set up by the Housewives' Union.

1987 Divorce legalised after 85 years of discussion and controversy. Formation of the Women's Committee of the provincial government of Buenos Aires to promote women's policies in the province.

1989 Peronist Carlos Menem is elected president as economy slides into crisis. Food rioting and supermarket looting hit Argentina's major cities. 3,000 women attend Fourth National Women's Meeting.

1991 New law makes it obligatory for political parties to include a minimum of thirty per cent of women candidates in elections.

5

The Home Front

Housewives and Community Health in Argentina

Maria Rosa: The dictatorship destroyed the spirit of the community. The military closed our neighbourhood organisations and people were afraid to meet. The security services would come day and night, searching houses and asking for documents, saying they were looking for someone. They took people away, whole families sometimes, and no one would ask any questions. Everyone kept themselves to themselves, no one wanted to get involved. All this left its mark on the community. When the military fell and people could go out and do things, they couldn't agree. Even when the people from the neighbourhood centres, the school, the church, all wanted the same things, they couldn't unite. They were all small, closed groups. There was no solidarity. It was a product of those years, when everyone went inside themselves and closed their eyes.

María Rosa lives in La Loma, a poor neighbourhood in the province of Buenos Aires. Just fifteen kilometres from the city of Buenos Aires, La Loma is a stark contrast to the elegant boulevards, theatres and fashionable shopping districts and cafes which earned the capital the title of 'the Paris of Latin America'. The half-finished brick and wooden houses and the cardboard and corrugated iron shacks of the adjacent shanty town, lacking even the most basic services, such as clean, safe water, a sewerage system, health facilities or paved roads, are the hidden face of a country once ranked among the ten richest in the world. Poor communities such as La Loma bore the brunt of the economic and political repression of military rule. Working-class organisations were targeted by the military and an estimated 54 per cent of the people who 'disappeared' were from working-class families. The regime's economic policies reduced social welfare programmes and opened the economy to free trade, devastating local industry and cutting jobs in manufacturing by more than a third. When the economic programme collapsed in the early 1980s, the situation became critical for a wide sector of society.

Yet, unlike Chile, there was no widespread movement amongst Argentine women in the poor neighbourhoods to find collective solutions to the problem of growing poverty. Communal kitchens and allotments, shopping collectives and other self-help survival strategies that were so common in other parts of Latin America, were virtually unknown in Argentina. Instead, the first reaction from women to falling living standards came from groups of middle-class Argentine housewives, who in 1982 took to the streets to protest. Two years later a housewives' trade union was formed, based on the idea not of the housewife as a consumer, but of the housewife as a worker. It was not until the economic crisis of 1989 that women's self-help organisations began to appear in significant numbers in Argentina.

Such organisations failed to develop earlier largely because Argentina had been unfamiliar with the levels of extreme poverty and hunger that had plagued other Latin American nations. The country's vast agricultural wealth not only provided the foundation for economic growth but also ensured that food was relatively cheap and standards of living relatively high. The state welfare system, developed during the 1940s under the presidency of General Juan Domingo Perón, was one of the most comprehensive in Latin America and, together with private charities, had traditionally taken care of the destitute.

Secondly, popular demands were traditionally channelled to the state via political parties and unions. Since the 1940s, despite years of repression and proscription, working-class aspirations have focused on the Peronist Party and its power-base, the trade unions. Working-class loyalty to Perón dates from his first presidency in the 1940s, when living standards rose by some twenty per cent and the state welfare system was established. Women were awarded political and labour rights and in 1947, with his wife Evita in charge of women's affairs, women won the right to vote. In the same year the Peronist Women's Party was formed as a branch of the Peronist movement on an equal footing with its political and union sections. By 1952 it had half a million members and 3,600 headquarters throughout the country. These headquarters not only dispensed charity but also organised women-only training in social and political organisation, giving working-class women their first real chance to take part in the world of politics.

Throughout the 18 years of the Peronist party's prohibition, from 1955 when Perón was toppled in a military coup, until 1973 when he returned as president, the working class retained its loyalty to Perón and the outlawed party maintained a level of grassroots organisation. Even after his death and the military overthrow of the disastrous government of Isabel, Perón's second wife, the majority of the working class continued to identify with Peronism.

A widespread self-help movement also failed to develop in Argentina due to the nature of the Church. From the late 1960s the Roman Catholic Church in many Latin American countries was influenced by the ideas of liberation theology, which stressed its responsibility for promoting social justice in addition to its spiritual function. In many countries the Church not only offered legal and humanitarian assistance to the victims of state violence and poverty but, with traditional political activity banned under military rule, promoted and sheltered many new community organisations. In Argentina, however, the Church has always been dominated by powerful conservative forces. The 'worker' priests and nuns who lived and worked among the poor during the 1960s and early 70s never received the support of the ecclesiastical authorities. The church hierarchy remained silent when at least thirty of these priests and nuns disappeared in the months following the coup and when an estimated 30,000 people disappeared into the torture camps of the military regime. As discussed in Chapter Four, instead of condemnation, prominent members of the Church co-operated with the regime.

Underlying the relationship between the military and the Church in Argentina was a shared belief in the importance of traditional family and Christian values. In the 1976 coup the military claimed to be 'reaffirming the family as the base of our society' and promoted the traditional image of women as guardians of the faith and defenders of the family. In this they were assisted by the oldest of Argentina's housewives' organisations, the League of Housewives.

The League was the initiative of a woman appointed Minister of Education in the provincial government of Buenos Aires in 1956 by a previous military regime. Its headquarters, a house in the centre of the capital, was donated by a woman from Argentina's aristocracy. Its original function was to advise the women of the middle and upper classes on household management and how to deal with their domestic servants. In 1981 Lita Lazarri, with 18 years experience as an executive secretary, was elected president of the organisation and converted it into a consumer-based pressure group. Working from an office whose walls are adorned with photographs of veterans of the Malvinas (Falkands) war and maps of Argentina, Lita is an ardent admirer of

Mrs Thatcher. The League addresses women primarily in their traditional role: 'Our objectives are the defence of the consumer, moral values and family and home life'.

For the League, defending consumer rights means defending the free market.

LITA: We are against price controls. We are in favour of freedom because free markets give us the possibility to comb the streets to find lower prices.

The League campaigns against the exploitation of women's bodies in advertising as part of a moral crusade against pornography, and has scored several successes thanks to its power as the representative of a wealthy sector of consumers.

LITA: If we speak of morality they call us mad old women, but if we hit the pockets of big business we have the power to stop them. We send a letter to a company saying that hundreds of thousands of housewives and their families won't buy a product until they get rid of the advert and they get rid of it.

Defending the family means encouraging women to stay at home.

LITA: We believe women should stay at home, especially when they have young children. Of course reality isn't like this and some women have to work, especially in this economic situation, but women shouldn't compete with men. Women were born for one thing and men for another.

The League's educational activities centre on a number of consumer schools set up throughout the country which deal with issues such as the use of natural resources, non-toxic products and advertising. They teach women how to shop.

LITA: In Argentina there have been price controls for forty years and with the opening of the economy housewives are defenceless. They don't know how to shop and this is what we teach them, that they've got to look for the cheapest prices and not buy the most expensive products.

In addition, the League offers workshops in a variety of traditional housewife's skills, such as flower-arranging, dress-making, cooking and knitting. The emphasis is recreational rather than on generating income, reflecting the priorities and concerns of this class of housewives.

LITA: We say, 'Señora, don't take pills, come and join us at the League'. The use of tranquilisers is a big problem, especially with older women because when the children have grown up, they have nothing to do, they get bored. They watch soap operas and cry because they're lonely.

In the workshops they can meet other women like them and join in an activity.

The League, like many other upper-class women's organisations, also performs a charitable role, although it makes a clear distinction between the deserving and undeserving poor.

LITA: We speak of consumers but we realise that there are people who can't consume so we open children's canteens in areas where there is little work. We feed 270 children every day in the province of Buenos Aires. We don't go to the shanty towns any more. Our experience has shown us that many people in the shanty towns don't like work, so we prefer to help the children.

As well as doing voluntary work in the canteens, members of the League donate toys to children's hospitals and support projects to assist elderly Mapuche Indians in the south of Argentina. Their other charitable activities include supporting veterans of the Malvinas war by paying for medical treatment and helping them raise funds for their own headquarters.

The war brought the organisation the closest it came to disagreement with the military government. While other women's organisations found themselves the object of persecution and prohibition, the League lived in peaceful co-existence with the military rulers.

LITA: We worked with the military government. I always argued with them, especially about the Malvinas. I couldn't believe that they let the boys come back from the war and no one went to see them in the hospitals. I argued so much that one day a colonel said, 'Look Lita, it won't happen again'. The military always respected us. We almost never took to the streets to protest. Those who do are making politics and you don't get what you want that way.

It was on the streets of Buenos Aires that a new housewives' organisation was formed in 1982, in the wake of the Falklands war. The war had provided a temporary respite for the military rulers, diverting public attention from the collapse of their economic programme to a popular nationalistic cause. During 1981 real wages had fallen by almost twenty per cent, affecting not only the pockets of the working class, but also causing a decline in the real income of middle-class families, particularly professionals and technical and clerical staff. Military defeat in the war opened the way for an eruption of discontent.

A few weeks after the end of the war a group of housewives from a middle-class district of Buenos Aires placed an advert in a newspaper calling for a 24-hour shopping strike. The newspapers dubbed it the 'popular movement of the empty shopping bags'. At the time, Marta was a housewife with young children living in Buenos Aires:

MARTA: In 1982 women began to form support groups for the soldiers fighting in the Malvinas. When the war finished, despite the fact that the military were still in power, new organisations began to be created. It was as if people had suddenly woken up after years of living in fear and silence. The military had lost the war, and they'd lost control of the economy too. Factories were closing, unemployment was growing and prices, especially food prices, were going up all the time. The unions began to reorganise and call strikes. People began openly to criticise the regime. When a group of women from our neighbourhood read in the papers that women in a district of Buenos Aires were meeting to protest against the high prices we went to see them.

The advert had been placed by Ana María Pissurno and a group of housewives from the middle-class district of San Martín in the province of Buenos Aires:

ANA MARIA: Prices were going up all the time and wages weren't. Prices would suddenly rise by 10 or 15 per cent so you didn't have enough money to get to the end of the month. I said to myself, protesting alone won't do any good, so I went to find other women in the neighbourhood to see if we could do something. What can a housewife do? If you go on strike in your house the only people who suffer are you and your family. We decided the only thing we could do was a shopping strike, as a form of protest and also with the aim of making women react and realise they weren't alone. We put an advert in just one newspaper, but that was enough. The next day there was a tremendous reaction. My telephone didn't stop ringing from seven in the morning, women calling from all over the province saying they were going to organise protests in local squares; the TV, the radio wanted to interview us and find out what these housewives were up to. We hadn't expected it. It was a completely spontaneous reaction.

In July 1982 the Buenos Aires Housewives' Movement was formed. Although it was a protest against the rising cost of living, it was also seen as a way of breaking the code of 'don't get involved', the philosophy by which most of the population had lived through the terror of the dictatorship. In the neighbourhoods of Buenos Aires province women distributed leaflets with the words 'No to fear, No to "don't get involved"' and called on housewives to bake their own bread and stop eating meat. Between July and November newspapers reported week-long bread strikes and meat boycotts in different districts of the province. As the women explained to reporters, their main concern was the deterioration in their families' standard of living.

'We are trying to help our husbands. Our politics are our husbands' wallets.' 'We need the country to work, for our husbands to work, so that we can educate our children and live in dignity. We are the authentic middle class who have got where we are with a lot of effort.' 'My son fought in the the South Atlantic conflict. For two months we lived the horror of not knowing what had happened to him. He came back weighing 16 pounds less and he can't find work. We are desperate.'

The housewives also attracted the attention of the military authorities.

ANA MARIA: In the beginning they tried to intimidate us. They tapped our phones, or as we were walking down the street they'd drive slowly alongside us in the green Ford Falcons without number plates that they used when they kidnapped people. One bank holiday my neighbours told me that three big men were asking for me, so I went up to one of them and said, 'listen, if you want to know anything about me, just ask, you're not going to scare us off like this.'

The 'war against prices' spread throughout the country. From a southern province came reports of 'empty pot' marches, petitions were handed to the government offices by demonstrators in the western city of Mendoza and in the northern province of Tucumán there were 'lights out' protests against the soaring price of electricity. In November 1982 the women launched a 'nationwide don't-buy-on-Thursdays' campaign and drew up a petition which they handed in to the Economy Ministry calling for price controls, subsidies for bread, meat and milk, free school meals and job security.

MARTA: We stood outside the local shops in groups with our placards, trying to convince people not to buy. We had a lot of arguments with the shopkeepers. You can imagine they weren't very happy about all those women picketing their shops. When you live in a small neighbourhood you know the grocer, the baker, the butcher and they know you so it makes it very difficult. 'This is a war against me, my family's got to eat too, I've got to pay electricity and rent as well!' and they showed us their bills. We told them they should be protesting to the government, not to us.

We weren't against the local shopkeepers. They're the last link in the chain. We knew the problem came from above, from the few big companies that control the market. That's why we called on the government to introduce price controls.

Their opposition to the free market economy was not the only factor which distinguished them from the League of Housewives. The Buenos

Aires Housewives' Movement was made up of young, lower-middle-class women whose families' living standards had plummeted with the crisis.

MARTA: They sent officials from the government with social workers to get information about us. They thought we lived in shanty towns. When they saw we were from middle-class districts they got a terrible shock. They called us middle-class but I'd say we're both middle-class and lower-class women. Women from shanty towns and domestic employees joined us, as well as some from better-off residential sectors.

We were all housewives and that was one of the differences with the League. Some of us worked outside the home but we still did the housework. To us, a housewife isn't a wealthy woman who doesn't work inside or outside the house, but only orders another woman to do it. We are housewives who do the work ourselves. It's a big difference.

ANA MARIA: I believe that because of our actions, people realised the housewife existed. There were other organisations, like the League, but at that time, no one knew about them. Women from the League came to talk to us. They wanted to work together. In the beginning we thought it was a good idea, thinking 'we're all housewives, we're all women', but then we saw that we didn't have the same objectives.

By 1983 thousands of women throughout the country had formed housewives' groups and were affiliating to the Buenos Aires organisation. They changed their name to the National Housewives' Movement (ACP), and developed an 18 point programme of demands for price controls on basic foodstuffs and urban services, subsidised school meals, cheap housing and unemployment benefit. Ana María Pissurno was elected president but the organisation retained its loose, informal structure and the individual groups worked with a great deal of independence. The main principle to which all groups had to adhere was that of independence from political parties.

MARTA: They called us communists and leftists but the majority of us didn't have any political experience. There weren't many young women who could have had experience because we spent our adolescence under a dictatorship. It was because we were so inexperienced that they were able to take advantage of us.

Housewives form over half the electorate and we're important as consumers, so politicians and the food industry are always trying to use us. Once when we were protesting about rising meat prices we called a two day meat buying strike. The International Trade department took advantage of the campaign. They printed posters promoting the meat strike — we'd never had posters before, we'd never had the money — and leaflets were being handed out using our name. But their aim wasn't to force a cut in prices. They wanted to reduce domestic demand and have more meat for export! Political parties offered us help but we preferred to keep our independence.

The movement's refusal to accept support from political or other organisations meant their only source of income was from voluntary membership subscriptions. They rented a small office where they organised workshops, sales of clothes, cheap medical treatment and legal advice. After a year the ACP could no longer afford the rent, the office closed and the organisation of campaigns and shopping strikes moved back to the homes of individual members.

The ACP took part in the massive demonstrations called by political parties and human rights organisations in the wake of the Malvinas (Falklands) debacle and supported the general strike of December 1982 when nine million Argentines downed tools and paralysed the whole economy. In February 1983 the regime called elections and ten months later the Radical Party leader, Raúl Alfonsín, was sworn in as Argentina's president.

ANA MARIA: We'd spoken to the politicians during the electoral campaigns and they'd all talked to us and made lots of promises. In electoral campaigns they're nice to everyone. They didn't keep their promises, at local or at national level. When Alfonsín came to power we thought we'd give him time, with all the problems he'd inherited from the military, but when a year went by and we saw that nothing had changed, we began our campaign again.

MARTA: It wasn't just that the economic situation didn't change; it got worse. Our members couldn't afford to go to supermarkets and fill up their trolleys at the beginning of the month. When inflation is thirty per cent a month, that's the only way you can survive. If you don't spend your money as soon as you get it, the next day it's worth half. Sometimes the price went up between going into the shop and getting to the cash desk.

Within 18 months of taking office, President Alfonsín turned to the International Monetary Fund to bail out the Argentine economy. The new government had inherited from the military a foreign debt estimated at $40 billion and an economy producing less in absolute terms than in 1974. By 1985 the annual inflation rate was running at 1,000 per cent. The IMF's condition for further loans to Argentina was a package of austerity measures including public spending cuts, monetary controls and a wage and price freeze, but the chief responsibility for monitoring prices was left to the general public. The ACP's calls for government intervention in wide sectors of the

economy and involving housewives in formulating price policies fell
on deaf ears.

Increasingly the ACP began to take up issues that were less
concerned with consumer rights and more related to the rights of
women in general. It was one of the founding members of the Women's
Multisectorial, an organisation set up in 1984 to commemorate
International Women's Day, composed of women from political
parties, trade unions, human rights organisations and feminist groups.
It also took part in the first of the annual National Women's Meetings
in 1986. In 1986 the ACP formally registered itself as a public
association and developed a twenty point programme which reflected
their contact with these diverse women's organisations. It included
demands for nursery schools, pensions for housewives, the legalisation
of divorce and free access to birth control.

> MARTA: We also became concerned about changing the traditional idea
> of a housewife. When we started out most of us were young women
> with small children, which made it difficult for us to meet. We had to
> take them with us. I didn't have problems with my husband but there
> were many men who didn't want their wives to go out. Only when we
> began to try and get women involved did we realise how trapped we
> were in our homes and that you had to deal with those problems too.
> Domestic work should be the responsibility of society as a whole, with
> canteens in the workplace and schools and universities, public laundries,
> creches, old people's centres, so a housewife can go out to work or study.
> Housework is isolating and when the children grow up and leave,
> women are left without a purpose and undervalued.
>
> We want to change the idea that housework is the responsibility of
> women, and to democratise home life. We have to learn to bring up our
> children in a different way.

> ANA MARIA: A housewife has to be involved in social and political issues
> too. The problem is that for years they've told us that being a housewife
> means to stay at home, looking after the children and your husband,
> dedicating yourself to cleaning and cooking. If you talk about politics,
> they just say 'what do you know?'. Our organisation is trying to change
> all that.

In 1984 a new housewives' organisation was formed with a very
different concept of the housewife and her interests, and with a very
different strategy for defending them. In that year the world's first
housewives' trade union was created, based on the principle not of
housewives as consumers, but as workers. The Housewives' Union
evolved from a women's group created in 1975 on the fringes of a
small left-wing political party, the Popular Left Front (FIP), which

allied itself with the Peronist party. Within a few years the group, the Centre of Social Studies of the Argentine Woman (CESMA), had established itself as an independent feminist collective. A number of such small feminist organisations had been formed in the early 1970s but most of them disintegrated after the military coup. Not only did they fall victim to the regime's prohibition on public meetings but also to military ideas about the proper role for women; feminism was seen as a subversive attempt to undermine the family. When CESMA, one of only two groups to survive the first years of military rule, tried to organise a public meeting in 1980, police occupied the building and arrested the women. In the early 1980s, when new feminist groups began to appear, CESMA disbanded to form the Union. They shed their feminist profile and adopted a position more closely identified with that of Evita Perón.

Evita has always been a controversial figure within the Argentine women's movement. At the beginning of the century an active and independent women's movement established itself in Argentina and successfully campaigned for changes in the law governing women's legal position. By 1946, when Juan Domingo Perón was elected president, their struggle for the vote was already well advanced. In general, however, the independent women's organisations were made up of women from the more affluent sectors of society; they failed to take account of the concerns of working-class women and underestimated the popular appeal of Peronism. The Peronist Women's Party, under Evita's leadership, effectively dislodged the women's movement's leaders and appropriated their cause. Under Peronism, women not only won the right to vote, but also made gains in labour legislation. The Peronists regulated domestic service, incorporated paid work carried out in the home into minumum wage legislation and introduced equal pay the textile industry. In the elections of 1951, the first in which women could vote, they voted overwhelmingly for Perón. Seven women senators and 24 deputies, all Peronist, were elected to parliament, a record for Latin America and never since equalled in Argentina. The Peronist Women's Party had won the mass support of women in a way the independent civil rights and female suffrage organisations had never managed to do.

The relationship between Evita and the early feminist organisations was one of mutual hostility. The feminists never supported her campaign for women's suffrage and saw Perón's adoption of their cause as a cynical attempt to gain women's support for his presidential ambitions. Evita was contemptuous of feminists, seeing them as masculine women of the aristocracy promoting a foreign doctrine, a movement 'led not by women, but those who aspire to be men'. Her own ideas about women were ambiguous. Under her leadership women had advanced in the worlds of politics and work and yet she never questioned the primacy of women's role as a housewife and mother. Her calls for women to participate in the public life of the country were expressed in terms of duty to the family, the home and to Perón; the women's movement could only accomplish great things if it was associated with a great man. She referred to her own relationship with Perón as, 'He the figure, I the shadow'.

After Evita's death in 1952 and the proscription of Peronism after 1955, the Women's Party began to lose its importance inside the movement. When Perón returned to power in 1973 his second wife, Isabel, tried to revive the organisation but it never regained its former influence. On Perón's death, Isabel assumed the presidency. The Peronist government's policies for women continued to be ambiguous. On the one hand it passed a law for the state provision of nursery schools, although it was never implemented, and increased maternity benefits. On the other hand Isabel banned the public sale of contraceptives and vetoed changes in family law which would have given women equal rights with men over their children. The traditional hostility towards feminism remained; when Isabel presided over a congress organised for International Women's Year, she had feminist groups forcibly removed.

Although the Housewives' Union was organised outside the official Peronist Party, it became the first significant attempt since the 1940s to rally women around the figure of Evita Perón. The starting point was the nature of the work women do inside the home. Elida now lives in the northern province of Misiones, where she was elected to local government as a deputy for a Peronist coalition. She was a member of CESMA and one of the founders of the Union.

ELIDA: In CESMA we reached the conclusion that housework was the key issue which affected all women, especially poor women. The crisis may force them to take on paid work, but they usually work on the black market, in low paid jobs with no social security cover, such as cleaning, cooking or looking after children, work which is low paid precisely because of the low value attached to housework. A middle-class woman who hires another woman to do the housework is a housewife too. Housework isn't just physical work. It's also teaching social, cultural, political and religious values to children.

This work seems to be individual, family work, carried out for love, but that conceals the fact that housework sustains Latin American societies. Without housework it's impossible to guarantee harmony and social continuity, yet its value isn't recognised.

From this theoretical discussion arose the proposal for wages for housework.

While domestic servants are commonly employed in middle— and upper-class households, in the vast majority of Argentine homes housework is unpaid work carried out by women. A study of 400 Argentine homes by the International Labour Organisation in 1984 showed that the average housewife worked ten hours a day, seven days a week while other members of the family contributed a daily average of 15 minutes. When the study calculated the cost of employing domestic servants to carry out this work, it concluded that housewives contributed $21 billion a year or 33 per cent of Argentina's gross domestic product. The study also found that women's responsibility for housework and childcare did not diminish when they entered paid employment, but rather they combined work inside and outside the home in what has been called the 'double day'. A typical 'double day' was found to be 13 hours, and rose still further as the economic crisis forced housewives to spend more time making and repairing clothes, shopping for the cheapest products and preparing food at home.

The idea of classifying unpaid work done in the home as a job like any other formed the basis for a series of demands made by the new housewives' union. As workers, housewives had a right to be paid a wage, form a union and be recognised as part of the labour movement.

Laura is married with six children. She works from the union's headquarters in the capital, Buenos Aires, in offices adorned with portraits of Evita and maps of Argentina. In the early 1980s she was a member of a women's study group.

LAURA: During the election campaign in 1983 we found that there was no party which offered any satisfactory policies for women. Then in the interior of the country a woman stood as a candidate for a very small party which had no electoral chance and she made women's rights the basis of her political campaign. She proposed a housewives' union and when she went on the radio to explain the proposal, the effect was extraordinary. At the exit to the radio station there were queues of women waiting to ask for details, how they could join. At that time I was part of a women's study centre and from that moment our group began to discuss the idea.

ELIDA: When in '83 we called for the formation of the Union, we did it with a declaration of principles which said very simply that we were the forgotten Argentines. That in spite of working all day, bringing up our children, guaranteeing their education, food, and health, and even though there were millions of us, our work had never been recognised. And that our work was so important that if we ever decided to organise a general strike, society would stop functioning, there would be no clean clothes to go out to work, no food for the children etc. First we demanded the right to organise a union, like all workers in Argentina. Secondly we wanted our work recognised through the payment of a salary, a pension and health benefits. This was read out over the radio and the response was overwhelming. By August 1984 we had formed the Housewives' Union of the Argentine Republic (SACRA).

SACRA is a unique attempt at drawing together a dispersed and scattered workforce that had no place in the traditional world of trade unions. The women registered the union as a legal association, charging a small monthly membership fee, and set up its headquarters in the capital.

The role of trade unions in Argentina is not confined to defending wages and working conditions; they also play an important role in the country's welfare system. Paid-up membership of a union entitles a member and his/her family to free medical treatment and subsidised medicines, benefits which can only otherwise be obtained through private health schemes or public hospitals. The state pensions system works through obligatory contributions by employees to a pension fund.

Both union and government schemes only cover those members of the population in legal paid work. The growth in unemployment and irregular forms of cash-in-hand work on the black market, together with cutbacks in state spending on public hospitals, has produced a crisis in social security and health provision, particularly for women. A considerable proportion of the increase in women's economic participation, from 25 per cent in 1974 to 30 per cent in 1984, was in part-time, casual jobs with no social benefits. Since this work is typically low-paid, women employed in this sector have little chance to contribute to a private health or pension scheme. Women often depend on their husband's pension fund and if their husbands did not contribute these women are left with no income on his death. Since the average woman in Argentina can expect to live seven years longer than the average man, the situation of elderly women in Argentina has become critical.

Since 1984 SACRA has led demonstrations throughout Argentina demanding recognition of domestic work, beginning with a law which authorises pensions for housewives.

LAURA: Because we are women without wages, we demanded automatic pensions, without having to pay contributions to a fund. When women have the opportunity, they contribute enthusiastically to pension funds but then they stop paying in, for many reasons — because they don't have the money, or because women are so undervalued they are always the last priority in the house. The situation of elderly women is very dramatic. If there are no children to support them, they're unable to stop work. They continue cleaning other people's houses until they drop. In Argentina's cities there are many women sleeping in the streets — old women who've worked all their lives and who are reduced to begging.

SACRA also set about developing its own union health scheme.

ELIDA: We proposed a union system of health cover to protect our members and their families. If you're not a member of a union health scheme you have to go to the public hospitals. If you can prove you're destitute you get free treatment. But for many years public hospitals have been in a very bad state. You have to go at five in the morning to get a ticket to be seen that day. In general women don't go to the hospital for their own health unless they're seriously ill. Even when they're pregnant, they may only go once or twice.

In 1986 the Union won one of its most important achievements, the creation of a government-approved, nationwide health insurance system. Paid-up members of SACRA are now entitled to free medical treatment and subsidised medicines. The Union has also launched a health education campaign specifically designed for women, which includes placing SACRA representatives in public hospitals where they supervise medical attention for women and distribute information on sex education and contraception.

SACRA has also developed an education programme aimed at improving women's work opportunities. They recently signed an agreement with the National Council of Adult Education, an autonomous organisation inside the national education programme, allowing them to create centres to provide literacy classes and the chance for women to finish both primary and secondary education, including skills training to improve their job prospects.

SACRA's spectacular increase in membership stems from the huge success of its health insurance scheme and its campaign for pensions for housewives. By 1989 it claimed some 200,000 members. The issue of wages for housework, however, has been much more controversial and has brought the Union into conflict with most other women's groups and in particular, with feminists. Many feminists argue that paying women to do housework reinforces their ties to the home and makes it more difficult for them to enter the work market or participate in public life. It also reinforces the traditional stereotypes about women which have influenced the kind of work they can find. Women are concentrated in a small range of jobs such as domestic service, teaching and nursing precisely because housework is seen to qualify them for these tasks. The union position is that economic independence will offer women more opportunities and that wages will lead to a greater recognition of their skills.

ELIDA: Our main demand is for wages, to be paid out by the state. We've prepared a parliamentary bill calling on the government to set up a fund to pay the wages. The idea is that wages would be paid to all those women who work only in the home and have no other job and where the family income doesn't exceed more than two minimum wages.

We don't know if it'll be more difficult to get a woman out of the house if she has a wage, because up to now she's never had one. Most housewives have never had the choice and they're forced to work in the home. With a wage a woman will be able to choose if she wants to be a housewife or if she wants to work outside. It means she will be able to do other things like study, have a social life and she'll have a different relationship with her partner because she won't depend on him or the eldest child to bring in the money. There will be more equality in family relations. Wages will give equality to women.

The Union emphasises social recognition of the value of housework rather than challenging the way society allocates such work to women. Although it supports the socialisation of domestic tasks and has presented a parliamentary bill calling on the government to provide communal facilities such as creches, public canteens and laundrettes to alleviate the burden of work in the home, SACRA's emphasis is on improving the working conditions of women as housewives, rather than questioning the traditional roles of men and women. There is little emphasis on transferring domestic responsibilities onto men. Indeed, inherent in the idea of wages for housework is that transforming traditional roles in the home could leave women redundant.

Perhaps because SACRA's proposals offer little threat to the traditional family structure, the Union has met with little resistance from men.

LAURA: There's a strong tradition here that people who work, affliliate to a union. In general men encourage their wives to join SACRA, partly because the union offers real benefits, such as health cover which is especially important in this time of economic crisis.

I've got six children and I began working after I'd had four. We worked at different times so my husband had to look after the children and wash the clothes. This has happened with many delegates. If the husband sees that what you're doing benefits him, he supports you. There are private struggles but we've never encouraged a conflict with men. We believe they're just as much workers as women and the idea is to strengthen the union movement and transform the whole of society, not to turn it into an individual struggle. Even if you have a perfect husband who does everything, it doesn't mean the situation of women in general will change.

If there has been little resistance from individual men to their wives joining the union, SACRA's relationship with the national trade union organisation, the CGT, has been more difficult. It is not easy to take work performed as part of a personal relationship and reduce it to a simple worker-employee relationship. Housework fails to fit neatly into conventional categories of work and work relations. Traditional trade union concerns such as unemployment, work contracts and conditions, selection procedures and conventional union strategies such as collective bargaining and strikes, take on a different meaning when applied to housework.

ELIDA: From the beginning we've supported and worked with the CGT but we still haven't got formal recognition as a union. According to the law covering the membership of professional associations, to be recognised as a union it's necessary to show a relationship of dependency. Supposedly housewives aren't dependent on an employer, so who pays the wages? We say that we don't work for our husbands — what we do is social work, so the state should pay it. So we're involved in a legal battle to prove we have a relationship of dependency. But this formal problem hasn't stopped us working with the CGT. We took part in strike rallies against the last government. We didn't tell the housewives to go on strike, but that's always a possibility.

While in times of economic crisis and falling affiliation rates a trade union organisation might be expected to welcome the arrival of a huge new membership, the heavily male-controlled union world has been reluctant to accept this potential challenge to their power. With a claimed membership of 450,000 by 1991, the union would rate among Argentina's largest.

LAURA: It's a struggle against the union world, which is a masculine world. Even unions where the majority of members are women, like textiles, are led by men. Now the only women leaders are the General Secretary of the teachers' union and us. We want to push for the inclusion of women in the CGT. We've got as many members now as the biggest trade union. They're afraid of being challenged for the leadership but we want to be there and we will.

Unlike many of the new women's organisations, which use informal structures and procedures, SACRA has adopted a traditional form of union organisation with decision-making concentrated in a central national council. The composition of the council has changed little in successive elections, provoking criticisms of the lack of democracy within the union. SACRA's leadership belongs to a minority current in the Peronist movement which fails to reflect the sympathies of the majority of the members. SACRA has, however, given thousands of women the chance to take part in public affairs.

ELIDA: Our organisation has been structured so that it's absolutely centralised, but at the same time it's a democratic centralism. It's got a National Council of thirty members who approve delegates responsible for the local branches. To be recognised as a delegate a woman must organise a group of women into a union branch. This is very important, because the majority of our housewives have forgotten how to write, they hardly read the newspaper. Their contact with public life is normally through the radio. The fact that a woman comes to lead a thousand women and is capable of organising activities, working with hospitals and schools etc. represents a revolutionary change for Argentine women. We've advanced enormously. We are organised in all provinces except the Malvinas.

In the late 1980s working-class women also began to organise outside the Union. By 1988 independent grassroots women's groups, virtually unknown in Argentina, began to appear in poor neighbourhoods in the province of Buenos Aires and the interior of the country. These groups arose not from a theoretical discussion of women's position in society, but from the daily struggle for survival in the face of rising unemployment, cuts in public services and growing poverty. By the late 1980s the country was in the depths of another economic crisis with prices rising at between 100-200 per cent a month and unemployment and under-employment standing at 16 per cent. An estimated 28 per cent of those with jobs were self-employed, mainly doing irregular, cash-in-hand work, with no social security cover. Few other South American countries have declined so dramatically as Argentina: by 1989 the economy was smaller in absolute terms than it had been in the early 1970s. The dimensions of the crisis became clear to stunned Argentines in May 1989, when food riots and supermarket looting broke out in several of the country's major cities. In Greater Buenos Aires observers told reporters that mothers told their children to eat stolen food in the supermarkets and run out past the cashiers. At the same time women began to set up self-help groups in their neighbourhoods, such as communal kitchens and allotments and community ovens. The Fourth National Women's Meeting in 1989 reflected the increase in women's neighbourhood organisations; nearly 3,000 women took part and for the first time there was a mass attendance by poor and working-class women.

The Community Health Workers (ESC) of Lomas de Zamora, a district to the south-east of the capital in the province of Buenos Aires, are perhaps a unique example of working-class women's organisation in Argentina. As early as 1981, a small group of women from Villa Lamadrid, on the outskirts of the town centre of Lomas de Zamora, set about tackling the serious health problems in their community.

Edith's part-brick, part-corrugated iron house is typical of those in the poor neighbourhoods of the province. Water is pumped into the house from a well in the garden and household waste drains into a septic tank or into the ditches which line the edges of the uneven, muddy roads. The neighbourhood is prone to flooding and the lower section of her house is regularly three foot deep in filthy water. Before the military took power, small groups of residents had successfully campaigned for a local school and electricity, but there were no permanent neighbourhood organisations. During the dictatorship, when community organisations were closed down and public meetings banned, plans for the neighbourhood came to a standstill. With the support of a social worker who began working in Lamadrid in 1981, Edith, together with nine other women, started a campaign to improve community access to the newly-built neighbourhood health centre.

EDITH: We started to organise during the dictatorship, when it was very difficult to meet and everyone was still afraid. We took the precaution of working from our own houses and avoiding any public protest which might draw attention to ourselves. We began work on health issues, because that was the most serious problem. With no clean water, the children constantly had diarrhoea, hygiene was so poor that they got mange, and they weren't being vaccinated.

We had a community health centre, which was a small first aid post, but none of the community used it. It was built by the military and we didn't feel it had anything to do with us, or our neighbourhood. It was seen as an official institution and the community was afraid of it, and of the people who worked there. People would say, 'we can't go to the health centre, the *doctors* are there!' — as if doctors were extra-terrestrials! Instead they went, and still go, to Don Pedro, the spiritual healer, who was a poor person like the rest of us. He listens to us — it's very different from seeing a doctor in a white coat who doesn't listen to anything and just gives you a prescription. People wanted to be listened to and that's why he had so many patients.

The social worker in the neighbourhood, Elisa Pineda, had the idea of forming a group of women to go out into the community and explain about the health centre. We reached an agreement with Don Pedro that while he would attend to the spiritual health of the community, people would go doctors for other ailments. We put up a notice on his house explaining this. Next, we organised a party to inaugurate the centre — even though it had been open for some time, it hadn't been inaugurated

— and lots of people came. Then, slowly, people began to use it. We began to find out about courses and to train ourselves in healthcare, with the idea of passing on what we'd learnt to other women and getting them to join us. We believed that the community members themselves were best equipped to know the neighbourhood's problems, and with training, to deal with them.

The women soon had 98 delegates, one for every block in the neighbourhood, willing to monitor the health of their neighbours. Gradually they began to develop new self-help projects to improve services in the community. Word of their activities spread to other districts and by 1984, after the fall of the military regime, seven others had joined the organisation, including a nearby community, known as La Loma.

La Loma's neighbourhood committees, which had been closed down by the military, were re-opened in 1984 and a group of women formed a small health commission. Their first major battle was also over the community health centre, which had been completed for six months, but was still closed. María Rosa, who has lived in La Loma with her husband and four children for the last twelve years, was one of the committee members.

MARIA ROSA: They finally opened the centre, but only after we'd protested for months and threatened to take it over ourselves. They had no resources so we went to offer our help but they didn't want to know. They didn't trust us. We kept on pushing because there were a lot of problems. For example, there was a dentist but he wasn't working because he didn't have anaesthetic, gloves, needles or syringes. We managed to get some anaesthetic from a local hospital and we persuaded the dentist to see ten children a day. We arranged it with the school and then the dentist took twenty days off for stress — the thought of work must have frightened him! The first day he got back we were waiting for him with ten children. If we hadn't done this, I'm sure he'd still be sitting there doing nothing.

We spent two years fighting with the health centre to prove that we could do something and in the meantime we decided that if we trained ourselves, we'd be able to work better. Then we found out about the ESC.

By this time the ESC had persuaded a number of professionals to run free courses on working and teaching in the community, health, child development and citizens' rights. After finishing the courses, María Rosa and a group of women from La Loma set up their own ESC group in their neighbourhood. Delia was one of the members of the group.

DELIA: The most serious problem in La Loma is malnutrition. Many children eat just one meal a day. When a doctor recently asked a woman at the health centre if the children ate well, she said, 'Yes. They eat up to two plates of food at midday.' When the doctor asked her what they ate, she said, 'When they get up, they have *mate cocido* (a kind of herbal tea) with bread, at midday I make a soup with pasta and tomatoes — and they eat two plates — in the afternoon *mate cocido* with milk and bread and at night, nothing'. In other words they eat one meal every twenty four hours. Nothing they eat contains the amount of protein they need. So in that conversation about a day in the life of that family you can begin to see the problems of malnutrition. Working in the community gives us the chance to find these children before they get ill.

The women in La Loma were able to take advantage of a new local government scheme donating powdered milk to established neighbourhood organisations. The milk was distributed every two weeks from María Rosa's house.

MARIA ROSA: Getting the milk is always a battle. We have to ask for it every month and maybe one month we get a lot and the next, very little. It's just a small help — it's often not enough for the poorest families, where the children depend on *mate cocido* with milk every night and morning. They try and stretch out the milk powder by over-diluting it. There are about 300 children receiving milk. We weigh and measure them all and we decide by this who are the most needy. There are forty children who are under normal weight and height and we've referred them to the health centre.

We don't just give away the milk. We have meetings with the people who receive it where we teach them about basic child-care and we also demand some participation from them, that they help out on the allotment or the second-hand clothes stall, or take part in a nutrition course or one of our health campaigns.

After gaining the support of some of the health centre's staff, the women organised short courses on nutrition, child development and family planning. They developed a creative approach to promoting health education in the community. Cristina is in her late fifties and has lived in La Loma for ten years. After working most of her life as a domestic, she now works at home, looking after her daughter's three children:

CRISTINA: One year we were expecting an outbreak of measles and we wanted to make sure all the children were vaccinated. We worked with the children from the local school. We got them to draw pictures and they drew gruesome pictures of children with terrible red spots saying, 'Dad, it's all your fault, you didn't vaccinate me in time!' We filled the school and the whole neighbourhood with these pictures. The campaign was very successful. We learnt that it's important to involve children, because when they get home from school with a fixed idea that everyone has to be vaccinated, you're driven mad until you vaccinate them!

Women's health, and in particular the lack of ante-natal care and access to birth control, is also a serious problem in La Loma. The Catholic Church's opposition to artificial methods of birth control has created difficulties in several of the neighbourhoods where women have tried to broach the issue. La Loma was an exception.

MARIA ROSA: Women are the most neglected members of the community. The husband gets ill and they insist he goes to the doctor but they don't go themselves, because they waste a whole morning or they haven't got anywhere to leave the children. There are a lot of problems with pregnancies. Usually women don't go to the doctor until the sixth month or until the baby is about to be born. The health centre doesn't cover births and it was only last year that we managed to get an ante-natal surgery set up, but few women go. We've done health courses for women to try and make them aware of the need to look after their own health. We have weekly meetings in our homes where we teach other women about smear tests, how to check for breast cancer and the dangers of abortion and we encourage women to take courses and join the ESC.

Last year we also organised a family planning talk with one of the doctors. We did it in the church. A priest came and explained the rhythm method!

In Villa Albertina, the attitude of the local church is more typical.

ALICIA: The issue of birth control and sex education comes up at almost every meeting and we're planning to do some work on it. The problem is that the local priest is against it. I'm a lay preacher in our church and he's told us that if he finds out that any of the women preachers use contraception, he'll kick them out. The opposition of the Church makes it very difficult for us to do anything.

The other problem is money. Poor people can't afford contraception and that means there's a lot of abortions. Legal abortion is only possible in exceptional circumstances. As far as we're concerned it's illegal, but there are thousands of women who abort in terrible circumstances which end in death or infection. The women who arrive at the hospital haemorrhaging from an abortion are treated like dogs. In my neighbourhood a woman with five little children has just died trying to do an abortion on herself. There was another case of a fifteen year old who did an abortion with a parsley root, which is very common and very dangerous, because it rots inside and causes an infection. When her mother found out, it was too late because she was all poisoned. Women just can't afford contraception. It doesn't matter how much they might know about it, they haven't got the money to pay for it.

One of the most serious health hazards in all the neighbourhoods is the lack of clean water and safe sewerage systems. Most houses are not connected to the mains water supply, and of those that are, the majority are connected by makeshift, often home-made devices, which fail to meet recognised safety standards. In La Loma for example, only seven per cent of the inhabitants have running water, eighty per cent get their water from wells with hand or electric pumps and thirteen per cent have no water inside their houses. Wells, the main source of water for most of the residents of the neighbourhoods, are often self-built and prone to contamination by the septic tanks and the ditches of stagnant water which line the dirt roads, into which runs kitchen and bathroom waste.

In some cases the women of the ESC have led successful campaigns for clean water. Work began on connecting Villa Albertina to the mains after twenty women emptied jars of contaminated water onto the forecourt of local council offices. In general, however, the council has done little to improve services, even in the face of a cholera epidemic in Latin America which has affected Argentina's northern borders. Cholera spreads through polluted wells and ditches, making the poor neighbourhoods of Greater Buenos Aires a potentially fertile breeding ground for the disease. The women have been forced to rely on their own resources to improve hygiene and sanitation in their communities.

Tina, who is forty years old and has lived in La Loma for 25 years, helps to organise the sanitation campaign.

> TINA: We've managed to clean up the drainage ditches and the open spaces. When it rains, the ditches flood and the roads become muddy rivers of filth and rubbish. We pay taxes which are supposed to cover rubbish collection, but the rubbish was never collected, so we used to pay a man to do it. We organised a big campaign to convert him into a council employee, to force the council to assume its responsibilities. First we stopped paying him so that he also became interested in becoming a council employee and finally he did. Then we took photos of the ditches and all the rubbish in the neighbourhood and invited the neighbours to come. No one had realised the filth they were living in, even those with piles of rubbish outside their houses. María, who was in charge of the clean-up campaign, had several methods. The first was persuasion, then after the nice chats came the threats, saying she'd get the inspector to come (the inspector doesn't exist). It worked and we go round checking the neighbourhood regularly.
>
> It was the same with street lighting — people weren't interested, saying they had no money — so we organised a raffle in one block and

got the money for the cables and when the block lit up, the people in the next one got more interested. Now a large area of La Loma is lit up.

Increasingly poverty and hunger have become overriding problems in the neighbourhoods. The IMF economic package adopted by Alfonsín's government in 1985 cut real wages, increased unemployment and axed many welfare and social services. The government's distribution of food aid, in the form of boxes of non-perishables providing thirty per cent of the nutritional needs of a family of four, did little to relieve the plight of the poor; a series of 'shock adjustments', involving further austerity measures, only added to their hardship. By 1988 nearly one third of the population was unable to meet their basic needs and 15 per cent was destitute. Forty per cent of the population of the neighbourhoods surrounding the city of Buenos Aires was living in poverty.

In response to the crisis, the ESC set up a number of self-help projects to help women cut the costs of feeding their families. In La Loma they built a communal brick oven in the yard of Delia's house, which uses cheap fuel such as old clothes and wood. There is also a communal allotment and a second-hand clothes stall. They began to take advantage of new charities, such as the Popular Culture Service (SERCUPO), a Catholic lay association which supplies food at wholesale prices to community shops run voluntarily by groups of neighbours. Delia runs the shop from her home, selling basic foodstuffs, such as cooking oil, rice, sugar, pasta, flour and *yerba mate*.

ESC has found little support from the local council of Lomas de Zamora for their work. Apart from the powdered milk programme, help from the provincial Buenos Aires government has also been limited, although the ESC has always been quick to take advantage of any new government initiatives. When the Peronists took control in 1987, they began a scheme known as *Plan País* (Country Plan), donating money to groups of twenty poor families to enable them to buy food at wholesale prices. ESC are currently running six of these groups in La Loma. Government aid however, tends to be irregular and the milk programme was recently suspended due to a scandal over contaminated milk powder.

MARIA ROSA: Each party has its own projects and they start everything again from scratch. The health centre opened during the Radical government of the province. When the Peronists took over the province in 1987 they weren't interested in it and began another health programme, a system of mobile health units. There's no continuity so it's difficult to plan anything.

Now economic survival dominates everything. There's hyperinflation and they say, 'Let's open 200 soup kitchens', which puts the lid on the crisis but doesn't solve anything. The Radicals handed out boxes of food and the Peronists began by handing out food vouchers — which are all bad for the people because they have to go individually to ask for these things, not organise. We're trying to do the opposite.

Political parties have appeared more interested in winning votes than finding solutions to poverty.

ALICIA: Politicians always come. They can't believe that a group of women are doing all this. Sometimes they've tried to break the organisation but they've never managed it. They've tried to persuade people to leave us and join their parties. The women don't go because they want to do something to improve their neighbourhood and all the political people do is have barbeques and fight among themselves. They've done nothing to stop the spread of cholera. We're still not connected to the mains or sewerage systems and it's been left to us to educate people.

We don't want to depend on the politicians. Most of us don't believe in politics. We're all people from the neighbourhoods, doing what we can to make our lives better, so there's no false expectations. We don't have to trust others, only ourselves and our capacity to organise ourselves. That's why the organisation is growing and new people are coming to us all the time.

By 1989 women from more neighbourhoods had joined the ESC and they soon had a mass of new proposals for community projects. For eight years the ESC had worked with practically no external funding, depending on professionals to volunteer the services and small-scale fund-raising activities, such as raffles and local football tournaments. With few resources and little prospect of support from the authorities, they decided to create an institution with legal status that could apply for funds from national and international organisations. The Community Organisation Foundation (FOC) was founded in 1989 with a committee of five, made up of three members of the ESC and two professionals. María Rosa is currently FOC's director.

As many international aid agencies still consider Argentina a rich country, raising money abroad has been difficult, but FOC has enabled some of the projects to obtain small grants. With the help of UNICEF and a new local government scheme, Cristina now sells bread to the neighbourhood from a small bakery she helped set up. Tina, who from the age of twelve worked in knitting sweatshops, now knits in a small workshop with two other women. Even in the current economic climate, which has made it difficult to find sales outlets, their earnings have been an essential contribution towards their families' incomes.

TINA: My husband's wages don't last us two days. We buy our food through the *Plan País* scheme. If it wasn't for that we couldn't survive, but it's still not enough. Food is very expensive for us and I still can't buy shoes for my children. An unskilled worker earns very little, sometimes if they've got to travel to a job, their whole wage goes on the bus fare. So every penny I can earn counts, and lately we've had some success in persuading shops in the centre of Lomas de Zamora to take our sweaters.

For women, funds for setting up small businesses are not enough; to be able to work they also need childcare facilities.

EDITH: When the local factories closed it devastated our communities. Most of the men had worked in the factories or in the building trade. Today most of them do *changas*, odd building jobs that might last a day or two. It's only the minority that have proper jobs now. In many families the head of the household is now the woman. Women find it much easier to get work, mainly cooking and cleaning houses in the capital. If they're both working on the same day, the kids get left with the oldest child, who's probably no more than twelve. These youngsters don't go to school, they hang around the streets and they start taking drugs. I'd say seventy per cent of the young kids in Lamadrid take drugs.

Members of the ESC share childcare and some have been able to establish more permanent creches. Leo opened one of the ESC's first creches in 1987. Born in the northern province of Formosa, the daughter of Paraguayans, Leo came to Buenos Aires when she was 21, where she married and had two children. In 1987 she found out about the ESC and after taking childcare courses, she decided to turn her small backyard into a creche. A few years later, with money raised by FOC, the yard was converted into an extension of her house, creating a large room which is divided into two sections and a small kitchen area. The desks and toys are donations from the Dutch Embassy and the paper is reject stock from a local factory. The food for the children's meals is obtained by FOC from the provincial government.

Leo herself has only a primary school education and five years ago had no experience of community organisation.

LEO: I could see all the three and four year olds out on the streets, sick-looking children playing in the filth, because their mothers were out working. So I went with my sister to speak to their mothers about the idea of setting up a creche. They said, 'How much?', but when we saw the conditions they lived in, we knew we couldn't charge them. We said that when they were working they could pay us what they could afford. So we started the creche in my yard with ten children and each year we got more. The year before last we had 180 and last year we ended with a hundred. We had to cut the numbers because we just couldn't cope, what with the babies as well. We were out in the open air, with just plastic sheets for cover and we were cooking from my kitchen. Now there's eight of us working, all unpaid, including women who cook and a teacher. We're open from 7am to 8pm every weekday.

Some of the mothers formed a committee to help us raise money. The majority are single or separated and they mainly work cleaning private houses. We teach them how to take care of their children and we demand that they take part, at least to come and see the work we're doing with their children. We've got three groups: the three year olds and under, who are in the creche, the pre-school four and five year olds, and the seven to ten year olds who get extra help with their school lessons. We teach the little ones how to keep themselves clean and eat properly. We don't know much, but the little we know, we teach the children.

ESC groups have always tried to involve all community organisations in their work, including churches, health centres, schools and other neighbourhood groups. This has not been an easy task in communities still scarred by military rule and suspicious of the women's motives.

CRISTINA: After we'd struggled for years to get the gas put in, or the street lighting, people said, 'It's all thanks to you, Cristina'. But when we started they said, 'You're mad Cristina. The contractors will trick you and then what will you do?'. People didn't believe we could get things done. They're still afraid of getting involved. Not just because of the police, but also because they're afraid of failing.

TINA: There are people who say, 'If she's doing this, she must be getting something out of it'. Lots of people don't want to work together in the neighbourhood. It took years for the health centre, the church and the school to trust us. Some said we were liars like the politicians, because the politicians came here and promised a lot and did nothing. The other day I was trying to explain to a woman that we do things as best we can, but we're not perfect. If we do something wrong we want to be told because it helps us to improve. We've learned from experience.

The ESC's early experiences made them aware of the need to find ways to develop co-operation and a sense of solidarity in their groups. The difficulties of working with other community organisations, political party influences and the women's inexperience in public affairs have sometimes created problems inside groups. Leadership conflicts based on political differences which arose in the original Lamadrid organisation encouraged them to seek the help of professionals in devising courses aimed at strengthening the groups and reinforcing their independence from political parties. The regular neighbourhood and inter-neighbourhood meetings, for example, are often accompanied by singing and games; they encourage the open discussion of problems and receive training in decision-making, delegating responsibilities and evaluating projects. The positions of neighbourhood co-ordinator are rotated to prevent a concentration of power in one individual. All this perhaps explains the extremely low drop-out rate from the ESC groups and courses.

The courses also aim to boost women's self-esteem to help them deal with any opposition from men in the communities. The ESC was established as a women's organisation. The reactions of the men ranged from bemusement to hostility.

> ALICIA: We're a women's organisation because women spend more time in the neighbourhood. We're the most concerned about health and education because we spend more time with the children. Men are more interested in other activities, like sport and the neighbourhood committees, where they all argue about who's going to be the leader. Because we're an organisation of women, women are more interested in joining us.
>
> In the beginning *machismo* was very strong. Now we've got it more or less sorted out, although there are still some big fights to come. They used to say, 'those old women, let them get on with it', as if we were second-class, as if we were just messing about with all this. Now men are accepting women as leaders. Some have helped us out, but in the last instance it's the women who decide.

In 1989 the ESC decided to encourage men to take part in their work, but so far there has been little response.

> MARIA ROSA: I think we'd arrived at the point where we were established enough to feel that men weren't going to take us over. It didn't make sense with just us. Communities are made up of men and women and it's not only the women who are responsible for educating and caring for their members. But we always have to reinforce the women aspect in our training, to build women's confidence so that women can take decisions and lead men, otherwise we'd be just like any other organisation in Latin America, where the men lead and the women help. Here it's the opposite. The women lead and the men help.

> TINA: Most men aren't interested in joining us. Delia's husband is an exception. We use the shop for our meetings and he makes us really comfortable. He serves us with mate and looks after us. (*Mate* is usually drunk through a metal, straw-type filter from a small communal vessel which needs constant refilling with hot water. It is traditionally the job of women to serve *mate* to men) Delia goes to all the meetings she wants

and he never complains. He helps out — he helped build the communal oven. Some men help out because they see us working and they feel guilty. Or else after we've done all the hard work, when it's all set up, the men start getting interested.

It's important that they work with us. We don't want the men to fall apart. We don't want to be like Chile, where they say the men are destroying themselves with drink. It's very important that they don't destroy themselves — it's important for them, for us and for our communities.

Work in the community has inevitably meant that the women of the ESC spend less time in their homes and the majority have had to deal with the objections of their husbands.

EDITH: When you try and get a woman to take part in something, she says, 'I've got the washing and the ironing and the kids and I've got to be here to give my husband his *mate*'. Once you make make her understand that you're also a woman with a husband and kids, and you still work in the community, she starts thinking, 'I could do that too'. It might cause trouble in the family in the beginning, but as we've got lots of experience at all this, and our husbands are used to it, we get them to speak to the woman's husband.

DELIA: Unemployment is terrible for men because they are brought up to work outside the home and earn money and when they see that they can't support their families, they go through a big crisis. When the woman goes out to do something to help feed the family, they don't like it. It's not until you start leaving the house that you realise what problems you've got as a woman. Tina had to make her husband understand that her work paid the bus fares, for the children's books and pencils.

TINA: My husband is very good — as long as I'm at home. If I'm not there when he gets home from work, he sulks and won't speak to me. If he doesn't have a button on his shirt he says, 'You've got time to go to a meeting, but not to sew my shirt'. So I try to have everything ready at home and then go out. Lately I haven't been taking much notice of him. He helps me more than he used to. He washes the clothes at the weekend when he's not at work. That's great progress. Before, the typical *macho* male wouldn't be seen dead in the kitchen. They get used to it, but it's difficult. At least mine's young and he's got time to change.

CRISTINA: If he's young, you've got time to domesticate him. My husband's an old man and set in his ways. I always have to be there to serve his *mate*. He's used to having everything done for him. My mother-in-law lived with us for 22 years so if I couldn't do it for him, she would. Then when the children were older he'd say, 'daughter, get me a glass'. It upsets him when I'm not there to prepare his *mate* when he gets home. What can you do? We've been together 35 years. You can't just forget that.

For the women of ESC, working in the community has not only meant improving the quality of their families' lives, it has also given them the opportunity for personal development and an awareness of their common interests as women. Rafaela is an elderly woman from Fiori, one of the most recent neighbourhoods to join the ESC. She works in a children's canteen built on a piece of her garden which she donated to the organisation.

RAFAELA: I went to primary school for two years and then I had to leave to work as a domestic. When I got married I believed that I was only here to serve my family and never went outside my home. This happens to a lot of women. There are some who won't even take their children to see a doctor because they don't know how to get to the hospital. Now I'm older, and my children have grown up and got married, but in the last few years I've listened and learnt like a child. I've learnt to speak and to go to meetings with a lot of people. Before I was afraid if I saw a policeman or a man in a suit. Now women come to me and ask for help. In the hospital they say, 'We can't see you today', or you'd sit around waiting, feeling like a beggar. Now I say to people, 'go to the hospital and stand up for yourself'.

TINA: What's important to me is the company. You don't feel so alone. You feel supported and you don't suffer so much. You realise that a lot of your problems aren't just yours alone, that all women have got them and that means we can work together to change our lives.

In 1987 three ESC members became consultative members on the Women's Committee of the government of Buenos Aires province, a state body concerned with the legal, economic and civil rights of women. They have come into contact with the growing number of women's community organisations through the National Women's Meetings.

In 1987 the women of the ESC also received authorisation from the Housewives' Union, SACRA, to form a union branch in Lomas de Zamora and the majority of the ESC members have now joined the union health scheme and the campaign for pensions for housewives.

ALICIA: The majority of the women belong to SACRA. The union dues are low enough for most of us to join, although there are some women who still can't afford to pay. It's been very important to us. Most of us had no health cover — many of the women and men in the neighbourhoods are in casual work and aren't covered. Now we can go to the clinics and get X-rays, eye tests, smears and some dental treatment for our families. SACRA also organises cheap holidays, which gives some of us the chance to get away, when normally we'd never have a holiday. We believe in their campaign for women's rights, like the pensions for older women. When we look around our own neighbourhoods and see how many old, destitute women there are, of course we can see how important it is for us. The health scheme and the pensions are the main reason we're in SACRA. The wages issue — no one really believes we're going to win that one. And the leaders — we have differences with them. They seem a very closed group to us, who don't share our ideas.

In 1989, in the midst of economic chaos, President Alfonsín stepped down six months before his mandate was due to end and elections were called. The elections gave the Housewives' Union the chance to present their policies to the general public. Unlike the ESC and other new women's organisations, which have defended their political independence, SACRA, like the majority of trade unions, aligned itself with the Peronist party. The Union backed the presidential campaign of the Peronist candidate, Carlos Menem, who in turn supported their demands. Although not a formal part of the Peronist movement, SACRA played an important role in mobilising women behind the Peronist cause. The Union's general secretary stood as a candidate for a Peronist-dominated coalition in the northern province of Misiones.

ELIDA: As housewives we supported Carlos Menem as our candidate, although we aren't part of any one political party. During the election period we campaigned on two issues, the creation of a national Ministry of Women and the recognition of domestic work, starting with pensions for housewives. Dr Menem accepted our demands and SACRA organised throughout the country, which was very important because for the first time as housewives we could promote a candidate for our programme.

After Menem's election the issue of pensions for housewives was taken up by the Women's Secretariat, a state body set up under Alfonsín's government as part of the Ministry of Human Development and the Family. The Union, together with the two other national housewives' organisations, the ACP and the League, helped draw up a bill to be presented to parliament which would affect some 600,000 women estimated to have reached or be about to reach the retirement age of sixty. Their co-operation on the pensions project did not represent a coincidence of interests among the housewives' organisations. Ironically, in the case of the two largest groups, it was the government which brought them together. Menem was elected president on a populist platform which promised employment and improved living standards for the working class, yet on taking office he embraced a series of IMF and World Bank-backed austerity measures as well as a closer relationship with the United States. This turnabout produced an unusual configuration of alliances between the housewives organisations. The Union, despite its nationalistic and anti-free market stance and despite the falling standards of living of the majority of its members, has so far remained loyal to the government. The League, despite its identification with non-Peronist parties of the right, has wholeheartedly supported the government's free-market policies.

While for the Union pensions represent the recognition of a housewife as a worker, the two other housewives' organisations have different positions. The League, which claims a 350,000 membership, remains chiefly concerned with consumer rights and works primarily with consumer groups. Its considerable financial resources have guaranteed it a high public profile and access to the radio and TV to condemn price rises, poor quality goods and unfair advertising, and to publicise the cheapest prices. While they claim to receive no financial support from food and retailing companies, their stamp of approval is often used in the publicity campaigns of manufacturers and supermarket chains. They support a housewives' pensions scheme but are vehemently opposed to the idea of pensions for women who have not previously contributed to a fund.

The ACP supports the pension fund and the unconditional payment of pensions to destitute women, but its contacts with the Union are limited to the issue of pensions and it rejects the idea of a housewife as a worker and wages for housework.

MARTA: We are working for a pension for housewives but this is in recognition of the kind of lives the majority of older women have had. A woman of 50 or 55 who's worked all her life and never had the opportunity to contribute or do anything else should get a pension. But this doesn't mean we want the same lives for our daughters. The situation of a young woman who's just got married is different. We don't believe in wages for housework. The objective isn't to pay a woman to spend all her life in the house. What we are aiming for is more socialisation of domestic tasks and the sharing of domestic tasks within the family. We don't believe in union health cover for housewives. Our position is that public hospitals should be properly financed and well-equipped.

The ACP is the only one of the national housewives' organisation to work with other women's groups, both feminist and non-feminist alike. Although many women's organisations work on gender issues, the word 'feminist' is almost universally rejected. SACRA has no relations with the feminists, it is not a member of the Women's Multisectorial and takes no part in the National Women's Meetings.

LAURA: We're the biggest women's organisation in the country and we're not recognised by the feminists. They don't recognise our central demand for wages and and above all they question the idea that a housewife is a worker. Feminist groups in Argentina are very European based. I'm not putting down the struggle of European women but they live in a different world.

For example, the feminists wanted mass support for the divorce law and they didn't get it. Why not? Fundamentally it was about the division of property, the law didn't include obligatory alimony in the form of food payments by husbands. If you take the great majority of women from the middle class down, they live as concubines and they haven't got property to divide up, so food is always the most important part of any divorce settlement. So this divorce law, which seemed like a great advance to the feminists, was no use to the women who live as concubines and have no property. There's a group of women inside the union who believe in abortion, but it's not the official union position. Nor is it the priority. The most important issue is to guarantee safe births and that the mothers and children can have enough food and live a decent life. We need inhabitants. We're a huge country.

Feminism may help explain reality but it has to be adapted to the conditions of people. In some senses we are feminists but we want it to have its proper meaning — an Argentine feminism for the mass of Argentine women.

From their very different perspectives the two new national organisations have had significant effects on the lives of Argentine housewives. By organising themselves, housewives have used their huge potential power as consumers and voters to promote new gender-related demands. They have challenged the image of housewives as conservative, politically inactive women. The ACP remains a relatively small organisation, reaching some two or three thousand women throughout the country. They have had some success in setting up nursery and primary schools and local council markets which sell low-price food products. Through their participation in the Women's Multisectorial, the ACP can claim credit for the advances made in the laws affecting women. Divorce, reform of the law on *patria potestad*, ratification of the law on the state provision of nursery schools, the establishment of women's departments at local and central government level and a recent law guaranteeing women thirty per cent of candidates in elections are the major achievements of the Argentine women's movement to date.

SACRA's huge membership is the result of the tangible benefits the Union offers women, through its system of health cover and the Union's education and health campaigns. The principle of pensions for housewives has been established in several provinces, although at present they operate on the basis of previous contributions to a pension fund. One of the Union's most significant achievements has been in the northern province of Misiones, where the Union's general secretary, Elida, is a member of the local government. Misiones was the first province to introduce pensions without previous contributions, currently benefiting some 1,400 women.

The prospects for further legislative gains are not promising. The IMF-backed programme of wage controls and expenditure cuts adopted by the current government is not fundamentally questioned by any major political party and there is little hope of any significant change in economic direction. There has been no response to SACRA's proposal for wages for housework nor for the creation of a Ministry of Women. Rather, as part of the government's efforts to reduce state spending, the Secretariat of Women has been dissolved. Argentina's state pension fund is in crisis and the pension fails to meet the basic needs of the retired population. Trade unions in general have found themselves in a weak position in this political and economic scenario. Not only have growing unemployment and the increase in part-time, casual work and female employment cut away at their former power-base among male blue-collar workers, but the government also plans to curb union collective bargaining powers and their control over health insurance schemes. In addition, corruption scandals and undemocratic practices have led to public disenchantment with the unions and to the feeling that traditional organisations have failed the working class. While SACRA represents a unique way of bringing women into the scope of the organised working-class movement, as well as an opportunity to introduce women's issues into trade union policy, it has yet to move away from a traditional, centralist structure which restricts the mass participation of women in decision-making.

Some unions have already recognised the need to move beyond traditional areas of union action and to build new power bases by involving themselves in community issues and developing links with local organisations. The rapid growth of new grassroots groups such as the ESC contrasts markedly with the decline in public confidence in traditional union organisations. The ESC has achieved remarkable successes, both in improving the lives of men and women in its communities and in giving large numbers of women a role in the public life of their neighbourhoods. There are now ESC groups in 41 neighbourhoods, stretching beyond the boundaries of Lomas de Zamora. In La Loma alone, there are over a hundred trained members and over 400 women involved in ESC activities. In all, the ESC now has more than two hundred working projects, including shops, small businesses, creches, nursery schools and educational programmes, as well as senior citizens' clubs, young peoples' groups and projects for the disabled. The success of grassroots groups such as the ESC suggests that these organisations have an important role to play in democratising a political system that has so often failed working-class men and women.

Chile
Chronology

1949   Women win the vote.

1973   President Allende killed during the military coup which brings General Pinochet to power. The Association of Democratic Women is formed to support political prisoners and their families.

1974   The Association of the Relatives of the Detained and Disappeared is formed.

1980   150 women detained by police during Chile's first International Women's Day event.

1982   The Movement of Women Slum Dwellers (MOMUPO) is created to unite and co-ordinate the activities of grassroots women's groups.

1983   Women's organisations take part in the first mass street protests against the Pinochet regime. Manifesto of the Feminist Movement appears for the first time with the slogan 'Democracy in the Country and in the Home'. Several federations set up to co-ordinate women's opposition to military rule.

1984   Police attack the Feminist Movement's celebration of International Women's Day. Several feminist organisations, including the Women's Study Centre and the Women's Place of La Morada are set up.

1986   The Civil Assembly, made up of 200 grassroots organisations, includes a list of women's concerns in its 'Chile Demands' challenge to the dictatorship.

1989   In the first free elections for 19 years, only ten out of 164 deputies and senators elected are women. 20,000 women celebrate International Women's Day. The Women's Place opens in a northern Santiago shanty town.

1990   The government creates the National Women's Service (SERNAM) to develop and promote women's programmes.

6

'Democracy in the Country and Democracy in the Home'

Grassroots Feminism in Chile

SUSANA: I remember the first time we went out on the streets for the 8 March (International Women's Day). We'd only just become aware of feminism — before then we'd no idea what the 8 March meant. We all had stickers which said things against the dictatorship and the idea was to try and stick them wherever we could, on the buses, on lamp posts. There were various meeting points, one was the Congress building, which of course was still closed, and the idea was to organise a march, but the police were everywhere and we couldn't join up. Everyone dispersed in different directions. We pretended we were waiting in bus queues or that we'd just come from work or we were looking in shop windows, so we didn't get caught by the police. We were all wearing skirts and carrying handbags because you were less likely to be caught than if you wore trainers and trousers. The nice thing was you felt you weren't alone. Women would get off the bus and whisper to us. 'I've just come from work, is it good?' and we said 'it's terrible, they're beating us up' but they'd go all the same with their stickers, looking really calm and as they passed behind the bus they'd stick one on.

Susana lives in a *población*, one of the urban slums which surround Chile's capital, Santiago. Until the early 1980s she was a typical working-class wife and mother. She had been married for over twenty years, had never worked outside the home and had never been involved in community organisations. Like many women in the *poblaciones* she became involved with women's groups only after she was forced out of the house to search for work during the economic crisis of the early 1980s. Her husband, a mechanic, lost his job and she began selling second-hand clothes in a market. Today Susana calls herself a feminist. She is part of a working-class women's movement in Chile which has come to be known as 'popular' or grassroots feminism.

The early feminist movement in Chile was largely made up of women from the middle and upper classes and was mainly concerned with political and civil rights that working-class women often felt had little relevance to their lives. The struggle for access to higher education was seen as a middle-class affair; the rights of married women mattered little to women who often did not marry officially; improvements in labour legislation for women only benefited those who had jobs covered by work regulations in the first place. After women won the vote in 1949, the independent women's movement disintegrated and it was assumed that the political parties would take up the interests of their new female constituency. The party leaderships, however, continued to be dominated by men who failed to recognise the need for any specific policies for women. Political parties of both the left and the right tended to see women's interests and the interests of the family as one and the same thing.

Until the 1970s the only major Chilean organisations composed exclusively of women were the Mothers' Centres, set up in the *poblaciones* by the Church and charities to teach women craft skills. For most working-class women these centres, together with the Church, were their only opportunity for community participation. During President Allende's government of Popular Unity (1970-73) the Mothers' Centres played an important role in campaigns for improved housing, health and recreational services in the community. Even under Allende speeches about the importance of wives and daughters to the future of Chile were more in evidence than coherent public policies. Ideas about women and the family were also manipulated by right-wing parties and provided the justification for one of the first large scale opposition movements to Allende's government. *'El Poder Femenino'* ('Female Power') was the name of a middle- and upper-class housewives' movement which organised 'empty pot' marches in protest at food shortages and the 'threat of communism' in Chile.

Any progress which had been made in women's rights was swiftly overturned when General Augusto Pinochet seized power in 1973. In the military scheme of things the proper role of women was to defend the family, guard the faith and protect morality. With Pinochet's wife as head of a new National Secretariat of Women, the Mothers' Centres were reorganised and became the main vehicle for the diffusion of military ideology. Skills training workshops were set up and free medical and legal services were offered to attract poor women. The Mothers' Centres 'have stopped being a political entity' declared Señora Lucia Hiriart de Pinochet. The regime attempted to limit, if not eliminate, a public role for women. Many of the civil and labour gains women had won in the previous years were revoked. Employers were no longer required to provide or subsidise childcare for female employees and a new law made it possible for employers to sack pregnant employees. One law even tried to stop women wearing trousers, although the attempt was short-lived.

As discussed in Chapter One the military's strategy backfired. It was precisely in the name of defending the family and children that women began taking on a more public role in the life of the *poblaciones*. To combat widespread unemployment and growing poverty, women joined church initiatives like the children's canteens and skills workshops and began setting up their own community organisations, such as the communal kitchens. Many of these groups came to concern themselves not only with the immediate problems of feeding their families, but also with the specific needs of women. For some of these organisations, like the Movement of Women *Pobladoras* (MOMUPO), the needs of women became the priority.

MOMUPO was the initiative of a group of women from *poblaciones* in a district in the northern zone of Santiago. Before the military coup Flora and Matilde had worked with local church organisations. When they joined a church-initiated education programme with the trade unions in 1980 they became frustrated at the lack of interest in women's concerns. They formed a women's commission inside the main workshop but their work continued to be ignored and they began to contact other women in their neighbourhood, both union and non-union members.

FLORA: Why did we meet separately from the men? Because when we put forward ideas in the meetings, no one took any notice. The same idea that we'd suggested was then put forward by a man from a political party or a union, using different words and he'd get the applause. It was this frustration which made us break away. We got the addresses of their wives and got them to join us and it spread.

MATILDE: We organised a meeting in the *población* to talk about the things that were happening: the privatisations, what was happening to the health service and education. No one understood anything. We tried to find people who could come in and explain it to us and started regular discussion groups. Most of the women had been learning craft skills but no one ever saw what they made, so we had the idea of organising a market to sell them. Sometimes the Church bought the crafts to sell in the Vicariate (the Vicariate of Solidarity was set up by the Church in Santiago to provide humanitarian support for the victims of poverty and violence) or abroad, but they weren't seen in the neighbourhoods. Everyone was isolated and stuck in their own worlds. The market had various aims — for women to sell their work, but above all as a step into the outside world. It was organised in secret in the offices of the parish. The situation in those years was very dramatic. We were living under an implacable dictatorship — there was no expression, participation, no social movements so the fact that women were organising was something very novel. It was an important step towards showing our faces in public.

They began to establish links with women's groups in other *poblaciones* and gradually became more independent of both the Church and the union organisation. By 1982 they were working with 15 women's groups and in that year they formed MOMUPO. MOMUPO's first concern was to work with ordinary housewives, with no political or community experience, women who were considered vulnerable to the ideas being disseminated by the military-run Mothers' Centres.

MATILDE: The challenge was to build an independent movement, as much from the Church as from the political parties. The Church gave the groups some initial training but it often stayed with them and ended up leading them. When we started to organise outside the Church many women thought we were falling into the hands of the political parties; they didn't believe that it was possible to to have an independent social movement. We formed a provisional committee and got some foreign aid for training courses. We held a seminar on women and history and talked about the role of women in popular struggles. This was seen as 'political'. We got a lot of criticism; some people said it was wrong to take women out to the streets and get them involved in politics. Some women left because they thought we were feminists. And the other problem was the more political women, who said we were too soft, not political enough. They didn't understand that we wanted to give ordinary housewives, with no political experience, the confidence to participate in the world outside their homes and then let them choose their political party, if they wanted. There was a lot of fear about the word 'politics'. It was taboo. I remember it was a time when the political parties tried to get women together and organise activities for them and because they had a very political message, instead of attracting women, they put them off. We learnt that you have to go slowly and not scare them, that you have to generate an atmosphere of trust among women. We had to be very careful not to do anything which appeared very 'politicised'.

FLORA: We were all *pobladoras*, so it was very hard at first because we didn't even know where to start. We didn't have any experience in organising groups, we just wanted to help other women like us and give them the chance that we'd been given, to go out and do something. It was difficult to get the women out of their houses. Women were too busy thinking about how to find food — many had young children and had no time to take to the streets to shout. Many had husbands who wouldn't let them out to meetings. There was a lot of fear and a lot of depression in the *poblaciones*. But women were interested, they wanted to understand why everything had changed. There were lay-offs all the time and no new jobs, and the men stopped being the providers. Women had to go out to earn money — ironing, washing, cleaning or working in the communal kitchens. Men began to lose their authority and their confidence. They were around the house all the time and women felt they had men around them who were just ornaments and were asking themselves what was happening.

SUSANA: Even if you didn't suffer repression directly, you felt afraid and alone, you were psychologically damaged. Most women didn't work outside and spent all day at home. I'd been married twenty years and had no other experience except as a wife and mother. I'd never worked outside and I'd always been very submissive. We all had very serious economic difficulties because of unemployment but my neighbourhood is a very closed community and most people suffered in silence. A lot of the women had problems with tranquilisers because in Chile you can buy them as easily as a loaf of bread. I was hospitalised twice with depression and all the doctors did was give me pills — pills to sleep, pills to wake up and pills to work. Fear paralysed everything. No one talked about politics. I got involved in MOMUPO when my husband lost his job. He used to teach car mechanics. It was very difficult for him too. He went right under. He spent entire days sitting around, he didn't want to do anything. It happened to many men. I began to work and then my cousin told me that there were groups of women meeting secretly in Flora's house. It was illegal for more than two or three people to meet and it was dangerous if people saw you, they could accuse you of something. I went to a meeting and found women talking about politics. I remember there was one woman, an elderly woman, who was saying that women had to take to the streets and give the police a good hiding. I was terrified. I thought, 'what have I let myself in for?' I'd spent twenty years inside my four walls with only the radio to listen to. I'd never heard conversations like this before. I went home and I didn't tell anyone where I'd been. My husband would have said I was crazy.

MOMUPO's aim was both to develop activities which helped to solve the immediate economic needs of the women and their families, to involve them in a process of self-education which would increase their awareness of the social and political situation in Chile and encourage them to take a more active role in grassroots organisations. Since craft workshops had been common in the *poblaciones* they were unlikely to be considered political by the military or by the *pobladoras*.

MATILDE: We wanted to set up workshops to train housewives and to give them skills which could help them solve their economic problems. We all needed money. We organised workshops like knitting, sewing and leatherwork. There's a cultural aspect to these workshops. Before the coup there were Mothers' Centres which were mainly organised for the *pobladoras* and reinforced the idea that they were places to train women to be better housewives. Almost all of them had manual activities and even today when a group tries to organise it has to have these activities to attract women, something practical and then later they may learn that other things are important, too.

FLORA: We also had workshops on mental health, unemployment, the disintegration of the family. We'd start with our family problems — and then we'd talk about what was happening to education, health, with all the privatisations — that now you had to pay for everything, that it wasn't like that before. The idea was to show that it wasn't just an individual problem — that if the husband was unemployed it didn't mean he wasn't capable of supporting the family or that he was bad at his job, and that if women were neurotic it wasn't because they were born with neurosis; to show that the problems had a political explanation, that it was a repercussion of the society we were living in. So it was a question of translating the problems from the private to the public sphere. That was our task. Of course we didn't have all the answers. We weren't pretending to be prophets or anything. We were all learning together and sometimes we asked professionals to come and explain very specific issues, like the changes in the education system, or we'd ask psychologists to explain about neurosis.

As the economic crisis deepened MOMUPO found itself increasingly involved with the overriding problems of unemployment, poverty and hunger. In 1984 MOMUPO launched the Hunger Campaign. Dozens of women dressed in black and carrying empty saucepans marched on local council offices in silent protest against the indifference of the government to the plight of the *pobladores*. The women also organised a series of workshops on the causes of unemployment and poverty. When women began setting up communal kitchens, several groups turned to MOMUPO for support.

FLORA: We had no food in our houses, so women were starting up communal kitchens. But as they were small, isolated groups, with little co-ordination, they began to come to us to ask for help. At that time we were working from the chapel and we suddenly had to form two groups, one in a room working for the movement and the other in another room organising the kitchens. The kitchens took up a lot of time and resources because you had to spend a lot of time begging. This caused arguments in the movement because our own work came to a standstill. Also the kitchens were mixed and it wasn't always women in the leadership. We were losing our identity, which was with women's organisations. We weren't able to organise all this new work, which was enormous and we didn't know how to divide up the responsibilities. Everything had started spontaneously, nothing was written down. And of course we didn't have the resources we needed to do it properly. Until 1985 we were still using the church for our meetings. After the earthquake the chapel was condemned and we were out on the streets. We had meetings in the backyard of the church, sitting on the ground. We'd always had problems finding places to organise events. Sometimes people offered us a place to meet — they must have been thinking 'these old women can't be doing any harm' but when we wrote invitations saying 'The Movement of *Pobladoras* invites you to..' they'd change their minds, saying it was something political and we had to find somewhere else.

We couldn't take on everything or we'd have just fallen apart, so we decided to let the kitchens organise themselves and concentrate on the women's groups. We got help from Oxfam to set up our own premises. The first house was small, a cubby hole and falling apart and we filled it with old hairdryers, in case the police came, so we could say we were giving hairdressing courses. A lot of women came. We'd go in one at a time and we'd never leave all at the same time. A few here and a few there, we had to be very careful.

When MOMUPO went back to co-ordinating activities for their women's groups, its house became a focal point for the women's organisations of local *poblaciones*. In 1985 it organised a health campaign which it followed up with a campaign for women's reproductive rights and a summer school on women and politics.

It was the very success of MOMUPO which presented difficulties for the organisation. Not only did it lack the resources necessary to respond to the needs of its members but the re-emergence of the political parties and the beginning of the public protests against military rule in 1983 placed new demands on the movement. By this time MOMUPO had women of varying levels of political awareness and some wanted the organisation to play a more public role in the national opposition movement. There were also external pressures from political parties, middle-class feminist groups and professional organisations who wanted to take advantage of MOMUPO's organisational strength in the *poblaciones*. As demands for MOMUPO's presence at social and political events increased, their grassroots work with women's groups began to suffer.

> FLORA: The biggest problem was that we didn't have the resources to follow anything up. Four hundred women took part in the health campaign, but women from other *poblaciones* were asking why we didn't invite them. They were all desperate to learn. People couldn't afford to go to the doctor any more, they couldn't afford medicines, the health system had abandoned the pobladores. They began to ask us to bring in professionals to give breast cancer examinations and smears but we weren't able to. At the same time, the protests were going on and there was the problem of finding the balance between the demands of the women's groups and the things that were going on around us.
>
> On top of this it was a very hard time for us as individuals. It was a time when we were all in a bad way. We all had family problems, some were having to take their children out of school to help support the family, or they had husbands who were ill or unemployed, or relatives in prison. I remember one Mother's Day we had the idea of organising activities with women from other zones. We invited mothers of victims of the protests. It began to dawn on us that something could happen to one of us and we began to realise that we weren't doing anything about our own security. And with such bad communications — we had one telephone between us and had to walk everywhere to find out if someone was all right. We used to go to the prisons to visit the women political prisoners and this had a terrible impact on us. It was a time of tragedy after tragedy, a young boy here, a man there, a child somewhere else, young people being taken prisoner... A large part of our meetings was taken up talking about the terrible things we'd seen or heard about, the dead bodies, the bodies with their throats cut...
>
> We had to do a hundred things at the same time: requests for MOMUPO to attend events and demonstrations, people bringing us information and wanting us to organise things and it all made supporting the groups more difficult. And not being part of a political party we had no back-up and we didn't understand anything. There was a problem of language, because we didn't understand the concepts, including the word 'concept'. We didn't understand what the parties stood for, what communism was. The majority of us were women without any political experience and when the political parties began reorganising and asking us to join them, we didn't know who they were or what they stood for.

MATILDE: The question of political parties was very important when the demonstrations started: one group would say to meet in a certain place and another group would say to meet in another place and those of us from the social movements were left in the middle. They all had different strategies and sometimes groups joined together, one lot went with the Socialists, the Christian Democrats on the other side, and we didn't know where we were. If you stick with one political group what does that mean? That you're taking the women to identify with something they've got no idea about. And the *pobladoras*, for whom it had cost so much to take to the streets, found themselves in the middle of a terrible mess. So there was this question of where we stood and whether we had to do things independently of the political parties.

FLORA: The militants in the organisation knew very well that if we went to a demonstration we could get beaten, soaked by the water cannons, smothered by tear gas or even shot at. What would the women who'd come for the first time think? The young ones were asking to be taught how to make a barricade, how to run and defend ourselves, how to climb a barricade — imagine if I went to my group and said 'today we're going to learn how to build a barricade' — the old dears would have taken me by the arms and thrown me out! We had to be very careful about what to take part in and to respect their level of politicisation.

MOMUPO was also being called on to take part in women's events. By the mid 1980s several women's federations had been formed to rally women around the fight for human rights and democracy. Women from all sectors of society had become involved not only in the movement against military rule but also in the struggle to ensure a place for themselves in any future democracy. Inside political parties, trade unions and professional associations, in human rights groups and universities, women had begun raising their own demands within the movement for social change. At the same time new groups began pressing for changes in the very heart of Chilean society, inside the family itself. Many of these were influenced by the first wave of women exiles who returned to Chile with the ideas of the feminist movements of Europe and the United States. On 11 August 1983, on the fourth day of protests, about sixty women staged a five minute sit-in on the steps of Santiago's National Library under a banner which read 'Democracy Now! — The Feminist Movement of Chile'. The slogan 'Democracy in the Country and in the Home' began to appear on demonstrations against military rule.

Until 1985 MOMUPO, like many of the other women's groups in the *poblaciones*, had not considered itself a feminist organisation.

FLORA: The feminists approached us and we did a workshop with them. I remember Julieta (Julieta Kirkwood, a Chilean feminist academic and writer) spoke about feminism, about witches and all that, and our hair stood on end and we said that we weren't feminists and that our organisation was class-based.

The reaction of MOMUPO members reflects the widespread suspicions held by working-class and poor women about feminism. Censorship meant that very little real information about the new movements abroad reached Chile. The popular press not only ridiculed the new women's movement as a man-hating, bra-burning, foreign fad but also, under a military dictatorship which extolled the virtues of motherhood, as something more sinister and subversive which aimed to undermine the family and the very foundations of Chilean society. To the traditional working-class organisations, feminism was seen as a Made-in-the-USA, middle-class strategy designed to split the working-class movement. MOMUPO identified itself with the working-class struggle but also shared with feminism a concern for the specific needs of women.

FLORA: The only thing that we were sure about was that MOMUPO was a social movement, independent of political parties and that we were bringing together both politicised and non-politicised housewives within the democratic movement. We wanted to play a part in the working-class struggle for democracy but we also wanted to fight for our needs, as women. We wanted a cultural transformation, a society with many changes in values. It wasn't just that we wanted democracy, full stop. We didn't want women to go back to their houses when the struggle against the dictatorship ended.

We had a couple of other meetings with the feminists and we began to realise that we were something different from the kind of feminism they were talking about — that ours was a grassroots kind of feminism.

Grassroots feminism not only challenged the assertion that trade unions and political parties speak for all the working class but also questioned the idea that 'traditional' feminism speaks for all women. Feminist groups in Chile were closely identified with the anti-dictatorship struggle and with the Left but, like the old women's movement before them, they were composed mainly of middle-class women. To the women of MOMUPO these groups ignored many of the issues which affected the lives of working-class women and failed to take into account their educational levels and their lack of economic options. They saw the discrimination they faced in their own lives as cruder than that suffered by middle-class women who could often soften the roughest edges of *machismo* by paying for better health services, private education and childcare and by employing maids to do their housework. The style of the feminists was seen as too confrontational for the *poblaciones*.

SYLVIA: We played a big part in the women's opposition movement. We joined the demonstrations called by other women's organisations. On International Women's Day we went on marches with the other groups. At the demonstrations they gave us placards and never asked us what we thought. We were there to make up the numbers, nothing else. There were some middle-class women who were interested in what we were doing. There were also professional women who wanted to work with MOMUPO but we were always very wary that we would lose our independence if we let middle-class women in.

FLORA: The difference is that we work with our class identity and middle-class feminism doesn't, they work only with gender. They say women's problems are common to all women. We have things in common with middle-class women but we also have other problems that middle-class women don't have, like the housing shortage, debt problems, unemployment, and we're not going to advance as women if the two things aren't closely linked.

Gender discrimination may be the same but the class situation is different. Working-class culture is more rigid — we've got more brakes. Perhaps because of the influence of religion and perhaps because we've got less choice — we haven't got the economic freedom to do what we want.

LUZ MARIA: Feminism of the upper class or middle class is a long way from our feminism. We've tried to work with middle-class feminists but they talk about a different world from ours. For example, they did a workshop where they told us we've got to value ourselves, stop serving the biggest steak to the men. Of course poor women like us aren't very familiar with steaks! Once we went to a feminist meeting where they told us we should watch blue films to improve our sex lives. That was very shocking to our women. We've been to their women's centres because they have the resources to offer legal advice or psychologists for battered women. It's another world, all carpeted, with pictures on the wall, everything brand new. We felt uncomfortable. The only time we'd been in houses like that was as domestic servants. We are the ones these women use as their servants.

By 1986 MOMUPO had defined itself as a 'popular' or grassroots feminist organisation. The question of the kind of relations it should have with other women's organisations, professional, political and feminist, caused division inside the organisation, reflecting a wider debate going on within social movements about their relations with political parties. In September 1986 the military regime declared a state of siege in an attempt to quash the struggle for democracy in the *poblaciones* and began conditional talks with a few chosen representatives of centre and right-wing political parties. The failure of the protests to oust Pinochet and the recriminations between political parties which followed caused disillusionment in the social movements. Many began to rethink their positions and reinforce their independence from the political parties. In MOMUPO the changing political situation brought into question the future role of the movement. Its growing public role had separated the organisation from grassroots women's groups and its main activity had become its yearly summer school. In 1987 Luz María, a member of MOMUPO's co-ordinating committee, left the organisation to concentrate on her women's group in her *población*.

The group had developed out of a small, church-backed sewing workshop which had produced the appliqué work known as *arpilleras*. Luz María, keen to give more women the chance to learn the skill and earn some extra money, broke away from the Church and formed her own workshop. The women had no place of their own to meet and had to organise their meetings in different houses, carrying their materials around with them. They began to organise activities to raise funds for a women's centre in the *población*. Luz María recalls, 'I imagined a women's house, a place of tranquillity, where women could relax and chat while they were sewing, but instead it's turned out to be a centre of education and training workshops. All the women who came here wanted to learn something'.

At the end of 1988 Luz María and her group opened the Women's Place in their *población*, which they bought with the support of some nuns from the local chapel, donations from community organisations and neighbourhood collections. The wooden building is typical of the *poblaciones'* houses which are often shared by more than one family. It has one large and two small rooms and a small kitchen and bathroom. Only the huge feminist insignia painted on the front wall and the constant stream of women visitors distinguishes it from the other houses of the *población*.

LUZ MARIA: The first year it turned out to be very small because as it was an ordinary family house you couldn't squeeze more than thirty women in. The first thing we did was something on domestic violence. So many women came that half of them had to stand out in the street. The building next door was abandoned and falling apart and we began asking who the owners were. We'd met a German woman who'd come to do her thesis here. We'd helped her and she'd promised to make contacts with a Christian women's group in Germany. When we were least expecting it, we received a letter offering help. They offered shoes and clothes, but we said no, our priority was space and they organised activities with Chilean exiles in Germany to get the money. It arrived just when we were asking about the house. They sent us just over half what we needed, $1,000, and we raised the rest selling *arpilleras*, making bread and with donations. We'd managed to get the wood from the Vicariate and our husbands built the big room where 120 women can fit in, squashed, standing up, not sitting. The nuns were away. After we inaugurated the first house they went away, one for three months and one for six and when they came back they found that instead of one house we had two. This house has also become too small, especially for the domestic violence groups — it's a very big problem in this *población*.

The money from the *arpillera* sales goes to the person who makes the *arpillera* but we take a small percentage which we put towards the expenses of the Place. With the bread-making we've managed to buy a roof, hire a teacher and do some repairs to the houses. We sell the bread to the people in the *población* — the same women who come to the workshops. Every week 150 women attend the workshops and if each one buys a kilo of bread we can make enough to cover some of the costs.

In both the Women's Place and MOMUPO a major priority has been teaching new skills to improve women's job opportunities and their chance of financial independence. Many of their members have unemployed husbands, care for elderly parents or are single mothers. Their home commitments mean they have had little experience of paid work and their lack of formal education means they have few job opportunities apart from part-time cleaning, caring for children or selling home-made food and clothes. Most have little confidence in their abilities to deal with the world outside their homes.

The Women's Place has set up accredited two-year courses on hairdressing and fashion, as well as a number of other workshops on sewing, bread-making and alternative medicine.

LUZ MARIA: When a woman earns money, even if it's a very small amount, it's as if it's a hundred times more than what the man earns because the women knows how to use it better. The man puts his necessities first — if he smokes he keeps some back for his cigarettes, for his beer, or to go to the football. What's left is for the house and what's left is the smallest part. The other thing is that we see ourselves first as mothers, then wives, and then as women — so all the money goes on the family and not on us. We talk about it — trying to change our mentality — that we have to buy things for ourselves. A woman has to recognise herself as a person because no one is going to value you unless you do it first. So far we've had no courses to teach women 'men's' skills. The idea of women working as mechanics or carpenters is something new for us. It would be thought strange if the men who come here to repair the house taught the women — the man knows how to nail, cut wood. We've begun to change all this because the men have learnt to sew and they do it perfectly and they help us at home with the *arpilleras* but if people outside saw, they'd say, what a pansy! We say that if the man gets home first he should be able to serve his own food and to share in the childcare, but changing the whole culture of the *poblaciones* is a slow process. All our lives they've been telling us that men are good at brute force things and can't produce a plate of food, or wash or iron or sew. It's very difficult because the man says, 'I come home tired from work and I want my woman to serve my food'.

FLORA: Middle-class women can go out to work and employ other women to do their housework and look after the children. Because they have an automatic washing machine and everything automatic and maybe the men help, the housework is easier and doesn't stop them doing anything else. The men from the *poblaciones* are the most *macho*; they won't work in the house. An important part of our workshops and courses is to encourage women to value ourselves so that we understand that there's no reason why we have to serve the children and the husband or bring up our daughters to serve, that we are people with equal rights in the home and that we should be respected.

We also want the government to socialise domestic work, for example by setting up cheap launderettes and creches. We don't want this to be left to us as it was with the communal kitchens.

Childcare provision is a crucial issue for women in the *poblaciones*. The privatisation of education under the military government reduced the number of daycare centres and increased the cost of those which remained. Childcare, in any case, had rarely been accessible to working-class women.

LUZ MARIA: We have to depend on relatives or friends to look after the children. Many women have to work in other people's houses, taking care of the children while their own children are alone at home. In the beginning we thought the Place would have a place for the children, a little room with toys and the mother in another room working. It's nice in theory but in practice it doesn't work. The children needed to run around, they called their mothers, if the mother was sewing they wanted to sew, they wanted the scissors — it was a madhouse! Then we got swings for the yard, just two but there are fifty children and they fought, 'they won't let me on', or one fell off, they played with the taps and got soaked. It was crazy.

Now we've managed to get a room in the local school and someone to watch the children while their mothers are in the workshops, but there's such a demand that one room isn't enough. We're asking for creches from the government. We can't solve everything ourselves.

Grassroots feminism, however, is not just a way of adapting the family to economic change. Courses at the Women's Place are free of charge but all women taking part must attend 'awareness-raising' workshops where they discuss issues such as domestic violence, sexuality and political and labour rights. Grassroots feminism emphasises a slow, gradual educational process to avoid alienating women who are usually religious, see themselves above all as mothers and wives and are suspicious of anything that might be considered 'political'.

Domestic violence is one of the greatest concerns of women in the *poblaciones*. When women left their homes to take part in the communal kitchens the extent of domestic violence came out into the open for the first time. For 15 years Lucella, who attends courses at the Women's Place, was herself a battered wife.

LUCELLA: If a man hits a woman from the middle class, of course the punch hurts the same, but the woman's reaction is different because her options, her freedom to leave, are much greater. She can go to her mother or sister's house, but we can't because our mothers haven't got anywhere to put us. She can call a friend who's got a flat, or she sells something and can start a new life. We are not professionals earning a good wage, we can't rent a room, we can't even sleep in separate beds because there are no other beds. If a man hits one of us and we go to the police — and the situation has to be very bad for us to go the police — the first thing the policeman does is make fun of you, and the poorer you are, the more they make fun of you. 'If your husband hits you it must be for a reason. Go home.' She has to go back to the same house and continue living with the man and if it goes to court the case takes a long time and in all that time she has to put up with more violence, because her economic situation doesn't allow her the luxury of leaving. Where's she going to go if her neighbour doesn't have enough to eat, or enough beds for her own family?

Our culture is different from middle-class culture. Men don't respect us. They grow up with this violence and they see it as normal and many women accept it as normal that their husbands hit them. They don't see it as mistreatment or they justify it, saying he's an alcoholic, or unemployed, or he's under a lot of stress. He treats her like a piece of furniture — which is what happened to me. He took me when he wanted, when he needed it. It didn't matter whether I wanted to have sex or not.

We are asking for a law to protect women and to punish the man. We don't think the solution is to put men in prison. Our aim is to make women aware that we shouldn't allow it and to learn about the law to know what we can do. The more aware a woman gets, the more she breaks with her situation, but it's a long slow process. We believe there should also be help for the men, to rehabilitate them. In my own case my husband learnt his bad ways from his father. His father chased his mother with a knife and she had to sleep on the streets with the children; that was the education my husband had. Violence was the only form of communication he knew. When we got married my husband repeated all this. I was battered for 15 years, badly beaten. The last time he hit me he split my upper lip and drove my teeth into my palate. I'm not ashamed to talk about it because all my life I've felt very proud that I was able to put a stop to it. He left me looking like a monster and I said, 'this is the last time'. I was lucky that time because someone let me have a house where I could stay with my children and that gave me the time I needed to report the case and to sort out the legal things. I didn't press charges because I felt it was still possible to change him.

I'd always been able to contribute to the household income by sewing, selling things and making things, so I'd always felt I'd be able to support my children. I took the time I needed and then I went back, but with everything very clear and he knew that if he raised his hand again I'd get him arrested immediately. He never hit me again. The experience made me stronger and more determined to help other women realise that they can also put an end to violence.

A lot of studies have been done, they've used us a lot. We don't want to talk to any more people doing research or studies on battered women, taking testimonies and photographs. Some women from this house have appeared on TV, giving their testimonies and then the researchers have never come back. We need a place where women can get psychological and legal advice. The Santiago City Council set up a project, but only for the city centre; it's difficult for the women in the *poblaciones* to get there. We're asking for a house where a beaten woman can stay for the first few days, while she reports the crime and where she can sort herself out — look for work, training and something new so she can survive on her own.

Since the 1980s contraception has become more widely available in Chile and is no longer the privilege of the rich. In general, however, women in the *poblaciones* have little information about contraceptive methods. They receive no sex education in school and the subject is not generally talked about by parents. A major influence on women's ideas about sex is the teaching of the traditional Roman Catholic Church which often portrays ignorance as a moral virtue. While some sectors of the Church are now more flexible about contraception, sometimes quietly contravening the official position of vehement condemnation of artificial methods of birth control, under the military regime government policies made women's access to contraception harder. The privatisation of health services put medical attention out of the reach of many poor women and serious abuses were committed in public hospitals under military rule.

> LUZ MARIA: They bring the worst forms of contraception here, everything that's rejected by other countries. They put them in and take them out when they want. Under Pinochet's government women went to the public hospitals for check-ups and they took out their IUDs without telling them. Women got cancer or other illnesses because they were terrified to go for check-ups saying, 'I'd rather die than have them take out my coil'. The state clinics aren't much good but there are some alternative clinics set up by foreign bodies which offer women contraception, including other more expensive methods like the pill. There are also clinics connected to the Church. We send women there and they put in IUDs and give them health education. On this issue some sectors of the Church have understood very well what we're saying — that it's preferable to avoid a child instead of a child being born to suffer. The Church has helped us with contraception but it can't do it publicly. What it doesn't accept at all is abortion.

While some sections of the Church have relaxed their attitude towards contraception, it remains united in its opposition to abortion. Abortion is illegal in Chile except to save a mother's life and women who have them can face prison sentences of between three and five years. Nevertheless it has been estimated that in the early 1970s nearly half of all pregnancies in Chile ended in abortion. Only a small minority of these were carried out by trained medical staff in safe, hygienic conditions. Working-class women have little choice but to use backstreet practitioners, and botched operations were responsible for forty per cent of all maternal deaths. Although huge numbers of women undergo abortions, it remains a taboo subject.

> FLORA: Women don't want to talk about abortion because it's against the teachings of the Church and also because it's against the law, but nearly all women have them. The difference is that the women from the *poblaciones* use a knitting needle, parsley twigs or rubber tubes and many end up in hospital or die, while the middle class go to a clinic and walk home afterwards. When we go to the hospital with haemorrhages the doctors slap our faces; they send their wives to the best clinics but they slap the faces of poor women.
>
> We have to handle this issue very carefully. We've never openly supported abortion in MOMUPO because this only brings rejection from the women.

LUCELLA: The question of abortion is very tricky because many women, practically all I'd say, are against it. The last time we had a seminar on abortion many women said 'abortion, no, it's a sin'. When I asked what happens to women who've been raped, mentally deficient girls who are thrown out onto the streets from the orphanages when they're 18 and then get pregnant — it's a sin what happens to *them*. Then the women started to open up a bit. Women are very familiar with abortions in the *poblaciones* because there's a lot done secretly, but less than there used to be. In the 1960s, when I was just married, I did many abortions on myself, without even telling my husband, using rubber tubes that they sell in the chemists which you insert in the uterus. Every time I did it I ended up in hospital but it was because at that time there were no contraceptives. Contraceptives didn't get here until about 1965 and they were only for the people with money.

Women's organisations have begun to respond to the deficiencies in the official educational system by creating their own workshops on sex education and sexuality. A major concern in the *poblaciones* is the huge rise in teenage pregnancies.

LUZ MARIA: In the workshops on health, the first thing we do is our body and its functions. Women have no idea, we don't even know how many orifices we've got, that we urinate from one place, a different place from where the menstruation comes and the babies are born. It was a great surprise when we discovered that there was a different place to urinate from.

Nor do the women or men know where the most sensitive parts of the body are, where you can feel pleasure. All we learnt is that sex is for the man's pleasure so many women endure sex because of their ignorance. You have to talk about all the myths you learn from a very young age, that the woman's just got to lie there without being able to express her feelings, perhaps you want to touch some part of his body but something stops you because the woman's not supposed to take the initiative, nor say 'I want to make love like this', because immediately comes the question from the man 'where did you learn that?' because they immediately assume there's another man who's teaching you these things.

It's hard for women to talk about sex. When we talk about it in the workshops they always start laughing. It's very difficult for them to take it seriously and we realise that the laughter is a result of ignorance. It's very deeply ingrained in us that you mustn't mention the sexual parts of the body. In the workshops we talk about it very carefully. It's not something we can talk about with women who've come here for the first time.

FLORA: It's very difficult for us to talk about sexual freedom. Many of us have only one or two rooms in our house and some of us share with other families. We don't have the privacy to develop a good sexual relationship with our husbands or with anyone else. In the summer, maybe, we can sleep on the patio but how can you talk about improving your sex life when you sleep in a room with the children?

In the *poblaciones* you don't hear anything about lesbianism. Perhaps it's something which exists, but it's always denied. Our culture is more rigid than in the middle class where there's more freedom and all the time they're seeking more pleasure, bodily and mentally. We can't openly have lovers or change partners all the time. It's never once come up in the sexuality workshops.

LUZ MARIA: We don't talk about freedom to choose different sexual partners, or if we do, it's as a joke. We've got it deeply ingrained that you get married and stay with your husband and a woman who goes with another man is very badly looked on. It's a very strong belief in the *población*. But the men, yes, they can have other women. These are things we're only just beginning to talk about, that we have the same rights to happiness as men. It's very difficult for a woman to understand this and not think you're being too extreme.

Feminist ideas are new to the *poblaciones* and *machismo* is deeply rooted. The possibilities of confrontation are high. One of the main concerns of the grassroots feminists is to minimise conflicts within the family and more specifically with their male partners. As with their participation in the communal kitchens, shopping collectives or health groups, women have often justified their actions in terms of defending the family. This is not just a strategy to appease male opposition, but also reflects the lack of possibilities that women have for economic independence; while one in five families were headed by a woman in 1988, these women are amongst the poorest in the *poblaciones* and single motherhood is not seen as an attractive option. It also reflects the importance women place on working together with men towards common goals.

Nevertheless, the ideas of popular feminism are a radical challenge to traditional family life and relations between men and women in the *poblaciones*.

SYLVIA: There have been a lot of crises with the husbands. Many of us have had to choose between our organisations and the home. Most of the women involved in MOMUPO go through this crisis. Before, you were a common housewife and here you suddenly come into contact with new things and for many reasons men have remained isolated, they haven't got the authority they had before. As you learn to value yourself you begin demanding things. You acquire a commitment to women's issues and you begin to participate more in things outside the home. I've had very serious problems with my family and I'm still trying to find a way to deal with the conflicts.

SUSANA: My husband used to hit me but not any more. I changed him by talking and talking. It's been very difficult for the men to accept that things have changed. Most of the women leaders are separated or going through a crisis in their relationships. It's happened to all of us — you discover a new world, you begin to value yourself and then you can't turn back. My husband changed. Now he stays at home and does the housework and looks after the children. He likes it. In fact, he likes it so much he's not interested in going out to work any more!

LUZ MARIA: The first stages are the hardest. The man is used to seeing the woman cooking, washing, ironing or watching TV, but the woman begins to change when she starts to read, to write, to talk about something different. On the question of sexuality for example, some husbands get scared or jealous because they think their wife is experimenting with something new and could achieve more than them.

In the Women's Place we want to rescue the family. We don't want women to be alone but to work together with men. This is an all-women's organisation but we try to work together with men. Every two weeks we have a couples' workshop with the husbands of women who are most involved in the Place. It's done in an informal way. For example, one issue might be the trade unions, because before we used to believe we had no reason to know about unions and we didn't understand anything about them. We saw it as the man's affair and it was never talked about at home. And we talk about what we're doing in the Place so that the men understand and will support us in our struggle as women. My husband's different now. He doesn't think I'm useless any more. He helps with odd jobs in the Place. Some of our husbands have turned out to be the best promoters of our work.

The relationship with middle-class feminism is still a delicate one. In the last few years several feminist study centres and campaigning groups have been established in the centre of Santiago, many offering advice and educational facilities. Many of these feminist groups work with grassroots organisations in the *poblaciones* and in the trade unions and offer leadership training and professional services in specific areas such as domestic violence. Like other women's organisations in the *poblaciones*, MOMUPO and the women of the *poblaciones* have used these services but they reject a close relationship with middle-class women, preferring to rely on their own abilities.

LUZ MARIA: Look, I feel a feminist, totally feminist, but not that feminism which defends only women, but the kind that defends the family. Feminism is a bad word for the women here, very bad. They associate feminism with lesbianism and being against men, but when you explain that feminism is about defending the rights of women and the family too, they begin to get interested. It's the word they don't like because it's badly looked on. Although we speak about feminist issues here in the Place, that we're putting women first, strengthening her, valuing women and their rights, most of the women who come here don't see themselves as feminists.

We have no relationship with middle-class feminist groups. We're all *pobladoras*. No one here is a professional. There's no one in an office, we run the Place ourselves and that was our idea from the beginning. When we set up the Place we said it was for women from the *poblaciones* and it had to be led by the women themselves. We've worked a lot in our workshops and we've learnt a lot, we're capable of doing it and that's why we defend our autonomy. Learning to value ourselves and recognise our abilities helps us to help other women and say, 'look, we were in your position, we've lifted ourselves up and you can do it too'. Middle-class feminists don't come here because we almost never invite them. We've got a lot of resentment towards them because they themselves often exploit women. They pay their domestic employees a miserable wage while they're having their chats about equality. They don't let her take part in anything and treat her like a slave.

Sometimes we use their services. We might take battered women who need legal advice to see them. We celebrate 8 March together. Our invitations for International Women's Day used to arrive the day before, but now we take part in the planning of the event. But we're not just going to go along to increase the numbers on special days. What we demand from women of the upper class, psychologists and lawyers, is that they respond to the needs of ordinary women.

FLORA: We don't invite feminists to give workshops for MOMUPO. We co-ordinate with them when there are general activities. We may invite a professional from an institution for something specific, not just feminists. There was a time when they wanted to come here but we can do the work better ourselves. There are no conflicts, we know each other and there's not a bad relationship, we just don't have much to do with each other.

By the time elections took place in 1989, Chile's diverse women's movement had established itself as a social force and had managed to include some of its demands, ranging from equal civil and labour rights to programmes for poor women, in the manifesto of the main opposition coalition. Yet women made little progress, in the numbers of women in posts of responsibility in the new government. Of 158 members of parliament, there were only eight women deputies and two women senators. In terms of policy gains, women have faced strong opposition from right-wing political parties who have tried to block proposals for equal civil and labour rights which do no more than comply with international law. The Right is currently combining forces with the Church to thwart the introduction of divorce. More hopeful for the women's movement has been the creation of a state institution, the National Women's Service (SERNAM). SERNAM's role is to design and put forward public policies for women. It has set up programmes to support women's organisations, women heads of household and victims of domestic violence.

The limits of the transition to democracy and the lack of any significant break with the economic policies of the military government have restricted change at a local level. By 1991 most local councils were still under the control of Pinochet's appointees. For independent grassroots women's organisations democracy has also presented new challenges. As foreign agencies have begun channelling their funds through government institutions, they have had less direct access to international support. They have had to learn the ways of traditional politics which often involve more bureaucracy and formality in their procedures, while much of their work continues to depend on the personal sacrifices of their members.

LUZ MARIA: The politicians came to the *población* with their campaigns, candidates came to this Place and then, after the elections, we never saw them again. Not one representative of the government has ever come here. No one comes to explain, to ask for our opinions or to give us support. We still have the same council leader who was chosen by the military and we don't go to him because he's the same person who persecuted us during the dictatorship.

We used to send *arpilleras* to the US, but now they don't want them any more. People think that because the military has gone there are no more problems in Chile. We got help from a government institution in 1990 to help pay the teachers and the water and electricity bills. We don't know if they'll be able to help us again this year. It's still in the air.

Some of the institutions which support community groups have driven us to tears. We've got to fill in a 22-page form and every heading has a word that no one here understands. We've had to get legal status because now there's democracy we have to be recognised as a legal organisation and we didn't want to feel we were working underground any more.

The institutions don't want to contribute towards wages for the people who work here unless they're professionals. That's bad because we don't

want someone to come from outside and install herself in the office here
— we can do it ourselves. We're not asking for a wage but a contribution
so we can work better. It's as if you're working but without a wage so
it makes things very difficult. The electricity's been cut off in my house
for a year. I connect illegally, in secret, hiding myself away and keeping
my door locked in case the electricity man comes.

And now there's a new challenge. The economic situation is the same,
wages haven't gone up, there's still redundancies, factories closing and
unemployment. They've done some good things, the pensions have
gone up a bit, they've helped a bit with our debts. Women who were
locked up in their houses for 17 years are beginning to come out and
they come here looking for help, so we've got a great challenge to offer
them something. Today more than ever we need to continue our efforts
because no one else is going to help working-class women. We have to
learn about the new circumstances, the new organisations, like the
neighbourhood committees — we don't understand them. We have to
educate ourselves to be able to advance.

Women in the *poblaciones* have not confined themselves to learning
about the workings of local politics; they have also begun to make a
place for themselves inside local council structures. By the beginning
of 1992 elections had still not been held to bring democracy to local
councils in Santiago. Only five had changed hands and their
councillors had been appointed by the new government, rather than
elected by popular vote. Matilde, still a member of MOMUPO, was
one of those appointed to work on a district council, responsible for
several *poblaciones* in the area, and headed by a self-declared feminist.

The last time an election took place in the neighbourhood committee
of the *población* was 17 years ago. The committee, elected by local
población residents and normally concerned with improving
neighbourhood services, used to be composed exclusively of men. In
1990, Rosa, one of the women who helped set up the Women's Place,
stood as an independent candidate and was elected to the committee,
becoming its first ever woman member.

ROSA: At the moment I'm one of four directors in charge of the social
side of the *población*. The neighbourhood committee should represent the
interests of the *pobladores*; see what's needed and solve problems, to
improve life in the *población*. I'm trying to introduce women's issues,
trying to make sure we don't get forgotten and that they consider
women's needs. In the beginning I had a lot of trouble working with two
of the men. They're not interested in women's issues. When you talk to
them you end up fighting.

I got my experience from the years of organisation in this Place and
with the church and women's groups here. I have to go out to a lot of

meetings and solve problems but I've got the advantage that my husband respects me and looks after the children. He used to reject my work but now he's interested in the committee and is thinking about standing for election too.

The struggle for 'democracy in the country and democracy in the home' continues to develop in many different ways in Chile. In trade unions, political parties, in education and at home, traditional ideas about women are being challenged. In the *poblaciones* the number of women's groups continues to grow. MOMUPO is in the process of rebuilding and restructuring its relations with grassoots women's groups. The Women's Place is again proving too small for the the number of women who want to join workshops and their extremely popular summer school. Grassroots feminism has shown that there is more than one way of being a feminist. The long-term challenge for the women's movement in Chile is to recognise the diversity of women's interests and forge alliances between the huge variety of non-feminist and feminist organisations.

Conclusion

'Sometimes I wonder where all this is really leading. I take my young daughter to work with me in the communal kitchen. One day she said, "Why do I have to work in the kitchen? I don't want to work in the kitchen all my life. I want to be a lawyer".'

Luisa (Argentina)

For the majority of women who appear in this book 'democracy' has not delivered the improvement in economic conditions, nor their hoped for advances in status. While grassroots organisations represent women's continued lack of choice, limited power and continued hardship, they also represent a potential force for transforming women's lives, not only in terms of their immediate living conditions, but also longer term change to their position in society. The strength of the new women's movement, and a factor which distinguishes it from earlier ones in the Southern Cone, is the presence of working-class women and the variety of interests with which they are concerned.

Concern for the welfare of their families, rather than an awareness of discrimination drove working-class women into the political arena. Economic change and political repression were more important for these women than feminism in propelling them into the world of politics. With no trade unions to defend falling wages and employment, no community organisations to take up local concerns such as poor urban services, no political parties or state institutions to respond to the demands of the working class and poor, women went out to find their own solutions. They did so as women, with their actions firmly rooted in the belief that their actions were the 'natural' responses of good mothers and wives. 'We are trying to help our husbands. Our politics are our husbands' wallets', said militant housewives taking part in shopping strikes in Argentina. The Mothers of Plaza de Mayo of Argentina, for example, refused to accept their children were dead and persisted with a search that many of their husbands felt to be useless with, in the words of Hebe, 'the desperation of a lioness who has lost her cubs'. Most had little understanding of the situation they found themselves in, or of the dimensions of the task they were taking on.

It was precisely because they evoked the powerful image of motherhood and the family that they posed problems for dictatorships claiming to defend those same values. The military fell victim to the misconceptions of their own *machismo*, allowing women the breathing space they needed to set up their organisations. It was inconceivable to the military authorities that a threat to their rule could come from the sewing clubs, fashion shows and hairdressing courses the Mothers and the women in Chile used to disguise their activities. When the police became suspicious of Susana and her friends standing in a Santiago street, the women could easily divert their attention away from the strike leaflets they were handing out, by talking about children. Even when they protested publicly the military did not, in the beginning, take women as a serious challenge. In Argentina the military first dismissed the Mothers as 'madwomen', and then imagined that deceptions and intimidation would be enough to deter them.

The women were not deterred, even when confronted with the full force of the military repression. With political parties and trade unions crushed or weakened, the new groups became a focus for resistance to military rule. Women's new activities may have been extensions of the work they did in the home, but by doing them collectively they became a challenge to the militaries' objective of crushing working-class organisation. The everyday survival of working-class families, once the private concerns of individual families, took on a political significance. Communal kitchens were not just about feeding families; they became a collective stand against poverty and the economic policies of the regimes. The Chilean *arpilleras*, which depicted the deprivation of the everyday lives of the poor, became subversive material that had to be buried in the ground when the police raided neighbourhoods. The empty pot marches, shopping strikes, the banging of saucepans bore the distinctive hallmarks of women's participation. Unintentionally, women put themselves in the firing line of military repression and exposed the hypocrisy of the military proclamations about the sanctity of the family. They not only showed enormous energy and creativity but also great determination and courage in the face of arrests, harassment and, in the case of the Mothers, the disappearance of their members.

However much women saw their public participation as natural extensions of their family role, their new activities took them away from the home and transformed their daily lives. Domestic routines were disrupted by their absence and husbands, children and housework became obstacles to women's participation. In the words of Isabel, the Uruguayan trade unionist, 'You don't feel confident .... You have to fight against yourself because the experience you get from your life at home is an obstacle'. The organisations women created reflected these difficulties. They bore little resemblance to conventional ones, not only because of the dangers of working under dictatorships, but also because they had to be adapted to the needs of women. Meetings had to be arranged around the duties which punctuate a woman's day, collecting the children from school, making the dinner, or they simply took their children with them and improvised creches. They created loosely-knit groups, based on solidarity and mutual support rather than hierarchies, they wrote little down and spoke in the language of their everyday lives, instead of the language of conventional politics or football, which, as Celia of the Uruguayan trade union movement complains, only alienates women. Their lack of political experience meant they were unburdened by party differences and did not rely on traditional political methods, but were free to devise their own tactics and adopt actions that had not been tried before. Some, like the Mothers, were able to break down the class barriers that divide traditional political organisations, successfully rallying women of all social classes and political parties around a common, ethical cause. Their lack of resources and access to institutional power often led them to reject the bureaucratic procedures of which they had little experience and to invent creative forms of direct action.

The links women made with others in the same situation not only relieved the isolation and monotony of their domestic lives but also developed an awareness of their common identity and interests. Sharing problems was not only a source of mutual support, but also a first step towards the recognition that the roots of their problems were not individual but social, and towards the discovery of their potential for transforming their lives. 'You realise that a lot of your problems aren't just yours alone, that all women have got them and that means we can work together to change our lives', in the words of Tina from the Community Health Workers in Argentina. Women began to question their traditional role and to search for new ways of organising housework and childcare. Whether it was mothers in Argentina searching for their disappeared children, or housewives in Chile faced with the privatisation of health services and education, women realised they needed to educate themselves to understand what was happening around them. Women who went out to work for the first time became aware of the need not only for childcare facilities, but also for training.

To varying degrees, creches, shared childcare in the home, women's health, education and training all became issues for working-class women.

Growing frustration at the failure of traditional organisations to recognise these needs also led women working in church groups, trade unions and political parties to break away or to form separate women's sections. In Chile, for example, where many community groups were set up with the encouragement and support of the Church, the further women moved away from the confines of their traditional role, the more reluctant the Church became to continue its support. As trade unions and political parties began to reorganise, traditional political issues took first place in their discussions and women's concerns were ignored. Women, traditionally excluded from peasant movements, fought a long and difficult battle to convince the men of the Paraguayan Peasants Movement to allow their wives and daughters out of their homes to attend meetings. They finally decided that only a separate commission could deal effectively with the barriers to women's participation. When trade unionists like Sonia in Uruguay and Flora in Chile found their voices were ignored by their male colleagues, they too began setting up commissions where they could develop policies that responded to women's needs.

The Influence of Feminism

The concern for gender issues by working-class women was the most significant new feature of the women's organisations. But while women began to talk about *machismo*, they rarely used the word 'feminist'. In the beginning at least, feminism played a limited role in influencing their development. Any feminist groups which existed before the coups not only fell victim to the military ban on public meetings, but also to their view that feminism was a subversive attempt to destroy the family. Feminist events such as the celebrations of International Women's Day were broken up by the police and army in all four countries. Opinions about feminism were also influenced by the prejudices of the popular press and the suspicions of working-class organisations that feminism represented a middle-class attempt to divide and rule the labour movement.

Nevertheless women in the Southern Cone were not completely isolated from the ideas of the European and US feminist movements. The declaration by the United Nations of 1975 as International Women's Year, and 1975-85 as the Women's Decade, was important in opening public debate at governmental and non-governmental levels on the issue of discrimination. It led to a profusion of research into women's issues and to the creation of the first women's NGOs (non-governmental organisations), or women's sections of established NGOs, both inside and outside Latin America, which encouraged and supported women's projects in the region. Partly as a result of pressure on governments from international organisations and the effects of International Women's Year, the statutory position of women improved in the 1970s. Also, as is made clear by the testimonies from Uruguay and Chile, returning exiles played an important role in spreading information about the feminist movements abroad.

The label 'feminist', however, was almost unanimously rejected by working-class women. It was not just a question of semantics; they saw feminist organisations as middle-class and failing to take into account their concerns. A heterogeneous women's movement grew up, with diverse, sometimes incompatible demands, ranging from practical concerns, such as creches, improved social services, clean water, price controls or land, to longer-term ones, such as equality, the socialisation of domestic tasks and the right to choose. The former, practical concerns for immediate improvements in living conditions, are often associated with the grassroots women's movement whose demands are seen as growing naturally out of their domestic role and traditional concern for the family. Longer-term demands for women's equality and an end to discrimination, implying a more radical transformation of society, are associated with the feminist movement. The examples of grassroots women's organisations in this book, however, suggest a considerable degree of convergence in the concerns of the two movements. Argentine and Uruguayan women trade unionists are working with issues ranging from equal pay to abortion and housework; shared childcare and home life are issues for most of the organisations; and the common ground between the two movements is clearly shown in the development of grassroots feminism in Chile. Yet the studies also show how *machismo* and discrimination affect women in different social sectors in different ways and require different solutions. The extent to which working-class women and feminist organisations have been able to work together has depended to a large extent on the recognition of the diversity in women's situations, as well as the historical factors affecting the development of the women's movement in each country.

In Argentina, for example, the mutual hostility between the early feminist movement and the popular expression of working-class demands through Peronism continues to determine the development of the women's movement. Feminist groups played little part in the movement for democracy and developed few links with the women who led the struggle against the dictatorship. They continue to be seen as elitist by the more recently formed housewives' groups. Many of their campaigns, such as the battle for divorce, have been criticised for failing to take into the account the situation of working-class women.

Even though many women's organisations had no contact with feminist groups, many were still influenced by feminist ideas. In Paraguay where the tiny feminist movement was seen as not only middle class, but also concerned only with urban issues, peasant women elaborated a criticism of *machismo* and even incorporated many of the terms used by the feminist movement into their literature.

In countries where the feminists clearly identified with the struggle against the dictatorship and where they set out to make contact with working-class women's groups there was a greater exchange of ideas. In the mass demonstrations of both feminists and non-feminists in Chile and Uruguay, women introduced their own demands into the struggle for democracy. The Chilean women's movement's call for 'democracy in the country and democracy in the home' clearly influenced the development of grassroots feminism in the shanty towns of Santiago.

The Return to Democracy

In all countries, however, the return of political parties and trade unions meant the return of men to positions of power and the relegation of women to the sidelines. Even in Uruguay, where the process of transition to constitutional rule was the most open, involving social movements as well as political parties, women had to fight to win a place in the negotiations and to make women's issues a legitimate concern for the new government. While many political parties included women's demands in their electoral programmes, they failed to include women in their decision-making structures. The new parliaments were almost exclusively male affairs. Most obvious was Uruguay, where not a single woman sat in parliament.

The return of traditional politics not only showed the resistance of male-dominated organisations to concerns regarded as being outside their normal sphere of activity, but also women's lack of formal political experience. Women's informal organisations did little to prepare them for the competitive, male world of politics; they were unfamiliar or unhappy with bureaucratic procedures and they often clung to their non-partisan positions rather than enter a political scene many considered to be corrupt and unrepresentative. In addition, the differences between women, hidden by the common struggle against military rule, came to the surface during the election campaigns and made the construction of a unified women's movement difficult. There were debates about how far women's organisations should cooperate with the government, state or political parties in their projects for women and risk manipulation and how far they should remain autonomous and risk powerlessness. The differences not only hindered co-operation between women's organisations but also caused internal tensions and divisions.

Despite the absence of women from the parliaments and the difficulties of building a united women's front, the decisive role women played in the struggle against the dictatorship meant that political parties could not ignore them completely. Significant gains were made at the legal and institutional level and some of the more crude examples of discrimination were removed from the statute books. In Argentina the United Nations convention on discrimination against women and the law on nursery school education was ratified, patria potestad was reformed and divorce was legalised. Equal pay laws were introduced in Uruguay. In Uruguay, Argentina and Chile the new governments set up departments to develop policies for women. In Paraguay, at the time of writing, a parliamentary bill for the creation of a women's department has been approved by the Chamber of Deputies and is awaiting the approval of the Senate, and a three year battle by women for equality before the law was finally won in 1992. A new Argentine law makes it obligatory for political parties to include a minimum of thirty per cent women candidates in elections and similar legislation is being considered in Uruguay.

The gains women can make at the level of the state, whether for better health services, equal pay or jobs, are limited by the current economic and political climate in the Southern Cone. Government Women's departments may have certain powers but decisions about women are also taken in other ministries where they are scarcely represented. Within state structures women are often isolated and underfunded, no match for the powerful alliance of forces which they must sometimes confront. Recent accusations of moral degradation made by sections of the Church and right-wing parties in Chile put at risk the National Women's Service (SERNAM)'s campaigns for divorce, sex education and contraception. At a time of public spending cutbacks, women's issues can be seen as a luxury that the state can ill-afford. In Argentina for example, the Women's Secretariat had its budget slashed and was finally dissolved as part of a process of state 'rationalisation'.

The legacies of military rule were greater social inequality and massive social problems, as well as economies crippled by huge foreign debts. In none of the countries do major opposition parties propose real alternatives to the International Monetary Fund's adjustment packages adopted by constitutional governments. The ability of councils and local governments to respond to grassroots demands are constrained by central government's priority of debt repayment. In Argentina and Uruguay in particular, the state's abdication of its social responsibilities has increased poverty, forcing communities to rely on self-help and increasing the burden on women. Health, income-generating and communal projects may demonstrate women's creativity, but they also reflect their lack of choice, limited power and continuing hardship.

Although chronic poverty is still a major reason for the continued growth of women's organisations, it is not the only explanation. While some organisations have disintegrated as the conditions which prompted their formation have disappeared, or as members have drifted away in the expectation that constitutional governments would take up their concerns, the majority of the organisations considered here have continued to grow and many have successfully developed into new areas. Despite some improvements in the Chilean economy, for example, the number of communal kitchens is still increasing; women workers and housewives have formalised their activities in trade unions; health groups have extended their work to include other self-help and educational projects. Women's organisations have continued to grow not just because of the need to solve immediate practical problems but also because of other benefits they offer women, from friendship and company to the possibility of more far-reaching changes to their lives.

Many important benefits have been won by women working inside traditional working-class organisations. As well as extending health insurance cover to a vast section of the female population that previously had little access to medical services, the Housewives' Trade Union in Argentina (SACRA), with its demand for wages, has introduced the issue of housework into the union world. In Uruguay women's commissions have been instrumental in winning equal pay, health services and childcare facilities. They have challenged traditional practices which make trade unions inaccessible to women, and introduced new issues into political life, such as domestic violence, sex education and even abortion. The potential of separate commissions for changing women's lives is illustrated by the testimonies of Eulogia and the women of Limoy in Paraguay. In rural areas, where a union's organisational branch is both a person's workplace and community, the formal acceptance of the promotion of women in public affairs has immediate repercussions on all aspects of women's lives, forcing radical changes in the private sphere of the home.

From outside traditional working-class organisations the grassroots women's movement is also influencing politics, injecting new values into political systems seen as corrupt and dishonest. Mothers of the disappeared forced the Argentine government to prosecute members of the juntas, making it the first elected Latin American government to put its former military rulers in the dock. In all countries the human rights movement, dominated by women, inspired the creation of human rights committees within political parties and trade unions, a significant development in countries where authoritarianism still permeates political practices and structures and where the armed forces retain considerable power and influence over political events. Paraguay's president may have been elected, but he is still a general, commanding a military which retains its membership of the ruling Colorado party and has proved reluctant to withdraw from politics. In Chile, Pinochet remains commander-in-chief of the armed forces. In Uruguay, and particularly in Argentina, the military have regularly rattled their sabres and are increasingly being brought in to break up strikes and other industrial action.

The human rights struggle has also inspired other women to take up the issue of domestic violence. Women's refuges have been created, as well as police stations staffed by women for the victims of rape and domestic violence. By challenging the authoritarianism embedded in everyday life and personal relationships, women are contributing towards a more democratic future, making it more difficult for tyrannical regimes to win legitimacy. As Teresa in Chile points out, 'It was accepted that men were dictators and women were dictated to. Men and women were used to dictatorships. Until that changes, the conditions for more military coups will always exist in our societies.'

Women's organisations have not only challenged the agenda of traditional politics but also traditional 'ways of doing politics'. Critical of what they see as competitive and aggressive behaviour, most, although not all, women's groups prefer informal organisation. But even where women's groups have adopted more formal procedures in response to their expansion, internal difficulties or to the demands of external bodies such as funding agencies, they have not just duplicated traditional forms. Training and education have been seen as a priority to help women overcome the problems associated with their lack of political experience and have been an important contribution to their success. The Community Health Workers (ESC) of Argentina and the women's commission in Uruguay have brought in professionals to train women in confidence-building, decision-making, the distribution of duties and project evaluation. Concerned to preserve their independence from political parties, many groups have adopted imaginative ways of promoting internal democracy, encouraging all women to participate in public speaking and decision-making. The 'rotation' of local branch leaders of the ESC, like the six month tenure of leaders of local CMC groups in Paraguay, gives as many women as possible the chance to experience leadership. In Chile, feminist organisations have offered women from the *poblaciones* the opportunity to take part in leadership training courses, aimed at increasing their representation in local council politics.

Women and the Future

At a time when the political and economic outlook is bleak and dissatisfaction with trade unions and political parties is growing, the women's movement represents a force for revitalising working-class organisation. By bringing women into public life and introducing new issues into political parties and trade unions, women have democratised politics. Daily life has entered the vocabulary of the Left, as has the need for mass grassroots participation. In Argentina, unemployment has spurred sections of the labour movement to experiment with 'territorial' trade unionism, working together with grassroots organisations on day-to-day community issues.

Further research is needed on the relationship between women's groups and these new forms of organisation, commmunity and local council politics and local and national government initiatives for women. What is clear is that, despite an increase in their participation in the traditional world of politics, they still face many difficulties in gaining access to decision-making positions. In recent municipal elections in Chile only twelve per cent of elected councillors were women. The commission of the Uruguayan trade union movement has not yet achieved real independence or powers of decision-making. Commissions have had to guard against being relegated to a secondary position, or adopted as a token gesture by union leaders more concerned with winning the female vote or increasing membership figures. Men remain resistant to changes that might affect their privileged position, both in organisations and in the home.

Home and family life are still crucial determinants of whether or not a woman can take part in an organisation. Women tend to participate on a short-term basis, 'against the tide', in the words of Sonia from Uruguay. This is not only because they withdraw as their specific demands, for a creche or running water for example, are met, but because their partners often accept their absence from the home only as a temporary or emergency measure. What Sonia says about the membership of union women's commissions in Uruguay applies to the majority of the organisations in this study: most were set up by women who were single, separated, married to union or political militants or men described as 'exceptional'.

Anxious to avoid conflict and confrontation with men and with the working-class movement with which they identify, women's efforts to deal with male opposition have focused on a gradual process of re-educating their partners. Almost all began by winning the support of a few men by justifying their actions as defending their family and children, and in contributing to the working-class struggle. Later, groups like the ESC and the peasant women of CMC used their husbands to convince other men to allow their wives and daughters to join in. They place great importance on explaining their activities to their partners, both at home and, in the cases of the Women's Place in Santiago and the ESC, through more formal couples' workshops.

One of the most important achievements of the diverse women's movements has been their contributions towards transforming cultural values that government programmes and legislation alone cannot achieve. The small changes that have taken place in women's everyday lives may be difficult to measure but they clearly have a social influence disproportionate to the numbers of women involved. While many grassroots women's organisations' approach to the family jars with feminist calls for radical change in what is seen as a principal factor in perpetuating women's subordination, the grassroots movement has challenged women's traditional role in many important ways. Even the Mothers, whose pleas for the return of their children had evoked most powerfully the traditional image of women in the family, in the end refused to accept their dead bodies and made motherhood and family life the basis for an ethical critique of society and its values. All the organisations studied here are concerned with changing family life, introducing more democracy into the home and changing their relationships with their partners. They have challenged traditional images of the passive subservient housewife and mother and are bringing up their children in different ways. They have developed new relationships with women based on solidarity and co-operation and in the process have gained self-esteem, discovering that their abilities are not limited to housework and child-rearing.

Through their struggle against poverty and persecution women in the Southern Cone have begun to challenge *machismo* as it appears in many different areas of their lives, inside political parties, unions, communities and at home. To a large extent the potential of the diverse women's movements to transform women's lives will depend on the wider social, political and economic circumstances of each country. But equally the creation of a strong, broad-based movement is essential for a wider social awareness of women's subordination and for the promotion of women's varied interests. The challenge for the women's movement is to search for common ground and convert this diversity into a source of strength.

Countries — in brief

Argentina

1. Population (1990)	32.3m
2. Urban population (1990)	86%
3. GDP per capita (1990, 1988 dollars)	$2,623
4. Population with access to health services (1987-89)	72%
5. Population with access to safe water (1988-90)	n.a.
6. Adult literacy rate (1990)	95%
7. Number of women in parliament (1990)	5
8. Under-five mortality per 1,000 live births (1990)	35
9. Maternal mortality rate per 100,000 live births (1988)	140
10. Houses without electricity (1980)	n.a.
11. Contraceptive prevalence rate (1985-89)	74%

Chile

1. Population (1990)	13.2m
2. Urban population (1990)	86%
3. GDP per capita	$2,451
4. Population with access to health services (1987-89)	97%
5. Population with access to safe water (1988-90)	89%
6. Adult literacy rate (1990)	93%
7. Number of women in parliament (1990)	6
8. Under-five mortality per 1,000 live births (1990)	27
9. Maternal mortality rate per 100,000 live births (1988)	67
10. Houses without electricity (1980)	25%
11. Contraceptive prevalence rate (1985-89)	43%

Paraguay

1. Population (1990)	4.3m
2. Urban population (1990)	48%
3. GDP per capita	$1,493
4. Population with access to health services (1987-89)	63%
5. Population with access to safe water (1988-90)	35%
6. Adult literacy rate (1990)	90%
7. Number of women in parliament (1990)	6
8. Under-five mortality per 1,000 live births (1990)	60
9. Maternal mortality rate per 100,000 live births (1988)	200
10. Houses without electricity (1980)	83%
11. Contraceptive prevalence rate (1985-89)	45%

Uruguay

1. Population (1990) — 3.1m
2. Urban population (1990) — 86%
3. GDP per capita — $2,921
4. Population with access to health services (1987-89) — 82%
5. Population with access to safe water (1988-90) — 85%
6. Adult literacy rate (1990) — 96%
7. Number of women in parliament (1990) — 6
8. Under-five mortality per 1,000 live births (1990) — 25
9. Maternal mortality rate per 100,000 live births (1988) — 50
10. Houses without electricity (1980) — 19%
11. Contraceptive prevalence rate (1985-89) — n.a.

Sources: Human Development Report 1992, UNDP; Economic and Social Progress in Latin America 1991, Inter-American Development Bank

Acronyms

ACP	*Amas de Casa del País*	
	National Housewives' Movement (Argentina)	
APCT	*Asamblea Permanente de Campesinos sin Tierra*	
	Permanent Assembly of Landless Peasants (Paraguay)	
CECTEC	*Centro de Educación, Capacitación y Tecnología Campesina*	
	Centre for Peasant Education, Training and Technology (Paraguay)	
CESMA	*Centro de Estudios Sociales de la Mujer Argentina*	
	Centre of Social Studies of the Argentine Woman	
CGT	*Confederación General de Trabajadores*	
	General Labour Confederation	
CMC	*Coordinación de Mujeres Campesinas*	
	Peasant Women's Commission (Paraguay)	
CMU	*Comisión de Mujeres Uruguayas*	
	Commission of Uruguayan Women	
CNT	*Convención Nacional de Trabajadores*	
	National Labour Convention (Uruguay)	
CONADEP	*Comisión Nacional sobre la Desaparición de Personas*	
	National Commission on the Disappearances (Argentina)	
CONAPRO	*Concertación Nacional Programática*	
	National Consensus-Building Programme (Uruguay)	
ESC	*Educadoras Sanitarias Comunales*	
	Community Health Workers (Argentina)	
ESMA	*Escuela Superior Mecánica de la Armada*	
	Higher Engineering School (Argentina)	
FEUU	*Federación de Estudiantes Universitarios*	
	Federation of University Students (Uruguay)	
FIP	*Frente de Izquierda Popular*	
	Popular Left Front (Argentina)	
FOC	*Fundación de Organización Comunitaria*	
	Community Organisation Foundation (Argentina)	
GRECMU	*Grupo de Estudios sobre la Condición de la Mujer en el Uruguay*	
	Study Group on the Position of Women in Uruguay	

IBR	*Instituto de Bienestar Rural*
	Rural Welfare Institute (Paraguay)
MCP	*Movimiento Campesino Paraguayo*
	Paraguayan Peasants Movement
MOMUPO	*Movimiento de Mujeres Pobladoras*
	Movement of Women Pobladoras (Chile)
PEM	*Programa de Empleo Mínimo*
	Minimum Employment Programme (Chile)
PIT	*Plenario Intersindical de Trabajadores*
	Inter-Union Plenary (Uruguay)
POJH	*Programa de Ocupación de Jefes de Hogar*
	Work Programme for Heads of Households
SACRA	*Sindicato de Amas de Casa de la República Argentina*
	Housewives' Union of the Republic of Argentina
SERCUPO	*Servicio a la Cultura Popular*
	Popular Culture Service (Argentina)
SERNAM	*Servicio Nacional de la Mujer*
	National Women's Service (Chile)

*

216

Further Reading

Amnesty International, *Extracts from the Report of an Amnesty International Mission to Argentina 6-15 November 1976*, London, 1977

Amnesty International, *Argentina, the Military Juntas and Human Rights, Report of the Trial of the former Junta Members, 1985*, London, 1987

Audrey Bronstein, *The Triple Struggle: Latin American Peasant Women*, London, WoW Campaigns, 1982

British Parliamentary Human Rights Group, *Report of a mission to Paraguay*, London, 1987

Lynne Brydon and Sylvia Chant, *Women in the Third World*, Aldershot, Edward Elgar, 1989

Jimmy Burns, *The Land that Lost its Heroes*, Bloomsbury Press, London, 1987

Marifran Carlson, *!Feminismo! The Woman's Movement in Argentina from its beginnings to Eva Perón*, Chicago, Academy Chicago Publishers, 1988

S. Charlton, J. Everett, & K. Staudt, eds., *Women, Development and the State*, State University of New York Press, New York, 1989

S. Eckstein, *Power and Popular Protest*, University of California Press, California, 1989

Jo Fisher, *Mothers of the Disappeared*, London, Zed Books, 1989

Jane S. Jaquette, ed., *The Women's Movement in Latin America, Feminism and the Transition to Democracy*, Unwin, Boston, 1989

Elizabeth Jelin (ed), *Women and Social Change in Latin America*, London, Zed Books, 1990

Elizabeth Jelin, *Family, Household and Gender Relations in Latin America*, London, Kegan, 1991

June Nash and Helen Safa, *Women and Change in Latin America*, New York, Bergin and Garvey, 1986

June Nash and Helen Safa, *Sex and Class in Latin America*, New York, Bergin and Garvey, 1980

Ronaldo Munck, *Latin America: The Transition to Democracy*, London, Zed Books, 1989

National Commission on Disappeared People, *Nunca Más*, London, Faber and Faber, 1986

George Philip, *The Military in South American Politics*, London, Croom Helm, 1985

David Slater, ed., *New Social Movements and the State in Latin America*, Amsterdam, CEDLA, 1985

William Smith, *Authoritarianism and the Crisis of Argentine Political Economy*, Stanford University Press, California, 1989.

Valenzuela, J. Samuel & Valenzuela, Arturo, *Military Rule in Chile: Dictatorship and Opposition*, Baltimore, John Hopkins, 1986

Sandy Vogelgesang, *American Dream, Global Nightmare, The Dilemma of US Human Rights Policy*, New York, Norton, 1980

Bibliography

General

Alvarez, Sonia, 'The Politics of Gender in Latin America: Comparative perspectives on women in the Brazilian transition to democracy', unpublished PhD dissertation, Yale University, 1986.

Alves, Maria Helena Moreira, 'Grassroots Organisations, Trade Unions, and the the Church, A Challenge to the Controlled Abertura in Brazil', *Latin American Perspectives*, Issue 40, Vo. 11, No. 1, Winter 1984.

Bronstein, Audrey, *The Triple Struggle: Latin American Peasant Women*, London, WoW Campaigns, 1982.

Brydon, Lynne & Chant, Sylvia, *Women in the Third World*, Aldershot, Edward Elgar, 1989.

Calderón, Fernando, ed., *Movimientos Sociales en el Uruguay de Hoy*, CIESU, Montevideo, 1985.
— *Los Movimientos Sociales ante la Crisis*, Consejo Latinoamericano de Ciencias Sociales (CLACSO), Buenos Aires, 1986.

CEPAL, *Los Grandes Cambios y la Crisis. Impacto sobre la mujer en América Latina y el Caribe*, Comisión Economica para América Latina y el Caribe (CEPAL), Santiago de Chile, 1990.
— *La Mujer en el sector popular urbano. América Latina y el Caribe*, Comisión Economica para América Latina y el Caribe (CEPAL), Santiago de Chile, 1984

Charlton, S., Everett, J., and Staudt, K., eds., *Women, Development and the State*, State University of New York Press, New York, 1989.

Deere, Carmen Diana & León, Magdalena, *Rural Women and State Policy*, Westview Press, Colorado, 1987.

Eckstein, S., *Power and Popular Protest*, University of California Press, California, 1989.

Evers, Tilman, 'Labor-Force Reproduction and Urban Movements. Illegal Subdivision of Land in Sao Paulo', *Latin American Perspectives*, Issue 53, Vo. 14, Spring 1987.

GRECMU, 'La mujer del Cono Sur frente a la crisis: desafíos y respuestas', Documentos Ocasionales, 15, Grupo de Estudios sobre la Condición de la Mujer en el Uruguay, (GRECMU) 1989.

Isis International, Ediciones de las Mujeres
— No 5, *Movimiento Feminista: Balance y Perspectivas*, Santiago, 1986.
— No 6 *Mujeres Campesinas*, Santiago, 1986.
— No 10 *Nuestra Memoria, Nuestro Futuro, Mujeres e Historia, America Latina y el Caribe*, 1988.
— No 13, *Transiciones: Mujeres en los Procesos Democraticos*, Santiago, 1990.
— *Women Organising for Change*, Santiago, 1988.

Jaquette, Jane S., ed., *The Women's Movement in Latin America, Feminism and the Transition to Democracy*, Unwin, Boston, 1989.
— 'Women, Feminism and the Transition to Democracy in Latin America', *Latin American and Caribbean Research Review* 1985.
— 'Women in Revolutionary Movements in Latin America', in *Journal of Marriage and the Family*, 35, 2, 1973.

Jelin, Elizabeth (ed), *Women and Social Change in Latin America*, London, Zed Books, 1990.
— *Family, Household and Gender Relations in Latin America*, Kegan, London 1991.

MacEwen Scott, Alison, 'Women in Latin America: Stereotypes and social science', *Bulletin of Latin American Research*, Vol.5, No.2, 1986.

Munck, Ronaldo, *Latin America: The Transition to Democracy*, London, Zed Books, 1989

Nash, June and Safa, Helen, *Women and Change in Latin America, Bergin and Garvey*, New York, 1986.
— *Sex and Class in Latin America*, Bergin and Garvey, New York, 1980.

Neuhouser, Kevin, 'Sources of Women's power and status among the urban poor in contemporary Brazil', *Signs: Journal of Women in Culture and Society*, Vol.14, No3, Spring 1989.

Philip, George, *The Military in South American Politics*, Croom Helm, London, 1985.

Schmink M. 'Women in Brasilian Apertura Politics', *Signs: Journal of Women in Culture and Society*, Vol.7, No.2, Aut., 1981.

Slater, David, ed., *New Social Movements and the State in Latin America*, CEDLA, Amsterdam, 1985.

Tabak, Fanny, *Autoritarismo e Participa ao Política da Mulher*, Edi oes Graal, Rio de Janeiro, 1983.

Valenzuela, J. Samuel & Valenzuela, Arturo, *Military Rule in Chile: Dictatorship and Opposition*, John Hopkins, Baltimore, 1986.

Zabaleta, Marta, 'Research on Latin American Women: in search of our political independence', *Bulletin of Latin American Research*, Vol.5, No.2, 1986.

Argentina

Abuelas de Plaza de Mayo, *Los Niños Desaparecidos y la Justicia*, Buenos Aires, 1988

Acuña, Carlos & Smulovitz, '?Ni Olvido, ni perdón? Derechos Humanos y Tensiones Civico-Militares en la Transición Argentina', Centro de Estudios de Estado y Sociedad (CEDES), Buenos Aires, 1991.

Amnesty International, *Extracts from the Report of an Amnesty International*

Mission to Argentina 6-15 November 1976, London, 1977

— *Argentina, the Military Juntas and Human Rights*, Report of the Trial of the former Junta Members, 1985, London, 1987

Archenti, Nélida, *Situación de la mujer en las sociedad argentina: formas de organización en Capital Federal*, Fundación Friedrich Naumann, Buenos Aires, 1987.

Asociación Madres de Plaza de Mayo, 'Historia de la Madres de Plaza de Mayo', Buenos Aires, 1988.

Bellotti, Magui, '1984/1989 El Feminismo y el Movimiento de Mujeres', Cuadernos del Sur, no 10, Tierra del Fuego, Buenos Aires, 1989.

Bombal, M. Inés González & Sondereguer, 'Derechos Humanos y Democracia', in Jelin, E., ed., *Movimientos Sociales y Democracia Emergente/1*, Centro Editor de América Latina, Buenos Aires, 1987.

Buchanan, Paul, 'Exorcising collective ghosts', *Latin American Research Review*, Vol. XXV, No.2, 1990.

Burns, Jimmy, *The Land that Lost its Heroes*, Bloomsbury Press, London, 1987.

Carlson, Marifran, *!Feminismo! The Woman's Movement in Argentina from its beginnings to Eva Perón*, Academy Chicago Publishers, Chicago, 1988.

Cortés, Rosalía, *Informe sobre el mercado de trabajo feminino en la Argentina*, Subsecretaría de la Mujer de la Nación/UNICEF, Buenos Aires, 1988.

Feijoo, María del Carmen, 'The challenge of constructing civilian peace: Women and democracy in Argentina', in Jaquette, Jane, ed., *The Women's Movement in Latin America, Feminism and the Transition to Democracy*, Unwin, Boston, 1989.

— & Mónica Gogna: 'Women in the transition to democracy', in Jelin, Elizabeth, (ed), *Women and Social Change in Latin America*, London, Zed Books, 1990.

Fisher, Jo, *Mothers of the Disappeared*, London, Zed Books, 1989

Herrera, Matilde & Tenembaum, Ernesto, *Identidad, despojo y restitución*, Abuelas de Plaza de Mayo, Contrapunto, Buenos Aires, 1989.

Hollander, Nancy Caro, 'Si Evita Viviera', in *Latin American Perspectives*, Vol. 1, No.3 (1974)

— 'Women Workers and the Class Struggle: The case of Argentina', *Latin American Perspectives*, Vol. IV, No.1/2 Jelin, E., 'Los Ausentes: Movimientos sociales y participación democrática en Argentina', in Calderón, *Los Conflictos por la constitución de un nuevo orden*, CLACSO

— 'Otros silencios, otras voces: el tiempo de la democratización en la Argentina', in Calderón,

— & Pereyra, Brenda, Caring and Coping, 'Households, communities and public services in the making of women's daily lives', Centro de Estudios de Estado y Sociedad (CEDES), Buenos Aires, 1990.

— & Feijoo, María del Carmen, 'Las mujeres del sector popular: recesión económica y democrácia política en la Argentina', in *Mujer y Sociedad, Perspectivos Metodológicas, Enfoques Peruanos, Temas Latinoamericanos,* Fundación Friedrich Naumann, Lima, 1987.

Lombardi, Alicia, 'Vida Cotidiana: Lucha Política y Movimientos de Mujeres', Asociación de trabajo y Estudio de la Mujer, (ATEM), Buenos Aires, 1985.

Maglie, Graciela, García Frinchaboy, Mónica, *Situación Educativa de las Mujeres en Argentina*, Subsecretaría de la Mujer de la Nación/UNICEF, Buenos Aires, 1988.

Midré, Georges, 'Bread or Solidarity?: Argentine Social Policies, 1983-1990', *Journal of Latin American Studies*, Vol.24, Pt.2, 1992.

Molyneux, Maxine, 'Anarchist Feminism in Nineteenth Century Argentina', in *Latin American Perspectives*, Vol. 13, No.1,1986.

National Commission on Disappeared People, *Nunca Más*, London, Faber and Faber, 1986

Organisation of American States, Inter-American Commission on Human Rights, 'Report on the Situation of Human Rights in Argentina', Washington, 1980.

Navarro, Marysa, 'The personal is political: Las Madres de Plaza de Mayo', in Eckstein, S., *Power and Popular Protest*, University of California Press, California, 1989.

Palomino, Héctor, 'El movimiento de democratización sindical /2', in Jelin, E. (ed), *Los nuevos movimientos sociales*, Centro Editor de America, Buenos Aires, 1985.

Peralta-Ramos, Monica & Waisman, Carlos H., *From Military Rule to Liberal Democracy in Argentina*, Westview Press, Colorado, 1987.

Recchini de Lattes, Zulma, 'Marital Status and Women's Work in Argentina', in *Genus*, Vol. 34, Nos.3-4, 1978.
— 'Dynamics of the Female Labour Force in Argentina', UNESCO 1983.
— & Wainerman, Catalina H., 'Marital Status and Women's Work in Argentina', *Genus*, Vol. XXXIV, No. 3-4 1978.

Smith, William, *Authoritarianism and the Crisis of Argentine Political Economy*, Stanford University Press, California, 1989.

Vogelgesang, Sandy, *American Dream, Global Nightmare, The Dilemma of U.S. Human Rights Policy*, New York, Norton, 1980.

Chile

Angell, Alan, 'Why is the Transition to Democracy proving so difficult in Chile?', *Bulletin of Latin American Research*, 5:1, 1986.

Fernando Calderón, *Los movimientos sociales ante la crisis*, Consejo Latinoamericano de Ciencias Sociales (CLACSO), Buenos Aires, 1986.

Campero, Guillermo, 'Luchas y movilizaciones sociales en la crisis: se constituyen movimiento social en Chile?', in Calderón, Fernando, *Los Movimientos Sociales ante la Crisis*, CLACSO, Buenos Aires, 1986.

Chaney, Elsa, 'The Mobilisation of women in Allendes's Chile, in Jaquette', Jane, ed., *Women in Politics*, John Wiley & Sons, New York, 1974.

Patricia Chuchryk, 'Protest, Politics and Personal Life: The emergence of feminism in a military dictatorship, Chile 1973-83', Unpublished PhD dissertation, York University, Toronto, 1984.

Chuchryk, Patricia, 'Subversive Mothers: The Women's Opposition to the Military Regime in Chile', in Charlton, S., Everett, J., and Staudt, K., eds., *Women, Development and the State*, State University of New York Press, New York, 1989.
— 'Feminist Anti-Authoritarian Politics: The role of women's organisations in the Chilean transition to democracy', in Jaquette, Jane, ed., *The Women's Movement in Latin America, Feminism and the Transition to Democracy*, Unwin, Boston, 1989.

Crumett, María de los Angeles, 'El Poder femenino: The Mobilisation of Women against socialism in Chile', *Latin American Perspectives*, 4:4, Fall,1977.

Dias, Ximena & Hola, Eugenia, 'Modos de inserción de la mujer de los sectores populares en el trabajo informal urbano', Santiago, Centro de Estudios de la Mujer, 1985.

Donoso, María de la Luz Silva, *La participacíon política de la mujer en Chile: Las organiziones de mujeres*, Fundación Friedrich Naumann, Buenos Aires, 1987.

Evers, Tilman & Muller-Platenberg, Clarita & Spessart, Stafanie, 'Movimientos barriales y estado. Luchas en la esfera de la reproducción', *Revista Mexicana de Sociología*, Vol.44, No.2, 1982.

Garretón, Manuel Antonio, 'Espacio Publico, Mundo Político y participación de la mujer en Chile', Facultad Latinoamericana de Ciencias Sociales, (FLACSO), Santiago, 1990.
— 'Las condiciones socio-políticas de la inauguración democratica en Chile', *Revista Paraguaya de Sociología*, Año 26, No. 76, Set.-Dic., 1989, Asunción.
— 'Political processes in an authoritarian regime: the dynamics of institutionalisation and oppoisition in Chile, 1973-1980', in Valenzuela, J. Samuel & Valenzuela, Arturo, *Military Rule in Chile: Dictatorship and Opposition*, John Hopkins, Baltimore, 1986.
— 'Popular mobilization and the military regime in Chile: The complexities of the invisible transition', in Eckstein, S., *Power and Popular Protest*, University of California Press, California, 1989.

Harding, Timothy, & Petras, James, 'Democratisation and the Class Struggle', *Latin American Perspectives*, 58, Vol.15, No3, 1988.

Hardy, Clarisa, 'Estrategias organizadas de subsistencia: Los sectores sociales frente a sus necessidades en Chile, Santiago', Documento de Trabajo, Programa de Economía del Trabajo, 1985.

Kirkwood, Julieta, 'El femenismo como negación del autoritarismo', Facultad Latinoamericana de Ciencias Sociales, (FLACSO), *Materia de Discusión*, No. 52, Santiago, 1983.

— *Ser Política en Chile: Las Feministas y los partidos*, Facultad Latinoamericana de Ciencias Sociales, (FLACSO), Santiago, 1986.

Larraín, Horacio Walker, 'Transformation of Practices in Grass Roots Organisations: A Case Study in Chile', PhD dissertation, Univ. of Toronto, Canada, 1986.

Leiva, Fernando Ignacio & Petras, James, 'Chile's poor in the struggle for democracy', *Latin American Perspectives*, Issue 51, Vol.13, No4, Fall 1986.

— 'Chile: New Urban Movements and the Transition to Democracy', *The Monthly Review*, July-Aug 1987.

Moulian, Tomás, 'Antecedentes y causas de la crisis de la democracia en Chile', Facultad Latinoamericana de Ciencias Sociales, (FLACSO), Santiago, 1990.

Razeto, Luis & Klenner, Arno, Ramírez, Apolonia and Urmeneta, Roberto, *Las organizaciones económicas populares 1973-1990*, Programa de Economía del Trabajo, Santiago, 1990.

Valdés, Teresa, 'Las Mujeres y la Dictadura Militar en Chile', Facultad Latinoamericana de Ciencias Sociales, (FLACSO), Santiago, 1987.

— & Weinstein, Marisa & Malinarich, A. María, 'Las coordinadoras de organizaciones populares. Cinco Experiencias', Facultad Latinoamericana de Ciencias Sociales, (FLACSO), Santiago, 1988.

— *Venid, Benditas de mi Padre, Las Pobladores, sus rutinas y sus sueños*, Facultad Latinoamericana de Ciencias Sociales, (FLACSO) Santiago, 1988.

Serrano Madrid, Claudia, 'Poor Women in Santiago, Women Organising for Change', *Isis International*, Ediciones de las Mujeres, Santiago, 1988.

Silva, Clotilde, 'Movimiento Social', paper presented at the International Conference of Women's Participation in the Southern Cone, Montevideo, 1986.

Valenzuela, J. Samuel, & Valenzuela, Arturo, eds., *Military Rule in Chile: Dictatorship and Opposition*, Baltimore, the John Hopkins University Press, 1986.

Walker, Horacio, 'Transformation of practices in grass roots organisations: a case study in Chile', unpublished PhD thesis, University of Toronto, 1986.

Paraguay

Arditi, Benjamin, 'Recesión y Estancamiento: La Economía Paraguaya durante el periodo post-"boom" (1981-1986)', Centro de Documentación y Estudios, (CDE), Asunción, 1987.

— 'Adiós a Stroessner, Nuevos espacios, viejos problemas', Centro de Documentación y Estudios, (CDE), Asunción, 1989.

Encuentro Nacional de Mujeres, 'Por Nuestro Igualdad ante la Ley', R.P. Ediciones, Asunción, 1987.

Latin America Bureau, *Paraguay, Power Game*, LAB, London, 1980.

Barreiro, Line & Escobar, Manuelita, 'Obstaculos para la participación política de las mujeres en el Paraguay', presented at Conferencia Internacional sobre la Participación Política de la Mujer en el Cono Sur, Montevideo, 1986.

British Parliamentary Human Rights Group, 'Report of a mission to Paraguay', London, 1987.

Carter, C., 'Role of the Church in Stroesnner's Downfall', *Journal of Interamerican Studies and World Affairs*, Vol.32, No.4, 1990.

Céspedes, Roberto Luís, 'Demanda social, política y autoritarismo en Paraguay (1986-1988). Senderos Paralelos frente a una dictadura prolongada', *Revista Paraguaya de Sociología*, Año 25, No. 73, Set.-Dic., 1988, Asunción.

Comisión Internacional de la Latin American Studies Association para Observación de las Elecciones Paraguayas, 'Las Elecciones del 1' de Mayo en el Paraguay: Rumbo a una nueva era de democracia?', *Revista Paraguaya de Sociología*, Año 27, No. 77, En.-Ab., 1990, Asunción.

Corvalán, Graziela, 'La acción colectiva de las mujeres urbanas en el Paraguay', Consejo Latinoamericano de Ciencias Sociales (CLACSO), Asunción, 1985.

Fogel, Ramón, 'Las invasiones de tierras: Una respuesta campesina a la crisis', in Rivarola, Domingo, ed., *Los Movimientos Sociales en el Paraguay*, Centro Paraguayo de Estudios Sociológicos, Asunción, 1986.

Galeano, Luis, 'Mujer y trabajo en el Paraguay', Centro Paraguayo de Estudios Sociológicos.
— 'Demandas Populares Urbanas y Propuestas para la Transición Democratica', *Revista Paraguaya de Sociología*, Año 26, No. 74, En.-Ab., 1989, Asunción.

Godoy Ziogas, Marilin, 'Condiciones de vida y estructuras domésticos campesinas del grupo doméstico guaraní a la familiar nuclear paraguaya', *Revista Paraguaya de Sociología*, Año 20, No. 56, En-Ab 83, Asunción.
— & Caballero Aquino, Olga & Escobar de Peña, Manuelita, *Pintadas por si mismas: Historia de Diez Vidas*, Las Autoras Independencia Nacional y Comuneros, Asunción,1986.

Lezcano, Carlos María, 'El Regimen Militar de Alfrredo Stroessner: Fuerzas Armadas y Política en el Paraguay (1954-1988)', *Revista Paraguaya de Sociología*, Año 26, No. 74, En.-Ab., 1989, Asunción.

Nickson, Andrew, 'The Overthrow of the Stroessner Regime: Re-establishing the Status Quo', *Bulletin of Latin American Research*, Vol.8, No.2, 1989.

Prieto, Esther, 'Mujer, Legislación y Penalización', Centro de Estudios Humanitarios, Asunción, 1989.

Rivarola, Domingo, ed., *Los Movimientos Sociales en el Paraguay*, Centro Paraguayo de Estudios Sociológicos, Asunción, 1986.

Roa, Angélica, 'Mujer y Violencia', Colectivo de Mujeres 25 de Noviembre, Asunción, 1990.

Rojas, Raquel, Kuña Paraguay, *La mujer en la domesticidad rural*, Centro Paraguayo de Estudios Sociológicos, Asunción, 1986.

Rossato, Verónica, 'Kuñáicha ha campesinaicha', *El Diario*, Asunción, 1986.

Viladesau, Tomás Palau, 'Participación campesina en el desarrollo rural', BASE, Investigaciones Sociales, Asunción, 1990.

Uruguay

Aguirre, 'Rosario, Los efectos de la crisis sobre la mujer en el Uruguay', Centro Interdiciplinario de Estudios sobre el Desarrollo, Uruguay, (CIEDUR), Montevideo, 1990.

— 'Relaciones de genero y trabajo en America Latina: Consideraciones teoricas y metodologicas', Centro Interdiciplinario de Estudios sobre el Desarrollo, Uruguay, (CIEDUR), Montevideo, 1989.

— 'La presencia de las mujeres uruguayas en el mercado de trabajo urbano: cambios y problemas', Centro Interdiciplinario de Estudios sobre el Desarrollo, Uruguay, (CIEDUR), Montevideo, 1988.

Alcoba, Julia, 'La Identidad Feminina en el Sindicato', Grupo de Estudios sobre la Condición de la Mujer en el Uruguay, (GRECMU), Montevideo, 1987.

Espino, Alma, '?Hay lugar para las mujeres en el movimiento sindical?', Grupo de Estudios sobre la Condición de la Mujer en el Uruguay, (GRECMU), Montevideo, 1990.

Filgueira, Carlos H., 'Movimientos sociales en la restauración del orden democrático: Uruguay 1985', in Calderón, Fernando, ed., *Los Movimientos Sociales ante la Crisis*, Consejo Latinoamericano de Ciencias Sociales (CLACSO), Buenos Aires,1986.

Lovesio, Beatriz, 'Las mujeres y sus trabajos', Grupo de Estudios sobre la Condición de la Mujer en el Uruguay, (GRECMU), Montevideo, 1988.

— 'Estado, Política y movimientos sociales en el nuevo orden democrático', in Filgueira, ed., Movimientos Sociales en el Uruguay de Hoy, CIESU, Montevideo, 1985.

Prates, Suzana, 'Documento: Autoritarismo y Democratización: actitudes y participación política de la mujer en el Uruguay', Grupo de Estudios sobre la Condición de la Mujer en el Uruguay, (GRECMU), 1986.

— & Rodríguez Villamil, Silvia: 'Los movimientos sociales de mujeres en la transición a la democracia', Grupo de Estudios sobre la Condición de la Mujer en el Uruguay, (GRECMU), Documentos Ocasionales 9, 1989.

Rodríguez Villamil, Silvia & Sapriza, Graciela: *Mujer, estado y política en el Uruguay del siglo XX* Montevideo, Ediciones de la Banda Oriental, 1984.

Sapriza, Graciela & Espino, Alma, *Hilamos una Historia: La Memoria sindical desde las mujeres*, Grupo de Estudios sobre la Condición de la Mujer en el Uruguay, (GRECMU), Montevideo, 1989.

Mujeres en la Industria de la Pesca, Seminario Nacional, 'Obreras que son Mujeres en la Planta y en el Sindicato', Grupo de Estudios sobre la Condición de la Mujer en el Uruguay, (GRECMU), Montevideo, 1990.

Sierra, Gerónimo, 'Los sindicatos en la transición uruguaya', Centro Interdiciplinario de Estudios sobre el Desarrollo, Uruguay, (CIEDUR), Montevideo, 1989.

Tornaría, Carmen, 'Las Mujeres y el Proyecto Democrático Uruguayo', in Isis International, Ediciones de las Mujeres, No 5, *Movimiento Feminista: Balance y Perspectivas*, Santiago, 1986.

Tricánico, Carmen Beretervide & Maynard, Celina Burmester, *Organizaciones femeninas en el Uruguay de hoy*, Fundación Friedrich Naumann, Buenos Aires, 1987.

Index

The Latin America Bureau is a small, independent, non-profit-making research organisation established in 1977. LAB is concerned with human rights and related social, political and economic issues in Central and South America and the Caribbean. We carry out research, publish books, and establish support links with Latin American groups. We also brief the media, run a small documentation centre and produce materials for teachers.